TRUDEAU AND FOREIGN POLICY

a study in decision-making

TRUDEAU AND FOREIGN POLICY

a study in decision-making

BRUCE THORDARSON

Toronto Oxford University Press 1972

TO MY PARENTS

ISBN 0-19-540197-2

© Oxford University Press (Canadian Branch) 1972

2 3 4 5 6 – 5 4 3 2 1

Printed in Canada by
Web Offset Publications Limited

Contents

Preface vii

1 Introduction 1

2 The Foreign-policy Setting 10

3 The Political Philosophy of Pierre Elliott Trudeau 54

4 The Decision to Review 105

5 The NATO Decision 121

6 The Foreign-policy Papers 167

7 Assessment 194

Bibliography 218

Index 226

Preface

The study of so recent an event as the foreign-policy review conducted between 1968 and 1970 by the Trudeau administration poses many problems for a researcher, chief among which is the lack of available written material. This has meant that I had to rely heavily—particularly in Chapters 4, 5, and 6—on interviews conducted in the summer of 1971. I talked with officials in the Departments of External Affairs and National Defence, Members of the House of Commons' Standing Committee on External Affairs and National Defence, Cabinet ministers, members of the Prime Minister's Office and the Privy Council Office, and officials of the Treasury Board, in an attempt to obtain as full a picture as possible of what really happened in the course of the review. For their patience and co-operation I am extremely grateful. With the exception of the Members of Parliament, all spoke to me in confidence, and it is therefore often impossible to attribute comments in the text to specific people. It may be frustrating for the reader not to know the source of some of the information presented in the text, but in the interests of clarifying so recent and controversial an issue it is probably not desirable to avoid using illuminating interview material when the source cannot be disclosed.

Two persons I can thank by name are former prime minister Lester B. Pearson and John Holmes, Director-General of the Canadian Institute of International Affairs. I am also grateful to eight of Canada's academic authorities on foreign policy for replying to my written questions, often in considerable detail: Ramsay Cook, James Eayrs, Jack Granatstein, Gilles Lalande, Albert Legault, Kenneth McNaught, Denis Stairs, and John Warnock. In most cases I have been able to attribute their comments to them, either in the text or the footnotes.

I would like to thank in particular Professor Peyton Lyon, for his belief that an examination of the Canadian foreign-policy review would be both feasible and useful. He was a constant source of helpful suggestions, first as my supervisor when this study was being prepared as a thesis for the School of International Affairs at Carleton University and later during its revision for publication.

Finally I am grateful to Mr William Toye and Mrs Tilly Crawley of the Oxford University Press for their editorial assistance, to Bob Tritt for his aid in proof-reading, and to Ellen Richardson for her helpful advice throughout my work on this study.

1

Introduction

Between 1948 and 1968 successive Canadian governments pursued a foreign policy that, with the exception of the period 1957–63, remained remarkably consistent in its orientation, goals, and underlying philosophy. Canadian foreign-policy-makers believed that contributing to collective security and world peace was their supreme task. These goals were to be attained through active support of the United Nations and, if the world organization was unable to provide these guarantees, through the regional security alliances of the North Atlantic Treaty Organization (NATO) and the North American Air Defence Agreement (NORAD).

With the accession to power of Pierre Elliott Trudeau in the spring of 1968, this foreign policy of twenty years' duration was suddenly thrown into question. Had the new prime minister merely wished to subject a few selected issues to review, there would have been little cause for surprise or alarm among the Canadian foreign-policy establishment. What Mr Trudeau proposed to undertake, however, was a reassessment not only of issues but also of the whole underlying philosophy of Canada's external relations. 'We wish', he said, 'to take a fresh look at the fundamentals of Canadian foreign policy to see whether there are ways in which we can serve more effectively Canada's current interests, objectives and priorities.'[1]

The result was that, between May 1968 and June 1970, the Canadian government undertook an extensive reassessment of its foreign and defence policies that for the first time went right back to basic principles. Indeed, it is unlikely that any government in any country has ever subjected its external relations to such scrutiny. During these twenty-five months foreign policy became in Canada what it had not been for years: a subject of contention and stimulated interest throughout much of the country. The government organized study sessions that enabled academics, journalists, and other interested people to discuss foreign-policy questions with senior government officials. The House of Commons' Standing Committee on External Affairs and National Defence entered the most active phase in its history, travelling across the country and abroad, listening to witnesses, and turning out reports on NATO and Canadian-American relations. Within the government, interdepartmental task forces proliferated, a new Policy Analysis Group was formed in the Department of External Affairs, and foreign-service officers were recalled to Ottawa to assist in the process of policy review. Finally, the Prime Minister and his Cabinet ministers held their own study sessions with university professors and others to exchange ideas on the changes that should be made.

When the dust had settled, the result of this two-year study was a document comprising six brightly coloured booklets called *Foreign Policy for Canadians*, in which the government set out what it referred to as the 'conceptual framework' that should guide Canada's foreign relations in the years ahead.[2] The fundamental premise was that foreign and domestic policies are determined by, and must be used to promote, the same national aims. This emphasis on national interests in turn provided the justification for Canada's new foreign-policy priorities: policies designed to promote economic growth, social justice, and quality of life were henceforth to be given greater emphasis than those related to peace and security, sovereignty and independence, and a 'harmonious natural environment'. Foreign policy, the government advised, must be based on national interests rather than on an assumption that Canada's natural role was to be the world's 'helpful fixer'.

Reaction to the foreign-policy review was not long in coming, and much of it centred on the theme that the papers were a clear repudiation by the government of the basic tenets of Canada's post-war foreign policy. Jack Granatstein of York University welcomed the government's recognition that 'Pearsonian diplomacy is out, and all we can do is operate within a strictly limited sphere of influence.'[3] On the other hand Professor Peyton Lyon noted that peace and security had been relegated to the second tier of priorities and deplored the abandonment of 'the constructive internationalism of St Laurent and Pearson'.[4]

The 'St Laurent-Pearson tradition in foreign policy' or 'Pearsonian diplomacy' are terms that were used frequently in the course of the two-year review, even by commentators who associated them only with some vague concept of the status quo and who would have been hard-pressed to define them with any precision. If there is one term that best summarizes what both Mr St Laurent and Mr Pearson sought in their approach to international affairs, it is 'collective security'. Having lived through two world wars caused by narrow nationalism and the refusal of states to cede part of their sovereignty to a universal peacekeeping organization, Mr Pearson in particular was a tireless crusader on behalf of collective security. 'We also know, or should know', he said in 1948, 'that there can be no political security except on the widest possible basis of co-operation. If that basis can be a universal one—so much the better. If it cannot, then on the broadest possible basis and inside the United Nations.'[5] The firm support given by Canadian governments to the United Nations and its peacekeeping activities was one application of this principle; another was the Canadian commitment to NATO and NORAD, which successive governments considered to be important regional collective security alliances.

Another key concept in the St Laurent-Pearson tradition was a firm commitment to internationalism. Both prime ministers believed that Canada's first foreign-policy goal was world peace and security, which could be attained only if countries put aside their own narrow interests. 'The last thing we Canadians should do', Mr Pearson said, 'is to shut ourselves up in our provinces, or, indeed, in our own country, or our own continent. If we are to be of service in the world and to ourselves and our own destiny, if we are to find our right place in the sun, we must look beyond our own national or local limits.'[6] In its dealings with other countries, Canada was to seek to gain their confidence by not giving undue publicity to differences of opinion (an aspect of Canada's so-called 'quiet diplomacy') and by making whatever contributions to regional collective security alliances that its allies considered appropriate. 'We can most effectively influence international affairs', Mr Pearson believed, 'not by aggressive nationalism but by earning the respect of the nations with whom we co-operate, and who will therefore be glad to discuss their international policies with us.'[7] Canada's natural allies in the quest for world peace were the countries of Western Europe and the United States. One of Mr Pearson's dreams was the establishment of a 'North Atlantic community' in which Canada, the United States, and Western Europe would co-operate in political, economic, social, and military matters. When this proved impossible to attain, he emphasized the creation of strong bilateral ties between Canada and these nations. In his dealings with the United States he spoke frequently of the special relationship that existed between the two countries, occasionally reminding the Americans that they must not, however, take their northern neighbour for granted.

This brief description indicates the main trends in Canadian foreign policy between 1948 and 1968: support for the UN, NATO, and NORAD in the quest for collective security; an internationalistic approach based on the premise that peace and security must be the foremost goal of any country's foreign policy; 'quiet diplomacy' in dealings with allies; and a belief that the United States and the countries of Western Europe were Canada's best and most natural friends. This is the foreign policy that Pierre Elliott Trudeau inherited in 1968 and that he decided to subject to intense scrutiny.

The purpose of this book is to study the evolution of Canada's new foreign and defence policies and to analyse the events that took place between 1968 and 1971. Above all it is a study in political decision-making that seeks to determine the major influences, or inputs, in the decisions that were reached by the Canadian government during this period. The study of decision-making has been largely ignored by students of Canadian foreign policy. Though they have described and debated the validity of the country's external relations in considerable detail, they have rarely attempted to explain how and why these policies were arrived at in the first place. This may be because decision-making theory has tended to originate in American universities, where it is applied to the kind of crisis situations that facilitate analysis but that have rarely occurred in Canada. Furthermore, until the accession of Pierre Elliott Trudeau, participation in the making of foreign policy by Canadians outside the government was very limited.

During the foreign-policy review there was much speculation about what factors would influence the final decisions. Some pointed to changes that had occurred in the external environment since 1948, saying that the principles that were valid then could not possibly form the basis of foreign policy twenty years later. Others emphasized influences for change *within* Canada, including military equipment that was becoming obsolete, economic problems that necessitated government cutbacks in spending, pressure from academics, Parliament, and public opinion, new attitudes within the civil service, and fresh faces in the Cabinet. Which of these possible sources of influence would be most significant in determining the direction of Canada's new foreign policy?

There was another possible influence—one that most observers instinctively felt was crucial—and this was the Prime Minister himself. Claude Ryan of *Le Devoir* described him as 'a man who doesn't truly exchange ideas with the other person; he sets out his own point of view', while political-analyst Peter Newman described the Prime Minister's general method of governing as one 'derived from the Jesuit principle of not imposing your views on others, but of letting people find their own way to your beliefs.'[8] When the foreign-policy papers were published in 1970, editorial writers and academics were quick to point out similarities between the papers and the known views of the Prime Minister. Professor Peyton Lyon even went so far as to call the foreign-policy papers 'the Trudeau Doctrine'.

In light of this, any study of foreign policy-making in the Trudeau administration can scarcely fail to pay particular attention to the personal influence of the Prime Minister. One of the aims of this book is to determine the nature of the role played by Mr Trudeau. Was he in fact the dominant factor, imposing his views on others, or did he find himself, in the words of Peter Newman, 'like a Gulliver immobilized with a thousand Lilliputian cords', frequently forced to 'diminish statesmanship with compromise, and even opportunism'[9]—as did leaders before him? Did he have specific views on foreign-policy issues? If he did, to what extent was he able to implement them?

A great many factors have to be considered if the influences that lie behind a country's foreign policy are to be properly analysed. The external environment is important, since decisions taken in London, Washington, or Moscow may have a severely limiting effect on the scope for international activity of a medium-sized country like Canada. Other factors—geographical position, natural resources, historic relationships, foreign-trade patterns, and ethnic composition—can also affect a nation's foreign policy significantly. The pressures for change expressed by diverse groups within the country must also be considered.

The organization of this mass of information for the purpose of this study is based on the decision-making model developed by Michael Brecher of McGill University, which has the virtue of combining both environmental and psychological factors.* (It is used, however, only as a framework for identifying the most important factors that must be examined in a study of foreign-policy decision-making. No attempt has been made to apply 'content analysis' to foreign-policy decisions, as Brecher did in his study.) Taking the external environment first, Brecher identifies three distinct levels at which its influence on decision-making should be considered. The first is the 'global system', which has been dominated in the post-war period by the relationship between the United States and the Soviet Union; the second is the

* Michael Brecher, Blema Steinberg, and Janice Stein, 'A Framework for Research on Foreign Policy Behaviour', *The Journal of Conflict Resolution*, Vol. XIII, No. 1, March 1969. Anyone familiar with the Brecher model will realize that I have taken considerable liberties in arranging the various components in the order most convenient for the purposes of this study, and also that I have greatly over-simplified it.

'subordinate system'—a regional grouping of prime importance that in Canada's case is the North Atlantic area; and the third is the 'bilateral system', which for Canada involves its relationship with the United States. In the internal environment Brecher identifies the most important sources of influence as a country's military and economic capability; its interest groups, including professors, members of parliament, journalists, and public opinion; and its foreign-policy élite, including civil-service departments and their ministers. All these factors are examined in Chapter 2.

Brecher has observed that it is also necessary to study closely key policy-makers themselves, for the way in which they interpret the external and internal environments may have just as much effect on policy, if not more, as the 'operational environment' itself. The renowned decision-making theorist, James Rosenau, has written: 'Busy public officials, bombarded by a myriad of messages, tend to select those that they wish to hear or distort them so that they fit preconceptions.'[10] For example, increased Soviet naval activity in the Mediterranean would be a source of considerable anxiety to someone who believed the Soviet Union was actively planning the destruction of the free world, whereas to a person convinced of the basically pacifist nature of the U.S.S.R. it would indicate only a Soviet search for greater influence or protection. Clearly the psychological element must be explored in depth, and for that reason Chapter 3 deals with the political thought of Mr Trudeau, examining both his general views and his approach to governing.

The foreign-policy review can be divided into three major 'decisions', each of which forms a chapter of this study. The first is the government's original decision in 1968 to conduct it; the second is the 1969 decision concerning Canada's contribution to NATO, the issue that dominated much of the first year of the review and that was probably the most controversial and difficult question with which the government had to grapple; and the third is the philosophy of foreign policy revealed in the six booklets that were published in 1970 and that comprised the government's statement of policy. Various factors are analysed in an attempt to determine which had most influence on each of the decisions.

It would be unrealistic not to acknowledge from the outset that any study of so recent and controversial an event as the foreign-policy review faces several limitations, the most serious of which is the lack of complete information. There is very little written material on this period. Only through interviews with government officials and others involved in the review could new information be obtained. However, even when an official was completely frank, the increasingly complex and interdepartmental nature of policy formulation in Canada meant that he was inevitably aware of only one part of the total decision-making process. And of course some information was confidential and therefore deliberately withheld. Decision-making theorists, moreover, have been unable to develop any accepted and proven method for weighing the influence of various inputs. James Rosenau admits that the precise impact of environmental factors on policy is not easy to determine and therefore resists coherent analysis. 'It is one thing', he says, 'to believe that a nation's foreign policy reflects its way of life and quite another to back up such a conviction conceptually and empirically.'[11]

Nevertheless, a study such as this can clarify some of the confusing events that occurred during the review process. It should be possible to assign relative weights to various influences and to say that one factor was more important than another, even if it may not be possible to say by how much. A description of the environment and of the political philosophy of Prime Minister Trudeau will perhaps demonstrate more clearly than has been done before the kind of role played by both in the foreign-policy review and also indicate areas that require greater study in the future. Finally, only by understanding the considerations that were involved in the process of policy formulation is it possible to understand the true nature of decisions arrived at by the government, and to predict what their impact will be on the future conduct of Canada's external relations.

Notes

[1] Canada, Department of External Affairs, *Statements and Speeches*. No. 68/17, May 29, 1968, p. 3.

[2] Canada, Department of External Affairs, *Foreign Policy for Canadians*. Ottawa: Queen's Printer for Canada, 1970.

[3] See 'Foreign Policy for Canadians: Comments on the White Paper', *Behind the Headlines*. Toronto: Canadian Institute of International Affairs, Vol. XXIX, Nos. 7-8, August 1970.

[4] *Loc. cit.*

[5] Lester B. Pearson, *Words and Occasions*. Toronto: University of Toronto Press, 1970, p. 69.

[6] *Ibid.*, p. 292.

[7] *Ibid.*, p. 69.

[8] Claude Ryan, 'The Changing Face of our Prime Minister', Toronto *Star*, May 2, 1969; Peter C. Newman, 'Pierre Trudeau: "A Bob Winters in Mod"', Toronto *Star*, June 25, 1969.

[9] Peter C. Newman, *Renegade in Power*. Toronto: McClelland and Stewart, 1963, p. 79.

[10] James N. Rosenau, ed., *Domestic Sources of Foreign Policy*. New York: The Free Press, 1967, p. 240.

[11] Rosenau, *op. cit.*, p. 2.

2

The Foreign-Policy Setting

I. The External Environment

1. THE GLOBAL SYSTEM

The Cuban Missile Crisis of 1962 marked a watershed in the history of the Cold War. Having led the world to the brink of Armageddon, both the United States and the Soviet Union became increasingly careful about avoiding high-risk situations in the years that followed. Although East-West tensions remained, the last half of the decade of the 1960s was noteworthy for a swing towards détente, in sharp contrast with the frequent confrontations that had marked the 1950s and early 1960s. Several events highlighted this gradual yet perceptible easing of tensions. In 1967 NATO's 'Harmel Report' stated that the future tasks of the NATO alliance lay largely in measures designed to further an improvement in East-West relations. From the U.S.S.R. came proposals for a European security conference that gave rise to the hope that the Soviets were engaged in a sincere quest for world stability. The opening, in November 1969, of the Strategic Arms Limitation Talks between the United States and the Soviet Union was another promising sign of détente, as was the decision announced the same year by the West German government to seek better relations with the countries of Eastern Europe. In December 1969, Canada's External Affairs Minister, Mitchell Sharp, returned from a NATO ministerial meeting in Brussels and reported to the House of Commons:

> There is a coming-together of events in Europe today that opens the way to profound change. Basic differences between East and West will not be resolved overnight, but there is reason to believe that a new era of genuine negotiation has begun.[1]

But, although the dominant global conditions throughout most of the period of the Canadian foreign-policy review were more in the direction of détente than of cold war, this trend was disturbed by one notable event: the Russian-led invasion of Czechoslovakia in August 1968. Throughout much of Western Europe and even in North America it aroused fears that the aggressive intentions of the Soviet Union were being renewed. For perhaps a six-month period at the end of 1968 and the beginning of 1969, there was a definite deterioration in relations between the two blocs as the West sought to determine the significance of the invasion. An official U.S. State Department announcement said that military intervention in West Germany by Russia or other Warsaw Pact nations would lead to an immediate allied response from NATO, while at the United Nations Canadian diplomats were reportedly feeling out other countries, especially those of Africa and Asia, to determine how much support there would be in the General Assembly for a resolution condemning the actions of the Soviet Union.[2] A NATO communiqué in November 1968 strongly condemned the invasion and warned that further interference in the internal affairs of another state would 'create an international crisis with grave consequences'.

Within the NATO councils the Canadian position was, as usual, to urge moderation. In the debate over the wording of the NATO response to the Russian invasion, Canada joined Denmark, Belgium, and France as the council 'doves' who opposed a strongly worded rebuke. Nevertheless, it is clear that the Canadian government was concerned about the invasion. Appearing before the House of Commons' Standing Committee on External Affairs and National Defence in December, Mr Sharp said that the Soviet Union's use of force in Czechoslovakia 'had not only jeopardized peace and international order but had also violated the basic right of the people of Czechoslovakia to shape their own future without outside interference.'[3] The one concrete response by the government was to delay its planned twenty-per-cent reduction in its air division in Europe on the grounds that, as Prime Minister Trudeau told the House,

> until there has been a better opportunity for the Canadian government to assess the aftermath of the Czech crisis, both in the light of this [NATO ministerial] meeting and in the light of our own review of defence policy, it would be prudent to defer a final decision on our part whether the air division should be maintained at its present levels or reduced.[4]

Although the foreign-policy review was conducted throughout a period of general détente, the part of it dealing with Canada's NATO policy took place in the midst of increased world tension that focussed public attention once more on Europe as the centre of the Cold War.

Changes in the external environment had altered Canada's relative power. During the period 1945-60, Canada had been among the six or seven most powerful and influential countries of the world. With the decade of the sixties, however, came the realization that Canada's influence had declined significantly. One observer described the situation in this way:

> By 1961 Canada's power had already been in decline for some years. . . . The recovery of the war-torn nations of Western Europe and Japan, and the increasing confidence of the newly independent peoples of Africa and Asia, had reduced Canada's relative importance. Canada's activity as a mediator, moreover, had accumulated grudges as well as gratitude, and restored harmony between London and Washington had eliminated, at least for the time, one of Canada's traditional functions.[5]

Despite impressive economic growth, it was clear that the country's relative influence was in decline and that its post-war position of power had been only a temporary phenomenon. Much of Canada's reputation as a useful middle power was based on its support of United Nations' peacekeeping missions; those who valued this role pointed with pride to the country's record of participation in all such ventures, and especially to Canada's part in the establishment of the United Nations' Emergency Force (UNEF) in 1956. During the 1960s, however, two of the major mediatory bodies of which Canada was a member encountered serious difficulties, and the whole future of 'peacekeeping' was thrown into question. The inability of the International Control Commission to play the role intended for it in South-East Asia, and President Nasser's eviction of UNEF from Egypt prior to the outbreak of hostilities between Israel and Egypt in 1967, highlighted the problems involved in mediatory activities. The Nigerian civil war of 1968-9 was another conflict in which the United Nations had been unwilling or unable to intervene, and the prospect of a growing number of internal disorders from which peacekeeping organizations would be excluded threw further doubts on the role of such institutions in the coming decade. Even External Affairs Minister Paul Martin, one of the most vocal supporters of Canadian peacekeeping activities, was led in 1967 to conclude: 'While we can expect some demands on the UN to undertake further peacekeeping operations we anticipate that, in the near future, the scope will be limited.'[6] It was in the midst of this decline in both the number and effectiveness of peacekeeping operations that the Canadian foreign-policy review was conducted.

2. THE NORTH ATLANTIC SYSTEM

During the 1960s many changes also occurred in the North Atlantic region and in the area's collective-security alliance, the North Atlantic Treaty Organization. When NATO was established in 1949, its European members were still recovering from the war and depended upon the American nuclear guarantee for protection against the Soviet Union. Fifteen years later, however, the Western European countries had recovered economically and were moving towards the establishment of a united Europe that would rank in economic power only behind the United States. At the same time there was a growing fear of American domination—particularly economic, but also political and cultural—which found expression in such bestsellers as Jean-Jacques Servan-Schreiber's *Le Défi Americain*. The combination of the war in South-East Asia and pressing domestic problems was giving rise to a feeling of isolationism in the United States that seemed to portend a decrease in American concern with Western Europe. Claiming that American nuclear power might not be used to defend Europe, France reacted by developing its own nuclear *force de frappe*, while others concluded that changing conditions made it inevitable that Europe would be required to contribute a larger proportion of NATO's conventional forces.

Coincident with these changing conditions, however, was a conviction within NATO that any reduction in the size of a member's military contribution should not be made unilaterally. The Harmel Report had been followed by the Reykjavik declaration of 1968, in which the member nations committed themselves to the goal of mutual and balanced force reductions (MBFR) with the Soviet Union. An important part of this communiqué was the implication that unilateral actions on the part of any member country would prejudice this search for arms limitations and détente in Europe. The communiqué contained the statement that the 'overall military capability of NATO' should not be weakened except as a part of MBFR, just as Article 7 of the Harmel Report had asserted that the chances for success in the search for détente 'will clearly be greatest if the Allies remain on parallel courses.' NATO officials believed that if the NATO countries began reducing their forces without insisting upon a similar move on the part of the Soviet Union, the Soviets would have less incentive to reduce the size of their own forces in Eastern Europe through a process of negotiation with the West. If, therefore, changing conditions in Europe made the withdrawal from the continent of some of the forces of the United States and Canada, the two non-European members of NATO, seem possible, these very conditions discouraged any Western withdrawals that were unilateral and did not bring about a similar reduction of Soviet forces.

3. THE NORTH AMERICAN SYSTEM

The second half of the 1960s was a time of confusion and trouble for the United States. Chief among its problems was the war in South-East Asia, which, as it grew from a relatively localized conflict into a massive war covering much of the sub-continent, led many Americans to question not only the basis and morality of their foreign policy but also the fundamentals of their whole society.

Many Canadians too were beginning to question the policies of their principal ally, and also to express uneasiness about the high degree of American control of the Canadian economy. Cultural as well as economic nationalism, directed primarily against the United States, was growing in the country. Segments developed within all the major political parties advocating greater government intervention to stop the 'Americanization' of Canada's economy and culture. (The NDP Waffle group was the most extreme manifestation of this trend.) One of many public-opinion polls taken on this issue showed that 59 per cent of Canadians surveyed felt that a growing concern for Canadian nationalism was a good thing.[7]

It was inevitable that the growing wave of anti-Americanism, whether implicit or explicit, would have an impact on Canadians' views of their own country's foreign policy, for this was predicated to a large extent on close relations with the United States and on membership in the two regional security alliances, NATO and NORAD, of which the U.S. was the dominant member. Growing disillusionment with American foreign policy, particularly in Viet Nam, led some Canadians to examine with new skepticism that of Canada. As one critic wrote:

> The war in Viet Nam persuaded many Canadians, as it persuaded many Americans, that the conventional interpretation of the cold war was long overdue for an agonizing appraisal. The Canadian role in Viet Nam was determined by the defence production-sharing agreement, under which millions of dollars worth of Canadian equipment was used by the Americans in Viet Nam. . . . Prime Minister Pearson, as loyal a friend as the Americans could ask for, was deeply troubled by American actions in Viet Nam. His helplessness encouraged many Canadians to take a critical look at Canadian foreign policy.[8]

II. The Internal Environment

1. MILITARY CAPABILITY[9]

During the first half of the 1950s the Canadian government was prepared to accept military responsibilities that required the most advanced weapons available: this would help to counter the threat of the Soviet Union and also allow Canada to exercise within the NATO alliance an influence that went far beyond specifically Canadian interests. The Arrow débâcle,* however, proved that only the largest countries were capable of producing the increasingly sophisticated and expensive weapons required for their own defence. Canada, like other medium and small powers, could not afford to play the big-power game.

An alternative approach was the one adopted by Canada with respect to North American air defence. It consisted of using American-made weapons systems—F-104 interceptors, SAGE detection equipment, Bomarc missiles, and eventually nuclear weapons—to enable the country to make an important contribution to the defence of the continent. There were, however, significant political problems in such an approach. The national pride of some Canadians was injured by reliance on American weapons. At one point in the 1950s the Diefenbaker government refused to accept a gift of sixty-six McDonell F-101 Voodoo jets from the United States to replace the cancelled Arrow for fear that such a gift would be cited as evidence of Canada's dependent position. The Canadian government eventually accepted the aircraft, but only on the condition that Canada pay its own way by assuming the operating costs of the Pinetree radar stations previously manned by the U.S. and by paying $50 million of the cost of providing F-104s for the European members of NATO. Even Lester Pearson, while Leader of the Opposition, expressed concern over the country's growing reliance upon the United States:

> Of course it [Bomarc] has to fit into the U.S. continental defence system, with Sage, otherwise it would not be of much use

* The government's contract to have interceptor aircraft manufactured in Canada was cancelled in February 1959.

> to us in Canada. In that sense, this arrangement is bound to tie us more closely to the U.S. production, U.S. industrial requirements. I wonder if that is why the U.S. is paying the cost of these Bomarc missiles in Canada. . . . Are we now, under this Bomarc arrangement, accepting for the first time mutual aid from the U.S., something which we did not do during the whole course of the war?[10]

The issue of nuclear weapons can also be traced back to the years of the Diefenbaker administration, for it was during this period that Canada acquired several weapons systems whose efficiency depended on the use of nuclear warheads. The Bomarc missile for North American air defence, the Lacrosse and Honest John missiles for the Canadian brigade group in Europe, and the air division's F-101 and F-104 jet fighters had all been purchased for use in Canada's two collective security alliances on the assumption (at least among Canada's allies) that they would be armed with nuclear warheads. Faced with the Diefenbaker administration's subsequent reluctance to acquire these warheads, Mr Pearson, abandoning his earlier position, pledged during the 1963 election to acquire the nuclear weapons to which Canada had committed itself, on the grounds that Canada must fulfil its international obligations. The result was that, in Europe, in tune with NATO's switch to a strategy of flexible response rather than massive retaliation, Canada's CF-104 strike reconnaissance aircraft had access to nuclear weapons, as did the Honest John artillery rocket; within Canada, both the Bomarc 'B' and the Voodoo interceptor were also armed with nuclear weapons.

The defence policy that existed in Canada at the time of the 1968-70 foreign-policy review was based essentially on the Defence White Paper of 1964 (which announced the government's unification of the armed forces, begun in August 1964). The dominant theme of this document was its emphasis on peacekeeping. There was no indication that the country's alliance commitments were to be diminished, but the forces were to be organized in such a way that alliance commitments would no longer determine the size and shape of the contingent available for peacekeeping duties. The speeches of Paul Martin confirmed that peacekeeping was now the government's first defence priority. At Radcliffe College, Cambridge, Massachusetts, in 1965, he said: 'There is very likely to be a continuing need for such [peacekeeping] operations. They are likely to enjoy fairly wide support. They can, in fact, be carried out efficiently and offer opportunities for durable settlements.'[11] General Allard conveyed a similar impression when, testifying before the Commons' Defence Committee, he said:

> Canada now wants, while remaining faithful to its existing commitments, to decide itself on the part it wishes to play in the new international society. . . . It is its duty to participate, to the best of its ability, in keeping the peace by supporting the organization which has made itself the champion of the smaller nations: the UN organization. In short, that is the transformation proposed by the white paper.[12]

Fulfilment of the country's NATO commitments was still a high priority, according to the Defence White Paper. Two units—the brigade group and the air division—were to remain based in Europe, giving Canada a combined force strength on the continent of approximately 10,000 men. The brigade group was given new equipment—armoured personnel carriers, tanks, anti-tank missiles, and heavier artillery—an indication that Canada's NATO contribution would continue to be based in Europe, at least until the equipment became obsolete in the early 1970s.

One of the major goals of the 1964 White Paper was the achievement of maximum flexibility within the armed forces in view of Canada's limited size and resources. All units were to be able to perform a wide variety of roles, permitting them to be deployed wherever they were most useful. But the two units in Europe performed functions so different from those of the forces stationed in Canada that such 'multiple-tasking' was impossible. The Defence White Paper had created six new commands for the Canadian Armed Forces, but the European brigade group and air division were so incompatible with the Canadian-based forces that they were placed outside the six-command structure and made directly responsible to the Chief of the Defence Staff—an indication of how out-of-place they really were in the government's new military organization. The heavy equipment of the mechanized brigade in Europe could not be used by the lightly armed air-portable combat groups of the Mobile Command in Canada; moreover, since there were no Canadian formations performing the functions of the European-based brigade, it was difficult to provide training in Canada for the men of the NATO force and to rotate units between Canada and Europe on a regular basis. Similarly, the air division in Europe was equipped with strike-attack aircraft for which there was no role in Canada, for North American defence was viewed in terms of anti-bomber defence requiring limited-range interceptor aircraft. All in all, the country's two units in Europe were becoming isolated from the forces at home.

While the White Paper gave high priority to peacekeeping and emphasized the importance of maintaining Canada's commitments to NATO, North American air defence was accorded somewhat less importance. On the assumption that the diminished threat from bomber attack would lead to a 'downward trend in continental air defence forces', several northern radar stations were closed, existing equipment was gradually phased out, and there was no indication that the acquisition of new equipment was being contemplated. There was no attempt on the part of the government to renege on its commitments to North American air defence, but its failure to acquire more modern weapons systems indicated that within a few years Canada would no longer be in a position to make a major contribution to NORAD.

Maritime Command was the organization responsible for the anti-submarine warfare operations (ASW) that formed part of Canada's contribution to NATO and in which the Canadian Armed Forces had acquired a reputation for considerable proficiency. The Command was well equipped with newly purchased destroyer escorts, maritime aircraft, and conventional submarines, and had been described as at least comparable in effectiveness to the forces of other nations engaged in ASW, including the United States.[13] As a Commons' Committee on Maritime Forces reported in June 1970:

> . . . a combination of forces with subsurface capabilities continues to be an appropriate and effective contribution of maritime

> forces which Canada can make to collective security. . . . Finally this role employs many similar forces to those required for the maintenance of sovereignty and the enforcement of extra-territorial jurisdiction.[14]

2. ECONOMIC CAPABILITY

During the last half of the 1960s the Canadian government encountered severe fiscal pressures. In 1966-7 there was speculation that Medicare would cost close to $1 billion and, although the Hall Commission determined that the cost would in fact be only a small part of that amount, the Pearson government was forced to delay its medicare scheme by a year because of lack of money. When the Trudeau administration assumed office in 1968, it was greatly concerned over the spiralling and almost uncontrolled costs resulting from the profusion of shared-cost and other social-security programs created by its predecessor in the mid-sixties.[15] Shared-cost programs had proliferated during the Pearson administration, and by 1968 the provinces were increasing their demands on Ottawa for additional revenue. With expenditures increasing at a much faster rate than revenues, the government was forced in 1967 to announce specific reductions in government spending in order to keep within the government's total expenditure target of $10.3 billion. At the same time Canadians were increasing the inflationary pressures on the economy by demanding more of the social-welfare programs to which they had become accustomed. By April 1969 Prime Minister Trudeau was stating flatly that the government had reached the limit of its spending power and that the public had to face up to the realities of what the country could and could not afford.[16] Faced on the one hand with pressures from both the public and the provinces for more money, and on the other with the belief that inflation could be halted only if the federal government limited its spending, Ottawa could see no alternative but to establish priorities in order to make the best use of its limited financial resources. The curtailment of some programs was inevitable. The problem confronting the government was how best to effect the required savings.

One possibility was to reduce the defence budget, particularly the part of it that maintained Canadian forces in Europe. When the North

Atlantic Treaty was signed, the Canadian government did not consider that membership in the alliance would involve Canada in an obligation to maintain large defence forces; it was the outbreak of the Korean War that prompted the Canadian decision to maintain a fairly large military force in peacetime and in 1954 caused the defence budget to soar to a peacetime high of 43 per cent of the total federal budget. Since that time defence expenditures decreased relative to other costs. By the end of the Pearson administration the defence budget was fixed at approximately $1.8 billion. In 1969 this figure amounted to almost 2.3 per cent of the country's GNP—a considerably lower percentage than the defence expenditure of most other countries.* Nevertheless the amount at which the defence budget was fixed by the Pearson administration—$1.815 billion—was, in absolute terms, a large and tempting sum. John Gellner, arguing against any NATO cutbacks, showed that even if all 10,000 of Canada's troops in Europe were discharged, the savings would amount to 'only $150 million' because of the cost of pensions and separation payments.[17] However, that was close to the amount that the Hall Commission had estimated to be the cost of Medicare. It was therefore natural for people both within and outside the government to speculate on ways in which some of the country's problems could be solved by a rechannelling of part of the defence budget.

Canada's economic problems were not dissociated from what many Canadians, and their leaders, thought was Canada's main challenge in the 1960s: national unity. In the economically underprivileged regions of the West and the Maritimes, people were expressing discontent with what they perceived to be a lack of attention on the part of the federal government to their particular interests. Of far greater danger to a united Canada, however, was the growth of nationalism, separatism, and even terrorism in the province of Québec as 'la révolution tranquille' of the early 1960s became less quiet and more threatening.

---

* Professor Peyton Lyon has determined that, out of fifty-five countries for which statistics are available, forty-one spent a greater percentage of their GNP on defence in 1968 than did Canada, eight spent less, and five spent approximately the same amount. (See Peyton V. Lyon, 'The Trudeau Doctrine', *International Journal*, Winter 1970-1.)

Faced with attempts by Québec to gain a greater voice in those foreign activities most relevant to the provincial government's main concerns, the Pearson administration initiated a policy of expanding Canada's contacts with French-speaking countries. Cultural agreements were signed, diplomatic missions established, and increased aid offered as Canada sought through its foreign policy to express the bilingual character of the country and to answer Québec's charges that Ottawa was the government of only English-speaking Canada. The foreign-policy changes instituted by the Pearson government, however, did not halt the growth of separatist sentiment in Québec, where the Parti Québecois won 24 per cent of the popular vote in the 1970 provincial election, and there was a feeling among some academics that a reduction in Canada's external activities was made necessary by the country's need to solve its internal problems. Professor James Eayrs expressed a rather extreme view:

> With the St Lawrence as turbid as it is today, it is blind to keep watch on the Rhine. What does it matter whether Canada remains in NATO, remains in NORAD, remains in the Commonwealth? What matters is that Canada remains. A decision to let Gaza or Laos or Cyprus stew in their own juice—the imperative of classic isolationism—can be justified if it means putting our house in order.[18]

3. THE PEARSON ADMINISTRATION

An examination of the foreign-policy élite within the Pearson administration indicates that the Prime Minister was not as much in favour of maintaining the status quo, especially with respect to NATO, as the failure of his government to take any major new initiatives would suggest. In 1963 Mr Pearson spoke of the need to review Canada's NATO policy, and especially of 'the necessity of building up NATO's conventional forces.'[19] The Defence White Paper of 1964 seemed to indicate a lessening of emphasis on the long-term importance attached by the government to Canada's alliance commitments, and by 1967 Mr Pearson had become quite outspoken in his criticism of NATO's preoccupation with its military role and its failure to develop common, unifying political institutions:

> NATO concentrated on the single, if vitally important task of collective military defence. It was not able to take effective measures for collective political action. National decisions were rarely subordinated to collective decisions, or national policy to collective policy. The United States, whose power dominated the alliance, largely determined the strategy and policy on which collective defence was based.[20]

Mr Pearson believed that NATO's main role in the future should include the search for détente, and be increasingly political.* He considered that there was no longer any military need for Canadian forces to be stationed in Europe at their existing strength and that Canada could withdraw some of its troops from the European theatre and change its strike-attack role in the air without harming its reputation among its allies, as long as this withdrawal was done with a minimum of publicity and after extensive consultation with Canada's allies. Mr Pearson is now convinced that that is the course his government would have followed by 1972 at the latest had he remained Prime Minister.

But while questioning Canada's military role in NATO, Mr Pearson appeared to have fewer qualms about Canada's defence relations with the United States, particularly with respect to the controversial Defence Production Sharing Agreement. In reply to a group of Toronto professors who accused the Canadian government of aiding the American war effort in Viet Nam, Mr Pearson wrote that

> the imposition of an embargo on the export of military equipment to the USA and concomitant termination of the Production Sharing Agreements would have far-reaching consequences which no Canadian government could contemplate with equanimity. It would be interpreted as a notice of withdrawal on our part from continental defence and even from the collective defence arrangements of the Atlantic alliance.[21]

Mr Pearson had publicly questioned the wisdom of the United States'

* This paragraph is based on an interview with the Rt Hon. L. B. Pearson in June 1971.

policy of bombing North Viet Nam, and afterwards frequently expressed pride at having been the first western leader to criticize openly American policy in Viet Nam. Nevertheless the war in South-East Asia does not seem to have changed his earlier conviction that the United States was Canada's principal ally and that Canadian interests were not endangered by Canada's adherence to two collective security alliances dominated by the United States.

As for the argument that Canada should divert part of its defence budget to foreign aid, Mr Pearson told the House in 1968 that Canada spent a smaller percentage of its GNP on defence than any NATO country except Denmark and Luxembourg, and that it could be reduced further only if Canada withdrew from its present commitments for collective and continental defence and became a non-committed power in world affairs.[22] Although a strong believer in the need for increased foreign aid—as evidenced both by his government's 1966 commitment to devote one per cent of the country's GNP to development assistance and by his later work for the World Bank—Mr Pearson clearly did not view foreign aid as an alternative to defence.

Prime Minister Pearson believed that the recognition of Communist China was a desirable step in theory, but impractical because of conditions both within and outside Canada. In an interview with the *United Church Observer* he stated that Canada was close to recognizing Peking when the Korean conflict broke out, but that afterwards public opinion was opposed to recognition and the attitude of the United States had also to be taken into consideration. 'When you have a division of public opinion inside your country', he explained 'and there is no great impelling urgency, morally or politically, to take action, then your relations with your neighbor, with the United States, become . . . a very important additional factor.'[23] After 1966 frustration over the UN's inability to bring China into the world community led Canada in the direction of bilateral recognition, but 'deterioration in the country itself [the Cultural Revolution] had postponed final action.'

Peacekeeping had been the cause of Mr Pearson's rise to world prominence in 1956, and he never lost his belief in the importance of a mediatory role for the United Nations. In 1964 he issued an appeal for the creation of a permanent international peacekeeping force that could be called into action on the request of the UN. For the most part, however, it was External Affairs Minister Paul Martin who made most of the Canadian speeches on behalf of peacekeeping in the 1963-8 period. A typical statement was his speech to the directors of the Canadian National Exhibition in August 1967. Mr Martin told them that, in spite of the precipitous fate of UNEF in the Middle East, he was convinced that when new peacekeeping forces were required, Canadians would want their government to participate if requested to do so by the UN.[24] At times, particularly in his references to Canada's role in Viet Nam, Mr Martin appeared to exaggerate the attention paid to Canadian views in situations where the country's involvement was marginal.[25] The Minister for External Affairs left the impression of trying to 'out-Pearson' Pearson with his almost unquestioning support for peacekeeping at a time when even officials in his department were adopting the view that mediatory roles should be accepted only when adequate terms of reference could be guaranteed. The absence of clearly defined terms of reference had contributed to the failure of both the International Control Commission and the United Nations Emergency Force to accomplish their goals, but Mr Martin appeared at times to be echoing the exaggerated rhetoric of his predecessor, Howard Green, who in the early 1960s frequently spoke of Canada as a world peacekeeper. The inference that many observers drew, perhaps unfairly, from Mr Martin's speeches was that it was Canada's duty to participate in any peacekeeping efforts, no matter how remote their chances of achieving a lasting political settlement.

By 1967 Prime Minister Pearson had become convinced that changing world conditions necessitated a reassessment of Canada's international role, particularly in connection with NATO. Two ideas dominated his thinking. One was that after twenty years it was perhaps time for the European members of NATO to assume greater responsibility for their own defence, which in turn implied a reduced military role for Canada in Europe; the other, which he regarded as especially important in view of his 1963 election pledge to review Canada's use of nuclear weapons, concerned the termination of the Canadian nuclear strike role in Europe.

At the same time, however, the Department of External Affairs, led by Mr Martin, was conducting a counterattack against the critics of Canadian foreign policy. While Mr Martin was defending existing Canadian policy in his speeches, his officials were arguing the case for continued Canadian participation in NATO in private conversations with newsmen and academics. The External Affairs Minister, sincere in his belief that Canada's policy was serving the country's best interests as well as contributing to international peace and stability, felt that any change in Canada's role in Europe would be a reflection on what the government had done in the past and, more important, on the policies that he himself had advocated. Hoping to take over the leadership of the Liberal Party when Mr Pearson retired, Martin was very sensitive to any criticism, implicit or explicit, of his policies, and was therefore, in the words of a senior government official, 'very reluctant' even to reconsider Canada's role in Europe. The government was not insensitive to the argument that Canada's contribution should be made from bases in Canada, he told the Senate External Affairs Committee in 1967, but until changes in technology or strategy made this feasible, Canada 'cannot fail to take into account the political consequences of unilateral action to withdraw forces from Europe.'[26]

By the fall of 1967 Prime Minister Pearson, still convinced of the desirability of a thorough reassessment of existing policy, reached an agreement with his External Affairs Minister. The government would carry out a full review of Canadian foreign and defence policy as the Prime Minister wished, but, in deference to Mr Martin, this would not be conducted by anyone from outside the government service. The task was assigned to one man, Mr Norman Robertson, then Director of the School of International Affairs at Carleton University and a former Undersecretary of State for External Affairs. Chosen to work with him were two experienced External Affairs officers, Geoffrey Murray and Geoffrey Pearson. The choice satisfied the Prime Minister for, as one observer put it, 'although "insiders", these were not the men whom anyone with knowledge would select if they merely wanted arguments to support the status quo.'[27]

The 'Robertson Review', conducted entirely within the Department of External Affairs, was completed in approximately three months. Mr

Martin was apparently pleased, for it did not call for any major changes in policy, while Mr Pearson also regarded it as 'extremely well done'. The review concentrated on the issues towards which Canadian academics and the press were devoting their main attention, particularly 'complicity' with the war in Viet Nam and Canada's relations with the United States. In these areas no alteration in existing policy was apparently recommended. The United Nations and peacekeeping were also considered, for it was felt that an unrealistic public faith in peacekeeping had resulted in an 'aberration' in Canada's attitude towards such activities. The Commonwealth was examined, with rather skeptical conclusions, but the most important recommendation was on the subject of NATO. The report apparently concluded that Canadian withdrawal at that time might lead to a chain reaction by smaller European countries and that the financial savings to be made by repatriating the forces would be more than offset by the cost of providing transport aircraft for a mobile force. The possibility of a future change in the nature of Canada's military commitment, perhaps by the early 1970s, was left open, but for the time being no major changes in Canada's NATO policy were recommended. The report concluded with a recommendation that the review of foreign policy should be more systematic in the future, and with some suggestions about how foreign-policy actions could be explained more adequately to the Canadian public.

Although it would be inaccurate to say that, by the spring of 1968, the Pearson administration's foreign-policy makers were completely committed to a status-quo approach, there was a consensus among the Prime Minister and top officials in the Departments of External Affairs and National Defence that no major changes were needed at that time. Mr Pearson was prepared to admit that the peacekeeping rhetoric had to be toned down, but not that any immediate changes in Canada's role in NATO, or with respect to recognition of Communist China, were necessary or desirable. Canada's relations with the United States were regarded as satisfactory, although the future role of the Commonwealth was in some doubt because of Britain's renewed bid for entry to the European Economic Community.

4. THE ACADEMIC COMMUNITY

The question of Canada's survival as a nation in the face of the American presence had become a dominant issue by 1966 and was largely responsible for a profusion of works on the hitherto relatively neglected subject of Canadian foreign policy. Given the fact that Canadian-American relations provided the theme for most of these books, it is not surprising that the majority tended to be critical of Canada's existing foreign policy. Professor Denis Stairs, in his summary of the approximately thirty books on the subject published between 1966 and 1970, has concluded that eighteen were critical, only six were favourable, and another six were more or less neutral.[28] One of the most widely read of these books was *An Independent Foreign Policy for Canada?*, a collection of essays edited by Stephen Clarkson.[29] With the exception of Denis Stairs, Peyton Lyon, and Harald von Riekhoff, the contributors to Clarkson's book were unanimous in their condemnation of existing Canadian foreign policy. These articles provide virtually the full range of opinion at that time and the book itself is probably the best summary available of what academics who were willing to stand up and speak were thinking about Canadian foreign policy.

Among the issues that provoked the most debate from academics during this period was the question of Canadian participation in NATO. While a few professors (notably Harald von Riekhoff and, more frequently, Peyton Lyon of Carleton University) emphasized the political function of the alliance, which gave the smaller powers such as Canada 'an unprecedented opportunity to influence international decisions in accordance with their own national interests,'[30] they were far outnumbered by the academics who, for a variety of reasons, were critical of Canada's role in NATO. Michael Brecher, John Warnock, and Kenneth McNaught were among those advocating a policy of non-alignment for Canada on the grounds that membership in NATO had both determined and hampered Canada's influence and relations with countries outside the North Atlantic alliance.[31] Even John Holmes, Director General of the Canadian Institute of International Affairs and long an advocate of Canadian participation in NATO, saw the desirability of change. He said that Canada should 'insist upon a redeployment of its forces to fit a situation that has shifted a good deal since 1949', implying that he favoured returning the forces from their 'distant places' overseas.[32]

Those who favoured a reduction in Canada's NATO commitments, however, were not agreed on the new priorities towards which Canadian foreign policy should be directed. For Kenneth McNaught and Jack Granatstein, Canada's principal objective was the enhancement of the United Nations and support of its peacekeeping activities.[33] But Thomas Hockin and Donald Gordon claimed that involvement in such a problematical undertaking as peacekeeping was unlikely to achieve lasting solutions.[34] Others associated peacekeeping with the Pearsonian approach to foreign policy, to which they objected, and opposed UN involvements on the grounds that they kept Canada (in the words of James Eayrs) on the 'lofty plateau of preoccupation with foreign policy to which we'd been led by L. B. Pearson—the pied piper of infantile internationalism—and where we had little business being.'[35] Even supporters of peacekeeping believed that Canadians had been suffering delusions of grandeur and an unhealthy preoccupation with role-playing, implying that emphasis on peacekeeping as Canada's main defence and foreign-policy priority would be unwise. 'Some corrective was required', wrote John Holmes, 'to the illusion of middle-sized superpower, and the recognition that foreign policy is more than a diplomatic high-wire act. . . .'[36]

More widespread was the view that the reduction of Canada's role in NATO should lead to increased spending on foreign aid. The main advocate of this approach was Escott Reid, a former senior official in the Department of External Affairs and then principal of Glendon College in Toronto. In several well-publicized articles and speeches, he argued for the establishment of new foreign-policy priorities:

> . . . expenditures on defence and expenditures on aid for the development of poor countries are both deterrents. One is a deterrent against armed attack. The other is a deterrent against anarchy, the anarchy into which much of the poor two-thirds of the world may be plunged if there is not a substantial speed-up in its rate of economic growth. . . . Canada now spends $2,100 million a year on deterrence, $1,800 million on deterrence

> against armed attack and $300 million for deterrence against anarchy. Canada should increase its share of the burden of deterrence to 3 billion dollars a year—a billion for defence, two billion for foreign aid and to deserving poor countries. To reduce our expenditures on defence to a billion dollars a year will involve withdrawing and disbanding our armed forces which are now in Europe. It will not require us to leave the North Atlantic Alliance.[37]

Anti-NATO arguments based on a desire to cut the defence budget were by no means unprecedented. As early as 1965 James Eayrs had argued for a cut in defence expenditures to $500 million on the grounds that (as virtually all observers agreed) Canada's armed forces were designed to serve political rather than military functions.[38] What was striking about the 'defence expenditure' argument in 1967-8 was that, instead of emphasizing domestic concerns, its advocates were pressing for a more active and energetic role for Canada on the world scene. In his introduction to *An Independent Foreign Policy for Canada?*, Stephen Clarkson said that two concerns had inspired his book: 'Canada's unrealized potential for effective international action; and the misconception of this potential by the Canadian people. . . .'[39] Rare were those academics who, like James Eayrs, advocated a less active role for Canada. Those who emphasized domestic concerns were primarily French Canadians such as Louis Sabourin, who stressed the need for 'a more balanced foreign policy' that would enhance national unity by reflecting the aspirations of both English and French Canadians.[40] Most observers, from Stephen Clarkson to Peyton Lyon, seemed to agree that a dynamic foreign policy was one of the most effective ways of strengthening Canada's national identity, even if they did not agree on what form this policy should take. Clarkson wrote: 'We cannot afford not to exploit the nation-building potential of our foreign policies, since the way others perceive us—dynamic and bicultural, or ineffectual and divided—can strengthen, or undermine, our own national identity.' On the other hand, according to Peyton Lyon, 'support for international organizations provides one of the best reasons for an independent Canadian foreign policy and is also one of the most effective means to augment Canadian identity and independence vis-à-vis the United States.'[41]

Included in most of this criticism was the idea that Canadian foreign policy had hitherto been too preoccupied with the North Atlantic and had all but ignored the Third World. John Holmes, for example, while opposed to Canada's withdrawal from its sub-system alliances, hoped that Canadians would accord Latin America 'a higher priority' in the future.[42] However, behind most of these arguments for increased connections with the Third World were humanitarian rather than political considerations. The idea that Canada could play a political role as a third force in inter-American politics was downplayed, as was Canadian membership in the OAS, which was seen by some observers as 'an essentially conservative organization that helps to legitimize U.S. hegemony in the Hemisphere' and one with which Canada should not become identified.[43]

A recurring theme in the academic criticism of Canadian foreign policy was the obsolescence of 'quite diplomacy', the slogan by which Pearsonian foreign policy was often identified. This epithet gave rise to criticism of the formulation of policy by people who said that neither Parliament nor the Canadian public could influence the foreign-policy-making process. 'Canada is notable', wrote one critic, 'for the extent to which a small group of politicians and civil servants dominates the foreign-policy-making process,'[44] while another complained that 'Canadian foreign policy is arrived at by ordinance.'[45] Stephen Clarkson said that the decision-making process should be 'opened up' through more intense public discussion of the issues and the activation of the Parliamentary Committee on External Affairs.[46]

Quiet diplomacy was also associated with the style and tactics of diplomacy that Mr Pearson articulated in 1967, in a defence of his government's policy towards the United States:

> . . . confidential and quiet arguments by a responsible government are usually more effective than public ones. . . . Statements and declarations by governments obviously have their place and their use in the international concert, but my own experience leads me to believe that their true significance is generally to be

> found not in initiating a given course of events but lies rather towards the end of the process, when they have been made possible by certain fundamental understandings or agreements reached by other means.[47]

This approach failed to satisfy critics such as Thomas Hockin and Stephen Clarkson, who argued that 'An independent foreign policy is not always a mediatory and flexible policy; it must also be a declaratory one', since 'a clear articulation of policy objectives' is needed to turn potentiality into reality. The Pearson approach, they said, tended to be overly reactive, for by not articulating clear policy positions Canada had become more concerned with organizational viability—maintaining the Commonwealth, NATO, NORAD, and the UN—than with determining where these organizations should be going or what they should be accomplishing.[48] Somehow, in a way that was not fully explained, these alleged weaknesses could be eradicated if only Canada would define its foreign-policy objectives for all to see.

For many commentators, however, the attack on quiet diplomacy was closely associated with what was probably the major academic criticism of Canadian foreign policy: its association with the policies of the United States. 'In its almost obsessive subservience to American policy', wrote James Steele, 'one can see the strategy of Quiet Diplomacy pushed to its practical absurdity.'[49] In spite of protestations to the contrary by John Holmes, Peyton Lyon, and Denis Stairs,[50] Canada was described by John Warnock as 'a meek spokesman for the U.S.' who could play an active role in the Third World only as a non-aligned power, and by Charles Hanly as a practitioner of 'branch-plant diplomacy'.[51] Disillusionment with the war in Viet Nam led to attacks on Canada's role in supplying weapons to the Americans through the Defence Production Sharing Agreement. Among the earliest expressions of concern over the degree of American control of the Canadian economy was Walter Gordon's book *A Choice for Canada*, whose subtitle implied that Canada had only two choices: complete economic independence or colonial status. Associated with the growing economic nationalist movement among Canadian academics was a concern that economic retaliation could be invoked by the United

States to prevent Canada from adopting policies contrary to its wishes. Statements by prominent Americans, such as George Ball, that 'commercial imperatives will lead to greater economic integration and eventually an area of common political decision' in North America[52] reinforced fears of American domination and led to intensified criticism of Canadian foreign policy on the grounds that it was not, in the most over-used and widely interpreted term of the debate, sufficiently 'independent'.

Concern over the predominant power of the United States was not, of course, a new phenomenon on the Canadian scene. During the 1958 Commons debate on the NORAD agreement, attention had been concentrated more on the provisions designed to protect Canadian sovereignty than on the actual contents of the agreement, while the 1962-3 controversy over nuclear weapons had produced a certain amount of unease in the minds of many Canadians about the state of Canadian-American relations. Newspapers such as the Toronto *Globe and Mail* had expressed concern that Canada was drifting into a position like that of certain Middle East and Latin American countries that draw their entire supply of modern weapons from one of the Great Powers. 'A nation in that position', it warned, 'may be independent in name, but it has no real independence in fact.'[53] What was new about the debate of the mid-sixties was its intensity, due largely to a growing revulsion to the war in Viet Nam, and the active part taken in this debate by Canadian academics, who a decade earlier had published relatively little on the subject of Canadian-American relations, or even on Canadian foreign policy in general. In the mid-sixties it was clear that the majority of academics who made known their views felt that Canada's relations with the United States—both bilateral and in the framework of the two countries' multilateral security alliances—were not only unsatisfactory but were preventing Canada from playing a more active and distinctive role on the international scene.

5. PUBLIC OPINION

While the availability of published sources makes it relatively easy to assess the attitude of academics towards foreign-policy issues, lack of adequate information hampers attempts to determine the views of the

Canadian public in general. Since no regular opinion polls are conducted in Canada on external policies, it is necessary to make the most of the few surveys that have been taken.

In 1960 a Canadian Institute of Public Opinion (CIPO) survey indicated that 72.3 per cent of Canadians who had heard of NATO approved of Canada's participation, while only 4.0 per cent disapproved.[54] More recent polls emphasized the nature of Canada's force commitments to NATO rather than the issue of adherence to the alliance. The most comprehensive survey conducted during the period of the foreign-policy review was a CIPO study that asked the Canadian public in the fall of 1968 whether Canadian troops should be withdrawn from Europe. The answer was reasonably conclusive, as Table 1 indicates.[55]

Table 1: CANADIAN MILITARY ROLE IN EUROPE

	National	*Québec*	*Ontario*	*West*
Continue in Europe	64	55	66	71
Call back troops	23	32	22	20
Qualified	3	—	1	5
Don't know	10	13	11	4

The most recent survey available is a questionnaire sent to his constituents in 1971 by Gordon Blair, MP for Grenville-Carleton, to which more than 7,200 replies were received. The proposition that Canada should reduce its commitments in NATO and NORAD was defeated by a majority of more than two to one (4,246 to 2,055). An increase in Canadian aid to underdeveloped countries was also rejected by a slight margin (3,091 to 3,002). Asked which expenditures should be reduced if the present level of taxation was considered too high, the respondents ranked defence fourth, following policies designed to promote bilingualism, equalization payments to the provinces, and welfare payments.

Evidence of the public's opinion of NORAD is even more sketchy than it is in the case of NATO. In 1961, 68.1 per cent of Canadians polled approved of 'Canada's defence becoming merged more and more with the U.S.', while by 1964 this percentage had decreased only slightly to 66.8 per cent; support for Canada's disarming and becoming a neutral nation was minimal (2.6 per cent); and only 2.7 per cent favoured leaving responsibility for the defence of Canada to the United States.[56] There are indications that the Canadian public favoured a foreign policy that was more 'independent' of the United States, for a 1966 survey indicated that 63 per cent of the respondents believed that Canada was not showing enough independence of the U.S. on both domestic and international questions. Nevertheless, the public's overwhelming support of Canadian participation in NATO and NORAD suggests a belief that greater independence could be achieved within the existing alliance structures.[57]

One of the very few foreign- and defence-policy issues in which there is evidence of a marked change of public opinion during the 1960s concerns the question of nuclear weapons. Between 1961 and 1966 there was a significant decrease in the acceptance of nuclear weapons by the Canadian public, suggesting that any dissatisfaction with Canadian defence policy was directed more against the acquisition of nuclear weapons by the Canadian Armed Forces than against the alliance systems within which these weapons were acquired.[58]

Table 2: ACCEPTANCE OF NUCLEAR WEAPONS BY THE CANADIAN PUBLIC, 1961–6 (%)

	Sept. 61	*Nov. 62*	*March 63*	*June 66*
Yes	61.4	54.4	48.6	34.4
No	30.5	31.6	31.0	43.8
No opinion	8.0	8.2	14.0	17.5
Qualified	—	5.6	3.5	4.1
Rejects	—	—	2.5	—

Finally, there seems to have been no opposition on the part of the general public to Canadian support for the peacekeeping ventures of the United Nations. As Jack Granatstein has written, the Diefenbaker government had little desire to participate in the UN's 1960 intervention in the Congo and eventually did so only because of the pressure exerted by external forces, and especially by the Canadian public, which was 'anxious to add to the Pearsonian laurels'.[59] When the Cyprus dispute occurred in 1964, 62.2 per cent of the public approved of sending troops, while only 32.9 per cent dissented.[60] There is no indication of the effect on public opinion of the expulsion of UNEF from Egypt in 1967, but a poll of delegates at the annual conference of the Canadian Institute of International Affairs in 1967 showed that they opposed decreasing Canada's existing emphasis on peacekeeping by a three-to-one margin.[61] Although the opinions of members of the attentive public do not always reflect those of the public in general, there is no evidence that the events of 1967 led to any significant disillusionment with peacekeeping on the part of the Canadian public.

Nevertheless the 1970 foreign-policy papers used the term 'public disenchantment' to justify the rejection of an international role for Canada in which it was cast as the 'helpful fixer', and said this resulted in part from 'an over-emphasis on role and influence. . . .'[62] Asked by the Commons' Committee on External Affairs to specify the nature of this disenchantment, one of the External Affairs officials responsible for drafting the main booklet of the foreign-policy papers gave as an example the 'great expectation built up out of our position and role in Viet Nam which never did materialize'—referring to Canada's membership in the rather powerless International Control Commission.[63] However, in a 1971 report to the House on the policy papers, the Committee expressed its views on the nature of Canadian public opinion in the following way:

> The Committee is inclined to agree that there may have been some 'public disenchantment' with the rather ritualistic character of some Canadian statements at the time and the defence of 'quiet diplomacy', which was sometimes seen as an excuse for doing nothing. It accepts that public expectations may have de-

> veloped to a point where there were bound to be disappointments because they were incapable of attainment, but the Committee doubts whether the interested public rejected—as the policy paper suggest[s]—a genuine mediatory role where Canada's position and authority equipped it to play such a role and where the parties involved were willing to see Canada involved.[64]

Most studies of public opinion agree that up to 90 per cent of the general public is usually uninterested in foreign policy; uninformed and without initiative, it lacks structured opinions, and its most intense feelings usually lie dormant, to be aroused only when some issue appeals more to its emotions than to its intellect.[65] Such, it could be argued, was the case with Biafra, the only foreign-policy issue that appeared to arouse the Canadian public during the period of the foreign-policy review. For the most part the public was preoccupied with internal matters. Opinion samples conducted by Peter Regenstreif show that during the 1968 election the major issues were taxes, housing costs, unemployment, and national unity; the only foreign-policy issue mentioned was Viet Nam, and that by only two per cent of the respondents.[66] The NDP (and, it can be assumed, the other parties as well) had conducted its own survey before the election to determine public attitudes and had discovered that only two per cent of the population expressed interest in international policy.[67] Lester Pearson has remarked that, in his experience, the Canadian public's only real and immediate interest in foreign policy is in connection with the United States.[68] Whatever the cause of this lack of public interest, it is apparent that foreign policy was not an issue of great public concern between 1968 and 1970, and that those Canadians who held opinions on such matters tended to approve of the general way in which Canadian foreign policy had been conducted by the Pearson administration.

Unlike the general public, Canada's editorial writers showed considerable interest in the foreign-policy review, but—as might be expected—they expressed many conflicting opinions. On the issue of NATO, for example, the Toronto *Star* and *Globe and Mail* advocated a transfer of resources from defence to foreign aid, but the Toronto *Telegram* strongly opposed any reduction in Canada's NATO commitment. On January 29, 1969 the *Montreal Star* stated its support for Eric Kierans' view that Canada could play a more positive world role by diverting part of its resources from 'sterile military commitments' to foreign aid, but three days later the Montreal *Gazette* commented that Canada could not abandon its NATO ties 'without ignoring the uncontestable realities of its position.' The Winnipeg *Free Press* expressed a common western-Canadian view when it stated that 'in light of prevailing tensions and the recent invasion of Czechoslovakia, it is impossible to conceive of pulling out of NATO at this crucial period.'

Most of the country's major newspapers seemed to feel that in its dealings with the United States the government should 'push Canada's independence to the limits of practicality and wisdom' (in the words of the Toronto *Star*), but few opposed Canada's continued participation in NORAD. In an editorial of June 28, 1969, the *Globe and Mail* urged an alteration in NORAD's regional divisions so that responsibility for the defence of southern Canada would be in Canadian hands, but it raised no objection to the use of nuclear weapons within the alliance.

One of the very few foreign-policy issues on which there was substantial editorial agreement during this period was the desirability of Canadian recognition of the People's Republic of China; this action was supported by the Toronto *Globe and Mail*, the Toronto *Star*, Montreal's *La Presse*, the Winnipeg *Free Press*, and the Vancouver *Province*, among others. All in all, however, Canada's editorial writers were so divided on most issues that it is highly unlikely their views were able to influence in any significant way either public opinion or Canada's foreign-policy formulators.[69]

6. MEMBERS OF PARLIAMENT

From the ranks of the Progressive Conservatives came two vigorous attacks on NATO in 1967. The first was by former External Affairs Minister Howard Green, who, in an article in the Vancouver *Sun*, questioned the necessity of stationing Canadian troops in Europe. He thought a mobile force based in Canada would still help defend Europe in case of war, while at the same time it could improve Canada's west-coast defences in the event of any threat emanating from Communist China.[70] More significant was the speech given by Dalton Camp, the party's national president, to the Policy Thinkers Conference at Montmorency in August of the same year.[71] Mr Camp stated that Canada's defence policy had dominated its foreign policy, and that by participating in military alliances as a partner of the United States, Canada was prevented from playing a constructive role in the Third World. National self-interest, he said, should determine the country's foreign policy, and it was in Canada's best interests to make its maximum contribution in the field of foreign aid rather than to organizations such as NATO, NORAD, or even the UN.

Although Mr Camp's proposals received a great deal of attention on editorial pages and university campuses, and may have helped shape opinion in these quarters, his own party's national policy conference was not willing to go as far as he had urged. The Conservative Party's official position in 1967-8 was similar to Mr Trudeau's: there should be a review of Canadian foreign policy in the light of changing conditions. Two days after the Prime Minister had called for a 'severe reassessment' of foreign policy in a pre-election press conference in 1968, Mr Stanfield made a similar speech, claiming that there was increasing dissatisfaction with Canada's international role and that it should be the purpose of government to resolve dissatisfaction, not merely to reflect it.[72] By November 1968 the Conservative Party was conducting its own 'fundamental reassessment' of defence and foreign policy, including an analysis of Canada's role in NATO and NORAD, which was to form the basis for debate in caucus and at the forthcoming policy conference in Niagara Falls.

An examination of the debates of the second session of the twenty-seventh Parliament (May 8, 1967 to April 23, 1968) shows that there was little support among Conservative MPs for the anti-NATO position articulated by Dalton Camp and Howard Green.* The majority appeared to agree wholeheartedly with the statement by former De-

* The second session is examined here in detail because, as it covered the period immediately prior to Mr Trudeau's becoming Prime Minister, it reflected the views that existed when he announced the policy review in May 1968 and that may have influenced his thinking.

fence Minister Douglas Harkness that the build-up of Soviet forces in Eastern Europe and the Mediterranean emphasized 'the necessity of maintaining military forces of NATO in a state of readiness so they will serve as a deterrent to any aggressive action.'[73] The major Conservative criticism of the government's policies concerned the emphasis placed on peacekeeping. The Tories became disillusioned with peacekeeping after the events of June 1967, when UNEF was expelled from Egypt. This disillusionment, coupled with a desire to embarrass the government, prompted John Diefenbaker's charge that 'The minister of National Defence built his policy on sand and Nasser brushed it away', as well as Gordon Churchill's warnings that Canada alone 'cannot be the peacekeeper of the world.'[74] The apparent failure of Canada's peacekeeping efforts gave the Conservatives ammunition with which to renew their attacks on the 1964 Defence White Paper and the unification legislation, which, they charged, had created a force that could not defend Canada. Gordon Churchill also attacked the 1964 Defence White Paper on the grounds that its priorities were misconceived:

> I believe Canada's defence policy should be primarily the defence of Canadian territory and Canadian waters. Second, it should be linked to the alliances that we have with the major powers (NATO and NORAD). . . . The disaster that has overfallen the peacekeeping effort on the border between Egypt and Israel should now bring about a reappraisal of Canada's defence policy and foreign policy.[75]

Any expectations that the Conservative Party's foreign-policy review would result in the advocacy of policies diametrically opposed to those of the Pearson years were dispelled with the publication of the party's report on foreign policy after its conference at Niagara Falls in October 1969.[76] Rejecting the argument that membership in NATO or NORAD limited Canada's freedom of action, it did not even raise the possibility of a new role for Canada within NATO, such as the Canadian-based mobile force that Robert Stanfield had mentioned in 1968.[77] The report recommended increases in Canada's foreign aid and closer relations with Latin America but did not tie these in any way to a reduction in Canada's alliance commitments. Its only major criticism of the government's foreign policy concerned the closing of several diplomatic missions in countries where Canada maintained a sizable aid program.

Not until June 1971 did the party's leader, Robert Stanfield, make a comprehensive statement of his own views on foreign and defence policy. In a speech in Kingston he showed himself to be very much an advocate of the main tenets of Pearsonian diplomacy.[78] While recognizing that in the past Canadians had expected too much from peacekeeping, he emphasized that 'we do have certain responsibilities that go beyond self-interest', and that for him 'it is the preservation of peace that must remain our first priority.' He defended membership in NATO on the grounds that it offered opportunities to increase Canadian influence and also acted as 'a useful counterbalance to our direct relations with the U.S. in continental defence.' In short, there seems to have been little pressure from the Conservative Party for a major change in the conduct of Canadian foreign policy during the period under study. The disillusionment with peacekeeping voiced in 1967-8 by some party members was noticeably absent from the 1969 policy report, suggesting that it had been largely a temporary reaction to the upsetting events in the Middle East in June 1967. There was a suggestion that Canada should concentrate more on its own defence, but the party's emphasis was on the idea that there is a clear distinction between Canada's domestic concerns and its international goals and obligations, and that there are some instances in which the latter should take precedence over the former.

The most vocal parliamentary critics of Canadian foreign policy during the 1967-8 period were the members of the New Democratic Party. Unlike the Conservatives, they tended to be critical of Canada's alliance commitments and to place great emphasis on its peacekeeping role. The party's position on NATO during this period was that Canada should remain in the alliance but that its contribution should take the form of a mobile conventional force based in Canada.[79] Not until the party's 1969 national convention did it officially advocate total Canadian withdrawal from NATO, and even then some of its most respected members, such as Andrew Brewin, the NDP spokesman on foreign affairs, continued to support the proposition that there was an important political role for Canada within the alliance.

The party seemed united, however, in its criticism of Canada's relations with the United States. More opposed to continentalism than the other parties, the NDP was critical of growing American investment in Canada, and especially of Canadian participation in NORAD. It advocated withdrawal from NORAD on the grounds that it was an expensive defence against a non-existent threat and the most blatant example of Canada's subservience to American foreign policy. Canada's policy with respect to Viet Nam was described by T. C. Douglas, then party leader, as 'one of timidity and hesitation which the Prime Minister calls quiet diplomacy', and Canadian arms sales to the U.S. through the Defence Production Sharing Agreement were deplored on the grounds that they undermined Canada's role as an international arbitrator and negotiator.[80] The party believed that Canada should not view its role as that of a principal ally of the United States, hesitating to criticize American policy openly for fear of losing diplomatic influence in Washington, but should adopt as independent a stance as possible and increase its influence in the Third World. The party remained unalterably opposed to Canada's possession of nuclear weapons and continued to be an ardent supporter of the United Nations. The fact that war broke out as soon as the peacekeeping force was withdrawn from Egypt was considered as proof, not that it was useless, but rather 'that the force is needed permanently.'[81]

One major argument used by the NDP in favour of a reduction in Canada's role in NATO and withdrawal from NORAD was that the resulting savings from the defence budget could be used in more worthwhile areas. Escott Reid's articles were frequently cited in the House to support the party's contention that foreign aid should receive a much larger share of the country's resources. Unlike most of the academic critics, however, both the NDP and the Créditistes tended to pay considerable attention to the ways in which these additional resources could benefit the citizens of Canada. Both David Lewis of the NDP and Créditiste leader Réal Caouette argued that the income tax surcharges introduced in 1967 would have been unnecessary had the defence budget been cut, while Grace MacInnis of the NDP said that any money saved in this way should be directed towards providing modern and comfortable homes for all Canadians.[82] At a time when there were economic problems in Canada it was perhaps inevitable that there would be pressure on the government to transfer funds from international ventures that seemed remote and relatively unimportant to many Canadians.

A final criticism voiced by the NDP, one that was often expressed by the Conservatives as well, was that information available to both Parliament and the public on the subject of Canada's external relations was inadequate. An extensive breakdown of the estimates of the Department of External Affairs and a more active role for the Parliamentary Defence Committee were thought to be necessary if Parliament was to exercise effective supervision over the government's conduct of foreign affairs. The Opposition complained that the government had failed to state the policies of the country with clarity, and was conducting foreign relations on the basis that it alone knew what was best for the nation.

Although it is difficult to ascertain the views of Liberal Members of Parliament (other than cabinet ministers), since few had given speeches on foreign affairs in the House of Commons, there are two available sources of information on the opinions of active party members. One is the survey conducted at the 1969 annual meeting of the Ontario Liberal Party, the other a questionnaire submitted to the party's 1970 national policy conference. The Ontario delegates were generally cautious about new departures in foreign policy.[83] The establishment of full diplomatic relations with the Vatican was favoured by only 35 per cent of the delegates, while a proposal that Canada join the OAS received the support of a mere 26 per cent of those questioned. Only on the matter of recognition of Communist China, approved by 59 per cent of the participants, did the delegates show the slightest inclination to depart from the policies of the Pearson administration. On the issue of NATO, 20 per cent advocated complete withdrawal while 31 per cent favoured a decrease in Canada's military commitment; on the other hand, 41 per cent of the delegates believed that the country's existing participation should be continued and 6 per cent desired an increased commitment to NATO. There was therefore a slight 'anti-NATO' majority (51 to 47 per cent), but the delegates who approved of the status quo nevertheless constituted the largest single group of voters (41 per cent). Although this survey did not reveal a conclusive trend in either direction, its results were communicated to the Prime Minister's office prior to the government's 1969 NATO decision.

At the party's 1970 national conference the delegates showed little sympathy with the major criticisms of Canadian foreign policy that had been made during the 1967-8 period. The argument that defence expenditures be reduced and channelled into foreign aid was rejected, even though approval was granted for another resolution advocating an increase in foreign aid. Resolutions calling for the suspension of Greece and Portugal from NATO and for a termination of Canada's trade with South Africa were both defeated, as was a motion that

Table 3: RESULT OF RESOLUTIONS VOTED ON AT THE 1970 ANNUAL MEETING OF THE LIBERAL PARTY

	Agree Strongly	*Agree*	*Not Sure*	*Disagree*	*Disagree Strongly*
Canada should continue its membership in both NATO and NORAD subject to a continuing review	189	393	45	76	60
Canada should reduce its defence budget and allocate all or part of such savings to increased foreign aid	102	108	133	277	184
The Canadian government should urge that Greece and Portugal be suspended from NATO	96	107	188	412	190
Canada should be independent in world affairs and first repatriate more control of its economy	275	317	114	171	102

Canada withdraw from all military alliances. A resolution was approved that Canada remain in its alliances 'subject to review'—an implication that some change was perhaps desired in the form of the Canadian commitment. The nature of this change was not specified, however, and in general the delegates seemed to support a 'Pearsonian' approach to foreign policy. Some of the most significant resolutions, as well as the results of the balloting, are shown in Table 3.[84]

7. THE TRUDEAU ADMINISTRATION

With the accession to power of Mr Trudeau in April 1968, only one member of the Pearson government's foreign-policy team remained in his previous portfolio. He was Léo Cadieux, the Minister of National Defence, whose personal commitment to both NATO and NORAD was beyond question. NATO, he told a luncheon meeting in Ottawa in early 1969, 'helped create a credible deterrent against aggression in Europe and at the same time allowed Canada to participate in efforts to create a détente between East and West.'[85] Although Europe was the geographical region where Mr Cadieux considered Canada's security to be in the greatest jeopardy, he also believed that the abandonment of NORAD's anti-bomber defences would encourage the Soviet Union to increase its bomber fleet and thus lead to a distortion in the strategic balance that served to maintain world peace.

On April 23, 1968 Mitchell Sharp was rewarded for supporting Mr Trudeau in his bid for the leadership of the Liberal Party by being appointed Secretary of State for External Affairs. In the light of his past experience it appeared that his main concern for, and interest in, foreign relations would be in the economic field. In the Pearson government he had at various times held both the Finance and Trade and Commerce portfolios; previously he had been Deputy Minister of Trade and Commerce; and he had left public life temporarily to serve as vice-president of the Brazilian Traction, Light and Power Company from 1958 to 1963. The new External Affairs Minister was committed to NATO. During the 1969 NATO debate Mr Sharp repeated his belief that Canada did not need to pull out of Europe in order to develop better relations with the Pacific and Latin America; participating in collective-security arrangements, he said, 'is not incompatible with assistance to developing countries or an active part in disarmament negotiations.'[86] Speaking to a CIIA conference at the University of Calgary in March 1969, he said:

> I have yet to hear any convincing argument that, if Canada wants to play a part in ensuring its own security, in the resolution of the security problems of Europe that directly affect our own fate, and in mitigating the confrontation between the superpowers, we could do so as effectively as within some such collective effort as NATO.[87]

The Trudeau cabinet, however, contained several members with views far different from those expressed by members of the Pearson government. Eric Kierans, then the Postmaster-General, was convinced that military alliances were the source of cold-war tensions in Europe and that a complete Canadian withdrawal from NATO would set a good example. The real danger in the world, Mr Kierans told a Liberal meeting in Nanaimo in 1969, was not the threat of Russian aggression but rather the division of the world into 'haves and have-nots'. NATO, far from being a genuine deterrent against a genuine threat, had become 'a self-justifying deterrent against a non-existent military threat'.[88] Mr Kierans had also questioned publicly Canada's relations with the United States. The time had come, he told a group of university students in Montreal in 1968, to cancel the Defence Production Sharing Agreement before Canada was pulled into a 'war economy'.[89] Less outspoken, but with views somewhat similar to those of Mr Kierans, was Donald Macdonald, then the government House Leader and President of the Privy Council, who favoured at the very least a withdrawal of all Canadian forces from Europe. He was skeptical of the value of armed forces; according to one official who knew him, he accepted the defence portfolio in 1969 when Mr Cadieux retired only because it presented more prospects for advancement than did the other three cabinet posts he was offered.

Two other cabinet ministers who belonged to the 'revisionist' school in matters of foreign and defence policy were Gérard Pelletier and Jean Marchand. As friends of the Prime Minister in their pre-Ottawa days, they were among his closest cabinet colleagues. Both advocated, if not complete withdrawal from NATO, at least a sizable redeployment or reduction of Canada's military contribution, and preferably a total withdrawal of Canadian forces from Europe.[90] Pelletier was also known to favour a more active Canadian role in Latin America.[91] As for the rest of the cabinet ministers, they appeared to want things to remain more or less as they were, or else did not feel strongly enough about them to express their views in public. Finance Minister Edgar Benson and Minister-without-Portfolio James Richardson may well have belonged to this latter group, for there are indications that both were critical of existing policy in private, and presumably also in Cabinet. Some ministers may even have chosen to remain silent in Cabinet rather than run the risk of differing openly with the Prime Minister and thereby endangering some of their own pet projects, especially if foreign policy was not a matter of great importance to them. As Eric Kierans stated after his resignation from the Cabinet, frequent opposition to the views of the Prime Minister was unwise, for 'After a while you lose credibility.'[92]

Although both the internal and external environments were far different by 1968 than they had been even five years earlier, these changes did not seem to be of a magnitude or character that would make alterations in Canada's foreign policy either inevitable or necessary. The trend towards détente and the recovery of Europe, which offered the possibility of a Canadian military withdrawal from Europe, were offset first by the resolution of NATO members to do nothing that would weaken the West's bargaining position with the Soviets, and second by the traumatic invasion of Czechoslovakia. There was a growing concern within Canada over the country's relations with the United States, but no indication of any popular opposition to continued participation in NATO or NORAD. The external environment in the 1960s revealed how modest Canada's power to influence world events really was, and indicated a decrease in the rhetoric of the Green-Martin years. No major policy changes were needed, however, for there was no evidence that other countries believed Canada to be seeking—whether within NATO or the United Nations—an unrealistic amount of influence.

The analysis of the internal environment presented in this chapter leads to the conclusion that the foreign policies inherited by the Trudeau government could have continued substantially intact. While the country did not have the resources to play a major military role, it was capable of making a contribution to Western security that its allies regarded as significant. The transport and technical capabilities of Canada's armed forces made it one of the countries best able to contribute to peacekeeping operations. Canada was experiencing reasonably severe economic problems by 1968, but there was no indication that its foreign activities were consuming a disproportionately large share of its national budget, or that substantial savings could be realized even if all Canadian troops were withdrawn from Europe. The opposition parties and the majority of interested academics were dissatisfied with existing policy, but there was no consensus about the changes that should be made. The Canadian public was uninterested. Any significant pressure within the civil service for such new policies as a gradual military withdrawal from Europe had been eased with the completion of the Robertson Report. Within the Trudeau Cabinet there were some ministers who desired greater emphasis on the economic aspects of foreign relations, the termination of the Defence Production Sharing Agreement, and increased contacts with Latin America, and there were at least four influential ministers who disapproved of the country's existing NATO policy; but the majority saw no need for drastic foreign-policy changes, and even those who opposed the status quo were far from advocating a Cabinet revolt if their ideas were not implemented. Pressure for change was certainly not strong, and could have been resisted with ease.

One person has been ignored, however, in this account of the internal environment: the Prime Minister himself. The fact that definite changes were made in both the articulation and content of Canadian foreign policy, and that none of the other possible sources of policy made such changes inevitable, suggests that it was the influence of Mr Trudeau, more than any other factor, that determined the course of the foreign-policy review. An extensive analysis of his views is necessary to substantiate such a contention, for it cannot be concluded that the influence of the Prime Minister is always decisive. Although John Diefenbaker, for example, tended to conduct foreign policy almost exclusively on the basis of his own views at the expense of his Foreign Minister, Sidney Smith, Prime Minister St Laurent frequently accorded the Department of External Affairs, under Lester Pearson, virtually a free hand in the determination of policy.[93] As the new administration assumed office in April 1968, officials in Ottawa must have speculated among themselves which of these two approaches would prevail. What were the views of this new Prime Minister who had effected so spectacular and rapid a rise to power? What were the techniques by which he intended to govern? And, above all, how determined was he to obtain his own way?

Notes

[1] Mitchell Sharp, 'An Era of Change for Europe and NATO', *Statements and Speeches*. No. 69/25, December 8, 1969.

[2] *Globe and Mail*, September 19, 1968; *Monthly Report on Canadian External Relations*. Toronto: Canadian Institute of International Affairs (hereafter referred to as *Monthly Report*), July-August 1968, pp. 72-3.

[3] Mitchell Sharp, 'Special NATO Ministerial Meeting', *Statements and Speeches*. No. 68/21, December 3, 1968.

[4] Canada, House of Commons, *Debates* (hereafter referred to as *Debates*), November 18, 1968, p. 2832.

[5] Peyton V. Lyon, *Canada in World Affairs, 1961-1963*. Toronto: Oxford University Press, 1968, Vol. XII, p. 2.

[6] *Monthly Report*, November 1967, p. 135.

[7] Ottawa *Citizen*, January 2, 1971, p. 7.

[8] Garth Stevenson, 'For a Real Review'. *Current Comment*. Ottawa: School of International Affairs, Carleton University, 1970, p. 17.

[9] Much of this section is based on the excellent analysis of Canadian defence policy by Jon B. McLin, *Canada's Changing Defense Policy, 1957-1963: The Problems of a Middle Power in Alliance*. Toronto: Copp Clark, 1967.

[10] Quoted in McLin, *op. cit.*, p. 88.

[11] Paul Martin, 'Prospects for Peacekeeping', *Statements and Speeches*. No. 65/27, November 17, 1965.

[12] *Debates*, June 8, 1967, p. 1329.

[13] McLin, *op. cit.*, p. 202.

[14] *International Canada*. Toronto: Canadian Institute of International Affairs, June 1970, p. 143.

[15] See Bruce C. Doern, 'Recent Changes in the Philosophy of Policy-making in Canada', *Canadian Journal of Political Science*, Vol. IV, No. 2, June 1971, p. 247.

[16] 'Trudeau says no more goodies for Canada', Saskatoon *Star-Phoenix*, April 25, 1969.

[17] John Gellner, 'What our new force would cost', *Globe and Mail*, April 12, 1969.

[18] James Eayrs, 'Dilettante in Power', *Saturday Night*, April 1971, p. 13.

[19] Lester B. Pearson, *Words and Occasions*. Toronto: University of Toronto Press, 1970, p. 204.

[20] Lester B. Pearson, 'An Era of Change for the Commonwealth and NATO', *Statements and Speeches*. No. 67/40, November 27, 1967, p. 3.

[21] Lester B. Pearson, 'Canada, the United States and Viet Nam', *Statements and Speeches*. No. 67/8, March 10, 1967, p. 4.

[22] *Debates*, March 12, 1968, p. 7535.

[23] *Monthly Report*, April 1968, p. 47.

[24] Quoted in *Monthly Report*, July-August 1967, p. 96.

[25] See Peyton V. Lyon, 'The Trudeau Doctrine', *International Journal*, Winter 1970–1, p. 25.

[26] Paul Martin, 'Canada and NATO', *Statements and Speeches*. No. 67/9, March 15, 1967, p. 5.

[27] Peyton V. Lyon, 'A Review of the Review', *Journal of Canadian Studies,* May 1970.

[28] Denis Stairs, 'Publics and Policy-Makers', *International Journal*, Winter 1970–1, pp. 229–34.

[29] Stephen Clarkson, ed., *An Independent Foreign Policy for Canada?* Toronto: McClelland and Stewart, 1968.

[30] Harald von Riekhoff, 'NATO: To Stay or not to Stay?', in Clarkson, *op. cit.*, p. 169; see also Peyton V. Lyon, *NATO as a Diplomatic Instrument*. Toronto: The Atlantic Council of Canada, 1971.

[31] See, for example, Kenneth McNaught, 'From Colony to Satellite', in Clarkson, *op. cit.*, p. 179.

[32] John Holmes, *The Better Part of Valour*. Toronto: McClelland and Stewart, 1970, p. 134.

[33] McNaught, *op. cit*., p. 181; see also Jack Granatstein, 'All Things to all Men: Tri-service Unification', in Clarkson, *op. cit.*, p. 141.

[34] Thomas Hockin, 'Federalist Style in International Politics', in Clarkson, *op. cit*., p. 126; and Donald Gordon in J. L. Granatstein, *Canadian Foreign Policy since 1945: Middle Power or Satellite?* Toronto: Copp Clark, 1969, p. 158.

[35] Eayrs, *op. cit*., p. 12.

[36] John W. Holmes, 'After 25 Years', *International Journal*, Winter 1970-1, p. 2.

[37] From a speech by Escott Reid to the Liberal Party of Ontario (*Monthly Report*, March 1969, p. 71) Mr Reid expressed similar views in two articles in the *International Journal*: 'Canadian Foreign Policy, 1967-1977: A Second Golden Decade?' (Spring 1967); and 'Canada and the Struggle against World Poverty' (Winter 1969-70).

[38] In J. King Gordon, ed., *Canada's Role as a Middle Power: Papers Given at the Third Annual Banff Conference on World Development, August 1965*. Toronto: Canadian Institute of International Affairs, 1966.

[39] Clarkson, *op. cit*., p. x.

[40] Louis Sabourin, 'Biculturalism and Canadian Foreign Policy', in Gordon, *op. cit*., p. 181.

[41] Clarkson, *op. cit*., p. 259; Peyton V. Lyon, *International Journal*, Winter 1970-1, p. 23.

[42] Holmes, *op. cit*., p. 230.

[43] See Holmes, *op. cit*., pp. 237-8; and Ian Lumsden, 'The "Free World" of Canada and Latin America', in Clarkson, *op. cit*., pp. 208-10.

[44] See Franklyn Griffiths, 'Opening up the Policy Process', in Clarkson, *op. cit*., p. 110.

[45] Introduction to Lewis Hertzman, et al., *Alliances and Illusions: Canada and the NATO-NORAD Question*. Edmonton: Hurtig, 1969, p. xii.

[46] Clarkson, *op. cit*.. p. 266.

[47] Lester B. Pearson, 'Canada, the United States and Viet Nam', *Statements and Speeches*. No. 67/8, March 10, 1967, p. 2.

[48] Clarkson, *op. cit*., pp. 121, 123, 268.

[49] James Steele, 'Canada's Viet Nam Policy: The Diplomacy of Escalation', in Clarkson, *op. cit*., pp. 79-80.

[50] See, for example, Denis Stairs' case studies of Canada's role in Korea and Cuba, in Clarkson, *op. cit.*, pp. 57-68.

[51] John Warnock, quoted in Granatstein, *op. cit.*, pp. 142-5; and Charles Hanly, in Clarkson, *op. cit.*, p. 28.

[52] Quoted in Granatstein, *op. cit.*, p. 200.

[53] Quoted in McLin, *op. cit.*, p. 88.

[54] For one of the few thorough examinations of the connection between Canadian foreign policy and public opinion, see R. B. Byers, *Canadian Foreign Policy and Attentive Publics*, a study prepared for the Department of External Affairs (DL 1), December 1967, p. 30.

[55] Quoted in *Monthly Report*, December 1968, p. 143.

[56] Byers, *op. cit.*, p. 67.

[57] *Ibid.*, p. 30.

[58] *Ibid.*, p. 68.

[59] *Behind the Headlines*, August 1970, p. 8.

[60] Byers, *op. cit.*, p. 84.

[61] *Ibid.*, p. 85.

[62] Canada, Department of External Affairs, *Foreign Policy for Canadians*. Ottawa: Queen's Printer for Canada, 1970, p. 8.

[63] Testimony by G. S. Murray, Department of External Affairs, November 24, 1970, p. 9.

[64] House of Commons, *Minutes of the Standing Committee on External Affairs and National Defence*, No. 31, June 1971, p. 23.

[65] See, for example, James N. Rosenau, *Public Opinion and Foreign Policy*. New York: Random House, 1961, pp. 26, 35.

[66] John Saywell, ed., *Canadian Annual Review, 1968*. Toronto: University of Toronto Press, 1969, p. 219.

[67] Interview with Andrew Brewin.

[68] Interview with Lester B. Pearson.

[69] For a brief summary of the foreign-policy stances of Canada's major newspapers in 1969, see Saywell, *Canadian Annual Review, 1969*, pp. 206-43.

[70] See Byers, *op. cit.*, p. 14.

[71] Excerpts from the speech are quoted in Granatstein, *op. cit.*, pp. 194-7.

[72] *Monthly Report*, April 1968, p. 42.

[73] *Debates*, December 18, 1967, p. 5520.

[74] *Debates*, June 8, 1967, p. 1301; and June 22, 1967, p. 1850.

[75] *Debates*, June 22, 1967, p. 1837.

[76] The report is quoted in the *Monthly Report*, October 1969, pp. 277-9.

[77] *Monthly Report*, April 1968, p. 45.

[78] Robert L. Stanfield, 'Notes for a Lecture', National Defence College, Kingston, Ontario, June 14, 1971. (Text released by the Progressive Conservative Party's national office.)

[79] Byers, *op. cit.*, p. 15; *Debates*, December 18, 1967, p. 5521 (Brewin).

[80] *Debates*, May 11, 1967, p. 74 (Douglas); March 18, 1968, p. 7742 (Brewin).

[81] *Debates*, June 22, 1967, p. 1851 (Brewin).

[82] *Debates*, December 6, 1967, p. 5126 (Lewis); March 12, 1968, p. 7561 (Caouette); October 2, 1967, p. 2714 (MacInnis).

[83] The results of this survey were made public in a news release issued by the Liberal Party of Ontario, April 9, 1969.

[84] *International Canada*, November 1970, pp. 257-62.

[85] Quoted in *Globe and Mail*, January 28, 1969, p. 3.

[86] *Globe and Mail*, February 21, 1969, p. 3.

[87] Mitchell Sharp, 'NATO in Canadian Perspective', *Statements and Speeches*. No. 69/4, March 1, 1969.

[88] *Globe and Mail*, January 28, 1969.

[89] *Monthly Report*, February 1968, p. 19.

[90] See Albert Legault, *Le Devoir*, 25 novembre 1969, p. 6.

[91] *Monthly Report*, April 1968, p. 42.

[92] *Maclean's*, July 1971, p. 63.

[93] See Peter C. Newman, *Renegade in Power*. Toronto: McClelland and Stewart, 1963, p. 253; and James Eayrs, *The Art of the Possible: Government and Foreign Policy in Canada*. Toronto: University of Toronto Press, 1961, p. 26.

3

The Political Philosophy of Pierre Elliott Trudeau

The statements made by Mr Trudeau before he entered politics in 1965 are the first and most important source for an analysis of his political philosophy, for it can be assumed that his essays and speeches in private life were written by him and not by civil servants or others. There is a second major source in some post-1965 comments that bear his personal imprint, including impromptu remarks made in interviews and press conferences as well as some of his prepared statements. These sources concern his 'philosophical beliefs'—his general philosophy as well as his attitude to specific foreign-policy issues. Finally there are his 'instrumental beliefs'*—his view of government as a means of attaining his philosophically motivated goals—and his technique of governing. Since the Prime Minister has never described this technique explicitly, it has to be inferred from the performance of his government since 1968.

---

* This useful phrase has been taken directly from David S. McLellan's article, 'The "Operational Code" Approach to the Study of Political Leaders: Dean Acheson's Philosophical and Instrumental Beliefs', in the *Canadian Journal of Political Science*, Vol. IV, March 1971.

I. Trudeau's Philosophical Beliefs

1. HIS BASIC VIEWS

Central to Mr Trudeau's philosophy is the idea that the basis of political society is the individual human being, possessing 'inalienable rights, over and above capital, the nation, tradition, the Church, and even the State.'[1] This concern with the individual—derived from the liberalism of John Stuart Mill—constituted one of the basic themes of the Montreal journal *Cité Libre*, which Trudeau helped found and for which he wrote several articles in the 1950s and early 1960s. Deeply disturbed by the combination of Duplessis authoritarianism and Catholic clericalism that had long stifled individual liberty in Québec, Trudeau later wrote, in an excellent capsulization of his basic tenets, that

> the state must take great care not to infringe on the conscience of the individual. I believe that, in the last analysis, a human being in the privacy of his own mind has the exclusive authority to choose his own scale of values and to decide which forces will take precedence over others. A good constitution is one that does not prejudge any of these questions, but leaves citizens free to orient their human destinies as they see fit.[2]

Mr Trudeau's actions in political life—particularly as Justice Minister, when it was relatively easy to determine his personal influence—have generally been consistent with his rhetoric on behalf of the individual and human dignity. He introduced the 'Omnibus Bill', which liberalized the law on abortion and homosexuality; was largely responsible for the concept of a new Bill of Rights that would be basic to a new constitution and in which linguistic guarantees would be entrenched in law; and was instrumental in introducing legislation for the broadening of the grounds for divorce. This last initiative Mr Trudeau defended in Parliament on the grounds that 'we are not entitled to impose the concepts which belong to a sacred society upon a civil or profane society.'[3] The whole tenor of his Criminal Code amendments, noted the *Montreal Star*, 'reflects the civilized humanity which has, since the appointment of Mr Trudeau, characterized the government's overall attitude to the law.'[4]

The goals of government, Mr Trudeau once told a parliamentary dinner in Australia that was expecting him to talk about the Commonwealth or trade, should be to realize 'maximum human dignity, maximum human welfare, maximum environmental quality, and minimum violence in human relationships.'[5] He has frequently stated that the first task of government, and Canadians' main expectation, was the development of policies to improve the 'quality of life' of the country's citizens. An interesting innovation in the 1968 Speech from the Throne was the stress on the need for facilities 'for the repose of the mind and restoration of the spirit, for support and for physical relaxation'—concepts typical of Trudeau.[6] Columnist George Bain has noted that Mr Trudeau's domestic policies have emphasized the creation of general conditions in which the position of the individual citizen can be improved rather than direct relief through subsidy or welfare payments; the result is that the Department of Health and Welfare was only a minor source of innovation in the Trudeau government compared to such departments as the Secretary of State and Regional Economic Expansion.[7]

For someone whose belief in the rights of the individual is so ardent that he once spent two hours in a Montreal jail for refusing to identify himself to a policeman who stopped him in front of his own home,[8] Mr Trudeau's decision to suspend basic individual liberties with the imposition of the War Measures Act in 1970 could not have been an easy one. It led, predictably, to charges by James Eayrs and others that Trudeau had reneged on his earlier beliefs and had brought about 'the collapse of liberalism in Canada'.[9] As Trudeau later noted, however, such action was not necessarily incompatible with the basic tenets of traditional liberalism. The role of the state, he told the Liberal Party policy conference,

> is limited to guaranteeing the fundamental rights of the individual, and placing no obstacle in the path of free competition between schools of thought. The state is nonetheless obligated to guarantee these fundamental rights of the person. The performance of this service justifies compulsion in specific circumstances.[10]

Whether or not the 'specific circumstances' of the October kidnapping crisis did in fact warrant such harsh measures is a question that is still being debated in Canada. They indicated to some that the Prime Minister was hypocritical and anti-liberal, though the majority of Canadians appear to have agreed with Mr Trudeau that the 'October crisis' was a serious challenge that required a strong response. In reply to critics such as Denis Smith of Trent University, who charged that the Prime Minister callously sacrificed the life of Pierre Laporte,[11] Mr Trudeau could well reply that in this 'specific circumstance' the interests of the nation had to receive first priority. Whatever the pros and cons of the imposition of the War Measures Act, it is surely an exaggeration to say that with this one deed the Prime Minister demonstrated a contempt of liberalism. Such a charge may be good polemics, and it may well be true that Mr Trudeau's deeds on behalf of the individual have not matched his earlier rhetoric, but it still ignores the many real reforms that he has been responsible for during his relatively short period in public life.

Another theme that emerges from an examination of Mr Trudeau's thought is his abhorrence of nationalism. 'My position in the Soviet Union or in Canada', he told reporters questioning him on his attitude to the persecution of Ukrainians by the Soviet government, 'is that anyone who breaks the law in order to assert his nationalism doesn't get much sympathy from me.'[12] Mr Trudeau's most articulate attack on nationalism is his 1964 article entitled 'Federalism, Nationalism, and Reason', in which he wrote:

> Nationalism, as an emotional stimulus directed at an entire community, can indeed let loose unforeseen powers. History is full of this, called variously chauvinism, racism, jingoism, and all manner of crusades, where right reasoning and thought are reduced to rudimentary proportions.[13]

It is not sufficient, however, to call Trudeau an anti-nationalist—he is one, but with important qualifications. His writings suggest that he objects not to the sovereign state, but rather to the use of emotionalism to provide the cohesive force that is required to hold a country together. It is this fear of emotionalism, not a dislike of states *per se*, that is emphasized in the above quotation. For Mr Trudeau, cohesion can be guaranteed in the last resort only by reason—an awareness by a people that their interests can best be served within their own country. In a statement that summarizes well his concept of functionalism and rationality, he says there is some hope that

> in advanced societies, the glue of nationalism will become as obsolete as the divine right of kings; the title of the state to govern and the extent of its authority will be conditional upon rational justification; a people's consensus based on reason will supply the cohesive force that societies require; and politics both within and without the state will follow a much more functional approach to the problems of government.[14]

Much of the confusion over Mr Trudeau's attitude towards nationalism arises from his unusual conception of the state and his somewhat careless mixing of terms. At times he uses 'nation', 'nation-state', and 'national state' almost interchangeably, to the confusion of his interpreters. A careful reading of his major essays, however, shows that he is very much aware of the differences in the ideas he discusses. The *nation-state*, a legal or juridical concept, serves the interests of all its inhabitants regardless of their ethnic origin.[15] This is what Trudeau usually means when he refers to the multi-national state, the territorial state, or simply the state;[16] he believes that this entity has a very positive role, provided it is held together by a consensus based on reason. The source of Trudeau's displeasure is the sociological concept of the *nation*: a collection of persons with a common ethnic origin. It gives rise to the *nationalist state*, which Trudeau describes as 'a nation-state with an ethnic flavour added'—one composed primarily of a particular ethnic group and whose government sees its basic function as the promotion of the interests of that group.[17] Trudeau usually thinks of *nationalism* as an ideology based on ethnic homogeneity: this concept offends his philosophy of liberalism, which is based on the rights of all citizens regardless of their ethnic origin.

Trudeau detests the 'nationalist state' (which unfortunately he has referred to as both a 'nation' and a 'nation-state'). His passionate opposition to this concept dominated his writings throughout the

1950s and early 1960s. In his 1962 article, 'La nouvelle trahison des clercs' ('The new treason of the intellectuals'), Trudeau delivered a stinging attack on 'nation-states' that contributed greatly to his reputation as an 'anti-nationalist'. The tiny portion of history marked by the emergence of the nation-states, he wrote, 'is also the scene of the most devastating wars, the worst atrocities, and the most degrading collective hatred the world has ever seen.' Then he added: 'There will be no end to wars between nations until . . . the nation ceases to be the basis of the state.'[18] What he means, in the terminology used above, is that wars between nation-states will end only when they are no longer nationalist states, each dominated by a single ethnic group. That it is the 'nationalist state' and not the 'nation-state' to which Trudeau objects emerges clearly in the same article:

> To insist that a particular nationality [i.e. nation in the ethnic sense] must have complete sovereign power is to pursue a self-destructive end. Because every national minority will find, at the very moment of liberation, a new minority within its bosom which in turn must be allowed the right to demand its freedom. And on and on would stretch the train of revolutions, until the last-born of nation states [i.e. nationalist states] turned to violence to put an end to the very principle that gave it birth. That is why the principle of nationality has brought to the world two centuries of war and not one single final solution.

Pursuing the same theme, Trudeau wrote in a 1965 article, 'Québec and the Constitutional Problem', that no state should see as its primary aim the promotion and glorification of a 'national fact', for any state that 'defined its function essentially in terms of ethnic attributes would inevitably become chauvinistic and intolerant.' A truly democratic government, he wrote, 'cannot be "nationalist", because it must pursue the good of all its citizens, without prejudice to the ethnic origin.'[19]

Trudeau is therefore an 'anti-nationalist' with respect to the 'nationalist state', but he could be called a 'nationalist' if one accepts his juridical conception of a 'nation-state', for he admires the latter as much as he abhors the former. To him the task facing countries such as

Canada is to create a true nation-state—a country based not on a dominant ethnic group but rather on polyethnic pluralism. We must separate once and for all, he has written, 'the concepts of state and nation, and make Canada a truly pluralistic and polyethnic society.'[20] The creation of such a multi-national state would, first of all, be a desirable thing in itself. Trudeau frequently quotes Lord Acton's comment that 'The co-existence of several nations under the same State is a test, as well as the best security of its freedom. It is also one of the chief instruments of civilization . . . [for] the combination of different nations in one State is as necessary a condition of civilized life as the combination of men in society.[21] This theme of unity in diversity recurs throughout Mr Trudeau's speeches and writings. During his 1971 tour of the U.S.S.R. he referred frequently to the multiplicity of races and cultures of which both countries were composed, emphasizing that 'We in Canada and you in the Soviet Union benefit from this enriched process and look upon the world from an understanding point of view.'[22]

Furthermore, to Mr Trudeau only the nation-state can satisfy all the economic, social, and cultural desires of its citizens. If Québec, he writes, were part of a Canadian federation grouping two linguistic communities, 'French Canadians would be supported by a country of more than eighteen million inhabitants [in 1965], with the second or third highest standard of living in the world, and with a degree of industrial maturity that promises to give it the most brilliant of futures.'[23] Mr Trudeau sees the nation-state not only as an instrument for promoting the well-being of its citizens, but also as a stabilizing element that lessens the danger of war on both the local and international scene:

> It would seem [he wrote in 1962] of considerable urgency for world peace and the success of the new [former colonial] states that the form of good government known as democratic federalism should be perfected and promoted, in the hope of solving to some extent the world-wide problems of ethnic pluralism. To this end . . . Canada could be called upon to serve as mentor,

provided she has sense enough to conceive her own future on a grand scale.[24]

He believes that the most important task facing Canada is the establishment of a solid federalism based on ethnic pluralism, for this is the best way in which Canada can solve its own problems, and also one of the most important contributions the country can make to the peace of the world.

'It is Trudeau's contention', Gad Horowitz has written, 'that the peace of the world is threatened primarily by nationalism. The necessary counterweights are internationalism and polyethnic federalism.'[25] This is a good example of how Mr Trudeau's ideas on nationalism have been frequently misinterpreted. For an anti-nationalist like Lester Pearson, internationalism is indeed a nostrum for the ills of the world because in Mr Pearson's mind the sovereign state itself is an anachronism. 'In any rational analysis,' he said in one of his Reith Lectures, 'we are surely entitled to say that sovereign power, exercised through the nation state [i.e. sovereign state], which comes into being to protect its citizens against insecurity and war, has failed in this century to give them that protection. The rationale for change has been established.'[26] This, it must be emphasized, is not Mr Trudeau's opinion. Far from deploring the existence of sovereign states, he sees them as a desirable and beneficial force in the modern world—but only if they are established on certain principles. His writings repeatedly express the idea that a state based on reason and designed to serve the fundamental interests of all its citizens is one of man's best creations; the difficulty lies in its attainment. In the world of tomorrow, he has written, the state will need 'political instruments which are sharper, stronger, and more finely controlled than anything based on mere emotionalism' if it is to transform the will of its members into a lasting consensus, which can be said to exist only when 'no group within the nation feels that its vital interests and particular characteristics could be better preserved by withdrawing from the nation than by remaining within.'[27] Properly conceived, such a nation-state can serve as the medium through which its citizens' basic aspirations are realized. Mr Trudeau's liberal philosophy constantly reminds us that men do not exist for states; 'states are created to make it easier for men to attain some of their common objectives.'[28] The nation-state, in short, has a very positive role in Mr Trudeau's thinking, for only within a given territorial area can a government promote the economic, social, and cultural ends that he sees to be desirable.

The question that arises at this point is: Why does Trudeau consider Canada to be a desirable nation-state? If he were truly an anti-nationalist in all respects, he would logically look beyond Canada and favour the creation of a larger federalist state of which Canada would be only one part. However, it is shown below that Mr Trudeau has never advocated the kind of internationalism, based on opposition to national sovereignty, that was the trademark of Lester Pearson. On the contrary, the continued existence of the Canadian nation-state is central to his whole political thought. In the first place a strong and united Canada must be maintained because it is the only available territorial area in which Trudeau's dreams of a society based on cultural dualism and ethnic pluralism can be attained. If Canada became part of the United States in a new federal state, the American 'melting pot' would almost certainly destroy the Canadian traits to which Trudeau attaches the greatest importance. 'If I don't think we can create some form of a bilingual country,' he announced bluntly in 1969, 'I am no longer interested in working in Ottawa. . . . What attaches me to this country is the belief that the French language can have certain rights.'[29] The Prime Minister also realizes that it is easier to shape the policies of relatively small countries along desirable lines than it is to alter those of larger ones. 'When a big society like the United States of America has moved in a direction', he has said, 'it takes a lot of energy to turn it around. How many miles does it take the *Queen Elizabeth* to turn around? Ten miles. It is true for the United States; it is less true for Canada.'[30]

Trudeau's conception of nationalism helps to explain his views on *sovereignty*. Just as casual observers have branded the Prime Minister an unqualified anti-nationalist, so have they described him as unalterably opposed to any manifestation of sovereignty. In April 1970, for example, he emphasized that the government's Arctic Water Pollution Prevention Bill was not an assertion of Canadian sovereignty over the waters within one hundred miles of Canada's shores; such a declaration, he noted, would satisfy national pride by proving we were masters in our own house, but would result in an immense economic loss to the country because it would deny passage to shipping that was of great importance to Canada.[31] Even more explicit was his 1964 article, 'Federalism, Nationalism, and Reason', in which he wrote:

> In the world of today, when whole groups of so-called sovereign states are experimenting with rational forms of integration, the exercise of sovereignty will not only be divided within federal states; it will have to be further divided between the states and the communities of states. If this tendency is accentuated the very idea of national sovereignty will recede and, with it, the need for an emotional justification such as nationalism.[32]

A closer examination of Trudeau's writings shows that his attacks on sovereignty are based on two main considerations. The first is his opposition to the idea that a national group must necessarily possess its own sovereign state. 'To insist', he writes, 'that a particular nationality must have complete sovereign power is to pursue a self-destructive end.' It is not the concept of 'nation' [i.e. an ethnic group] that is retrograde, but rather 'it is the idea that the nation must necessarily be sovereign.'[33] By far the majority of Trudeau's attacks on sovereignty centre on this theme, for much of his effort in the 1950s and early 1960s was devoted to attacks on the claims by Québec separatists that, with complete sovereignty, the Québec national state would progress and flourish. It is perhaps inevitable that Mr Trudeau tends to be instinctively hostile to the concept of sovereignty, since opposition to the sovereignty of Québec has dominated his thinking and efforts.

Mr Trudeau's criticism of the sovereignty of pluralistic nation-states has been, by comparison, both moderate and infrequent. It appears to be inspired by his fear that a country's preoccupation with sovereignty will lead to an increase of the irrational and extreme kind of nationalism that leads to inter-state rivalry and conflict. 'There will be no end to wars between nations', he writes, until states 'give up that obsession whose very essence makes them exclusive and intolerant: sovereignty.'[34] This in itself is not a bad thing; it becomes undesirable only when it is emphasized so greatly that it gives rise to emotional and nationalistic justifications for the existence of the state.

Although Mr Trudeau has described integration, particularly that of an economic nature, as the trend of the future,[35] he seems convinced that the sovereign state will continue to be the rule rather than the exception—at least for the time being—and that a moderate use of sovereignty is in the interests of most countries. He considers sovereignty as a means rather than an end, something to be applied judiciously and with moderation in cases where it can contribute towards the attainment of human objectives. In cases where it is not a useful device—in the waters of the Arctic archipelago, for example—it should be abandoned in favour of approaches more suited to the particular circumstances.

From his extensive readings of political philosophy, Mr Trudeau is well aware of Jean Bodin's concept of internal sovereignty—the power and authority of the government over a state's citizens. For Trudeau the true meaning of federalism is that 'sovereignty is really divided in its exercise between two levels of government'. When he opposed Québec's attempts to increase its international status in 1968, it was on the grounds that if a province were permitted to conduct its own foreign policy, 'an essential part of Canada's sovereignty would be withered away'.[36] Since a strong federal system is of supreme importance to Mr Trudeau, he regards the protection of the Canadian government's constitutional authority as one of the country's fundamental national goals.

Trudeau also refers to sovereignty in connection with another of his basic aims: the attainment of national unity and the fostering of a distinct Canadian identity. For him sovereignty is not a device to be used by an ethnic group seeking independence, but rather 'a legal concept meant to unite people of heterogeneous origins.'[37] He rejects complete economic integration with the United States on the grounds that it would have a detrimental effect on Canada's national identity. 'You realize', he said in 1968, 'that each country wants to keep its identity—or its sovereignty, to speak in legal terms— . . .to select those areas which are important for our independence.'[38] Like Canadian nationalism, Canadian sovereignty, both political and economic, cannot be sacrificed completely, for then the cultural diversity for which Trudeau has fought so ardently would be in danger of disappearing from the Canadian scene.

In an interview with the French daily, *Le Monde*, in 1970, Prime Minister Trudeau associated the concept of sovereignty with a country's freedom of action. American economic power and technological advances raised problems for Canada, he said, not in the strictly legal sense of sovereignty, but in terms of its 'liberté totale d'agir dans le monde suivant les priorités déterminées à l'intérieur du pays.'* Although aware of the difference between sovereignty and independence, Mr Trudeau tends to associate the two because in many cases a judicious use by Canada of the former is a means of attaining the latter.

2. TRUDEAU'S VIEW OF THE WORLD: THE ROLE OF THE UNITED STATES, THE SOVIET UNION, AND CANADA

Although Mr Trudeau has said little concerning Canada's political relations with the United States, his comments on Canadian-American commercial relations have been numerous. No one familiar with his writings and speeches could consider him an economic nationalist. Throughout his *Cité Libre* career, Trudeau stated that the world-wide trend towards economic integration should be encouraged, although not necessarily brought to completion, by free-trade policies that would improve the economic well-being of Canadians. He warned Québecois of the dangers of economic chauvinism, noting that 'Great industries cannot promote maximum efficiency by ethnocentric policies, any more than by nepotism', and went on to add that these objections were as valid for English Canadians as they were for his French compatriots.[39] Nor did his basic thesis seem to change upon accession to political power, despite a growing mood of economic nationalism throughout much of the country. There is a danger in Canada's becoming too possessive of its natural resources, he told a

* 'Complete freedom to act in the world according to priorities determined within the country.'

student audience in Ottawa shortly after President Nixon had given the State Department permission to continue negotiations with Canada on the creation of a continental resources policy. 'If we don't use them now', commented the Prime Minister, 'we won't be able to. . . . If we're not going to use them, why not sell them for good hard cash?'[40]

Mr Trudeau has consistently advocated that Canadians should be both moderate and selective in their approach to economic nationalism. Although he is on record as deploring the extra-territorial problems arising from the fact that Canada is '[le pays] le plus endetté vis-à-vis l'étranger',*[41] his cool attitude to the 1968 Watkins Report stemmed from his equally strong conviction that Canada should concentrate on developing new industries for the future rather than buying back existing ones. He has said more than once that to insist on Canadian control of all of the country's economy would result in an impoverishment of the nation. Instead, savings should be directed towards those specific areas 'which are areas of future potential greatness for Canada.'[42] An example of these strategic sectors is the uranium industry. Explaining his government's decision to block the sale of Denison Mines' stock to American investors, the Prime Minister said that 'Canada should have more than export control over uranium reserves in view of the possibly important part this energy resource will play in determining a future integrated resources pact between Canada and the United States.'[43] Only when foreign investment infringes on the basic interests and freedom of the Canadian 'nation-state' does the Prime Minister act as an economic nationalist.

In general Mr Trudeau views the United States as Canada's best friend and ally—certainly not as an imperialistic power against whom Canada must defend itself. He welcomes the good things of American society, saying that the art of living with the United States consists not in trying to remain distinct from the Americans in all things but in choosing 'those areas in which we think our values are superior.'[44] Cultural dualism and ethnic pluralism are undoubtedly two of those areas, and it is largely for this reason that Mr Trudeau sees a need to

* 'The country with the greatest foreign debt.'

defend the sovereignty of the Canadian nation-state. His 1971 visit to the Soviet Union, which was highlighted by the signing of a protocol that offered the prospect of increased contacts between the two countries, showed clearly his desire to create for Canada a foreign policy that was definitely distinct from, and 'roaming more freely' than, that of the United States. But he insisted that it was not inspired in the least by sentiments of anti-Americanism.[45] As the Prime Minister explained to reporters during the return flight to Ottawa:

> I made the points often enough and repeated that the Americans are not only our neighbours and ally but they are even our friends. And I think this was established quite clearly at the outset from our part that we weren't trying to weaken the [western] alliance in any sense, and from their side that they weren't trying to drive a wedge.[46]

As for Mr Trudeau's attitude to the Soviet Union and the Cold War, it is clear from his statements both before and after 1965 that he is doubtful whether the Soviet Union possesses any aggressive intentions against the West. Commenting on a chapter in a book by Maurice Lamontagne that had taken a 'hard-line' approach to the U.S.S.R., Trudeau condemned it as 'nothing but a collection of clichés on neutralism, the cold war, and communism; like most official arguments, these are rather unsatisfactory.'[47] In 1968 the Prime Minister observed that since the outbreak of the Cold War in the late 1940s, Communist China had developed into a great and imperial power. It is obvious, he said, that in the future Russia's greatest fear will be China and not the United States. 'And if you can develop this line of thinking,' he continued, 'then you cease to be as afraid of Russia in Europe as we are now.'[48]

The Prime Minister's failure to become particularly concerned over the Soviet-led invasion of Czechoslovakia in 1968 indicates that his perception of the U.S.S.R. as a country that did not threaten the West, at least in Europe, had become well established by that time. Although he cut short a holiday in Spain when the first reports of the invasion were received, he played down an official American State

Department announcement that any military intervention in West Germany by Russia would lead to an immediate allied response from NATO. The situation, he suggested, was not that serious. At a time when the other members of NATO were talking of the need to strengthen the alliance to deter further Soviet 'aggression', Mr Trudeau told the House that 'We are not led to the immediate reaction, after the Czechoslovakian events, to conclude that we should necessarily escalate in NATO.'[49] Barely a week after the invasion, the Prime Minister reiterated his view that détente was possible if all parties displayed a desire for it. 'We are hoping', he said, 'that Europe—and the world—will evolve beyond this political partition of spheres of influence, and our foreign-policy review is an attempt to go beyond that.'[50]

During his visit to the Soviet Union in 1971 the Prime Minister was visibly impressed by many changes that had taken place in the country since his first trip in 1952. He told reporters that the people were better dressed, that consumer goods seemed more readily available, and that the absence of pollution was particularly remarkable in a city the size of Moscow.[51] Clearly he did not share the hard-line view that the Russian people were suffering under an uncaring government. Mr Trudeau's speech at a luncheon given by the Soviet government seemed an apt summary of the sympathetic attitude he had consistently displayed towards the U.S.S.R.;

> I do not wish to leave the impression that Canada and the Soviet Union have no differences. . . . They relate to deep-seated concerns springing from historic, geographic, ideological, economic, social and military factors. Nevertheless, as governments, many of our objectives are similar. We seek for our peoples a world without war, a world in which governments are at the service of man—to raise the standard of living, to eliminate disease and want, to attempt to make life a happier experience.[52]

The Prime Minister told newsmen that during his Soviet visit he was frequently obliged to remind his hosts that Canada was a modest power and did not want the protocol to be compared to the one signed between the Soviet Union and France. 'I'm a bit surprised', he said, 'at the tone in which they are willing to deal with us as a great power. . . . To compare it to the protocol signed with France, for instance. . . . This is the kind of thing they wanted to see in our protocol, and I kept saying no, you know, we're a modest power; we're not going to try and pretend we're dealing with you as being a major power.'[53]

Mr Trudeau thus appears to have a well-defined image of Canada's appropriate position and role in the world. In the first place, he contends that Canada's relative strength has declined since the 1950s, but that the country's perception of its role has not altered to meet these new conditions. As early as April 1968 he was discussing Canada's international position in the following terms:

> We begin by reminding ourselves that we're perhaps more the largest of the small powers than the smallest of the large powers. And this is a complete change, I think, from our mentality of 20 years ago . . . [for] now we have to realize that Europe has developed itself; it is a great continent, it's strong, its currency is strong. And Canada, on the other hand, has fallen onto a more modest role, and it should reassess its foreign policy rather than trying to peace-keep everywhere, which, in a sense, means that we're trying to determine international situations.[54]

One of the comments Mr Trudeau made in Moscow revealed that this disinclination to talk in terms of an important role for Canada may be based to some degree on a misconception on his part of what is meant by a broker or mediatory role.[55] As the word 'broker' is commonly used, he said, it refers to Canada's 'playing a go-between between great powers', involving little more than 'carrying messages from one party to another.' He saw the real significance of Section 2 of the protocol to be the agreement that 'if areas of tensions arise, then both parties will consult and both parties will take whatever means they can to reduce these tensions', which in many cases 'would mean talking to our respective friends.' It is this latter approach, involving the taking by Canada of constructive initiatives, rather than the more passive former course, that most advocates of traditional Canadian foreign policy have seen as Canada's role.[56] Mr Trudeau, however, appears not to have realized this, and seems to associate previous Canadian policy with mere rhetoric, which he abhors, rather than with constructive action, which he applauds.

Canada's proper role, in short, is one that is both modest and effective. Just as Mr Trudeau believes that Canadian industry must concentrate on areas in which it has 'competitive strength', so he feels that Canada should specialize internationally. 'We should not think that we are a great power', he emphasizes. 'We should channel our efforts into that which we do best.'[57] Canada should concentrate on creating a just society at home so that it can reflect this image in its international activity. 'We shouldn't be trying to run the world,' Mr Trudeau says. 'We should be trying to make our own country a good place.'[58] Then, if Canada has some proposals for the solution of world problems, it can make them 'modestly' and can occasionally experiment with good ideas, which countries such as the United States are unable to do because of their position of power.[59] A strong economy and a just society, which should be Canada's first priorities, will provide the basis for Canada's distinctive contribution on the international scene.

3. TRUDEAU'S PERCEPTIONS OF ISSUES

Consistent with Trudeau's lack of hostility towards the Soviet Union is his often-expressed belief that the West should be afraid not of Communism but of the fact that people in the world are starving to death. The importance of foreign aid and the need for an improvement in Canada's foreign-aid program are recurring themes in Mr Trudeau's speeches. We must recognize, he said in May 1968, that in the long run the overwhelming threat to Canada will not be foreign investment, foreign ideology, or even nuclear war. 'It will come instead from the two-thirds of the peoples of the world who are steadily falling farther and farther behind in their search for a decent standard of living.'[60] After the Commonwealth Conference in Singapore in 1971, the Prime Minister told the House that Canada had to be more active in the Third World, not because it had some 'vague international role', but because it is in our national interest that there not be a general racial war in Africa.[61] The failure of Mr Trudeau's government to commit one per cent of the country's GNP to foreign aid, as recommended by both the United Nations and the Pearson Commission, is not an indication of the Prime Minister's declining interest in foreign aid but rather the result of the severe economic problems existing in Canada at the beginning of his administration and his desire not to promise more than can be delivered. In 1968 Mr Trudeau said that Canada's objective was to meet the one-per-cent goal as early as possible in the 1970s, a statement reaffirmed by Mr Sharp two years later.[62] At the same time, however, Canada's contribution towards international development was increasing as rapidly as the government felt internal economic conditions would permit. In 1969, when the budgets of most government departments were frozen in an economy move, the Canadian International Development Agency was one of the very few government organizations allowed to increase its spending in the next fiscal year.

With his belief that foreign aid was a more important concern than defending the West against Communism, Mr Trudeau understandably tended to downplay the importance of both NATO and Canada's contribution to it. One of the Prime Minister's major criticisms of NATO was that it was the main focus of, and had dominated, Canadian foreign policy in the post-war period. For twenty years or so, he told a BBC interviewer in the fall of 1968, 'Canada's foreign policy was largely its policy in NATO, through NATO, and perhaps a little bit through the United Nations and peacekeeping.'[63] Another major complaint, more frequently expressed, was that NATO was primarily a military organization at a time when there was no significant military threat to the West from the Soviet Union. Agreeing that when NATO was established a strong military presence was required to protect the prostrate countries of Western Europe from the Soviet Union, Mr Trudeau argued that conditions had now changed and that 'there must be a shift in emphasis from the military to cultural, political, and economic relations with Europe.'[64] NATO, the Prime Minister implied, was only a peacekeeping operation, not a peace-restoring one, and Canada should decrease its military role in Europe in order to improve its relations with the countries of both Western and Eastern Europe.

Despite speculation that Mr Trudeau personally favoured neutralism and a complete Canadian withdrawal from NATO, his statements both during and after the 1968 election campaign indicate that it was only Canada's military role in Europe that he seriously questioned. In July 1968 the Prime Minister stood by what was said during the campaign in May and June. 'We weren't contemplating pulling out of NATO politically or economically or socially,' but our 'military involvement in it was still under consideration.'[65] In interviews with the *New York Times* and *Le Monde*, the Prime Minister explained that he attributed to NATO an important political role, for it constituted a forum where Canada could discuss a variety of international matters with countries other than the United States. 'Face à ce géant, les Etats-Unis,' Mr Trudeau explained, 'nous sentons le besoin d'avoir des amis qui ont à peu près la même optique occidentale, des amis autres que les Etats-Unis, et c'est pourquoi nous donnons une haute priorité à nos relations avec l'Europe.'*[66]

Having apparently decided that 'the principle of collective security is an important one' for Canada, Mr Trudeau considered which alliances were most 'natural' to Canada.[67] This was largely a rhetorical question, for the Prime Minister clearly believed that it was NORAD and not NATO towards which Canada should devote its attention militarily. As early as March 1968 he told a rally in Moncton that Canada should withdraw its forces from Europe and play its role in the defence of the Western world in North America. Two months later, in Winnipeg, he explained why Canada should concentrate on defending the North American continent in collaboration with the United States:

> Canada's air space is between the United States and its potential enemies, China and the U.S.S.R. Because of that, I think we must play an active role in the defence of this continent, because that is the way in which we can assure that the defence of

* 'Face to face with this giant, the United States, we feel the need to have friends who have roughly the same western outlook, friends other than the United States, and that is why we give high priority to our relations with Europe.'

> Canada is, at least jointly, the concern of Canada and the United States. In other words, it is of some importance to us that the United States, when it sets up its defences against ICBMs or other missiles or even indeed nuclear armed bombers, it is of concern to us that the oncoming missiles be exploded, not over our cities, but as far away as possible to the north or up in the air.[68]

Mr Trudeau seemed to be saying that only by co-operating actively with the United States in the defence of North America could Canada gain enough influence to persuade Washington to organize its defences in such a way that, in the event of war, Canada would suffer as little as possible. For all his skepticism of the Cold War, Mr Trudeau still believed that nuclear war was a possibility, however remote, and that Canada was obliged to take steps to protect itself. Where he differed from Lester Pearson was in his belief that if war broke out it would not necessarily begin in Europe. 'Our military commitments', he told an Edmonton audience in June 1968, 'should, perhaps, be a little bit more North American, not for reasons of isolationism, but because this is where the next world war will take place . . . and we should have a little bit of something to say about what will happen here and the way in which we shall defend ourselves.'[69]

Only once did Mr Trudeau publicly question the wisdom of emphasizing defence of the North American continent in preference to Europe. In an exchange with students at the University of Manitoba in December 1968, he noted that a defence policy that concentrated on NORAD rather than NATO would be 'either much less efficient or much more expensive', since in NATO Canada was defending itself with 'a very small engagement over there'.[70] That the Prime Minister was speaking instinctively rather than on the basis of knowledge became apparent when he said that 'If we get into NORAD we get into ABM and anti-bomber defence and this is vastly more expensive'; nowhere did Mr Trudeau explain how emphasis on NORAD would involve Canada in the American Anti-Ballistic Missile program, since NORAD is an anti-bomber defence system only. The Prime Minister might have believed at the time he made this statement that concentration on continental defence would prove expensive for Canada, for if he did not know that the ABM program was not part of NORAD, he might have thought that Canada's anti-bomber capacity would need modernizing within a few years. In view of his government's 1969 statement of defence priorities, with their North American orientation, and the fact that this was the only occasion on which he expressed these views, it may be that the Prime Minister was indulging in his favourite past-time of attempting to stimulate public debate without really believing what he was saying. As he himself admitted, he did not have the answers to the questions he had raised.

Another factor in Mr Trudeau's belief that Canada's natural military role was in North America rather than in Europe was his concern that North American civilization was menaced more strongly by internal disorders than by external pressure. In a widely publicized question-and-answer session at Queen's University in November 1968, the Prime Minister said that he was 'less worried now by what might happen in Berlin than in Chicago or New York', for if riots and civil war broke out in the United States, 'there is no doubt that they would overflow the borders and link up with underprivileged Mexicans and Canadians.'[71] This was not the first time, George Bain reported, that Mr Trudeau had mentioned the danger of civil unrest in the United States in connection with Canadian defence policy. He had made very much the same point in an off-the-record dinner conversation with a number of correspondents at 24 Sussex Drive just a few nights earlier.[72] Mr Trudeau may also have expected that unrest within Canada, particularly in Québec, would provide an increasing threat to law and order. A series of terrorist bombings in Montreal in February 1969 led the Prime Minister to state that the government might have to be 'more severe' in the future.[73] Insiders reported that during much of 1969 the first priority of the Department of National Defence was 'aid to the civil authority'. As Canada's armed forces had relatively few troops available for large-scale 'peacekeeping' operations at home, it is highly probable that Mr Trudeau and his advisers desired a return of at least part of Canada's forces from Europe.[74] The government was also aware, long before it became public knowledge, of the impending voyage in 1969 of the American tanker *Manhattan* and realized the need for surveillance and control activities to protect Canada's jurisdiction in the Arctic.

Another international issue that concerned Mr Trudeau, even before his accession to power, was the danger caused by nuclear weapons. In 1961, responding to the resumption of nuclear testing by the United States and the Soviet Union, he penned a savage indictment of nuclear weapons and their effects that, by its very passion and eloquence, showed the extent to which he was appalled by the prospect of nuclear war:

> Massacres c'est trop peu dire. Tordus, calcinés, liquéfiés, volatilisés .... De toute une humanité, il ne restera que des traces d'ombres imprimées sur le béton des décombres, sur les pierres des champs, sur les falaises de la mer, comme autant de taches sur une mauvaise plaque photographique.*[75]

In 1963 Mr Trudeau delivered a blistering attack on Lester Pearson for his decision to accept American nuclear weapons, and in 1968 he told a press conference that he still objected to the 'proliferation' of nuclear arms on the grounds that the danger of nuclear war increased in direct proportion to the number of countries that had nuclear weapons on their soil.[76] Similarly, the Prime Minister viewed NATO's nuclear strike capability as dangerously provocative,[77] and something in which Canada should have no part (since the Soviets would be unable to distinguish between reconnaissance and strike flights).

Recognition of Communist China was another of the few foreign-policy issues on which Mr Trudeau wrote consistently and at length before entering federal politics. The failure of the West to attempt to improve relations with Communist China he viewed as doubly irrational—politically, he said, because we allow a question of prestige to prevent our recognizing the existence of the rulers of a quarter of the human race, and economically, since we hesitate to increase our trading

---

* 'Massacres is too weak a term. Twisted, charred, liquefied, vanished into thin air.... Of all humanity nothing will remain but traces of shadows stamped on the concrete débris, on the stones in the fields, on the cliffs of the ocean, as if they were so many stains on a bad photographic plate.'

relations with 'the most formidable reservoir of consumption and production that has ever existed.'[78] In his campaign for the leadership of the Liberal Party, Trudeau promised that his government would offer diplomatic recognition to Communist China on the understanding that Canada would continue to have relations with the government of Formosa. During the election campaign he tended to avoid direct references to Taiwan, saying that his goal was recognition of Mainland China 'on suitable terms'.[79] The issue of Taiwan seemed to be of secondary importance to the Prime Minister, although perhaps it had to be taken into consideration for political reasons. What mattered most to him was that Canada establish diplomatic relations with the Peking government.

The desire to establish closer relations with Communist China was only one aspect of Mr Trudeau's general belief that Canada should diversify its foreign relations and place greater emphasis on the countries of the Third World. It was during the election campaign of 1968 that the Prime Minister talked of making Canada a 'Pacific nation'. Historically, he said, most of Canada's immigration and overseas trade had travelled across the Atlantic. Canada could enlarge this incomplete perspective by taking advantage of its 'ringside seat on the Pacific' and, in matters of trade and transportation, 'face both ways at once'.[80] Similary he called for increased Canadian attention to Latin America. On the subject of Canadian membership in the Organization of American States, however, he told delegates to the Liberal leadership conference that Canada should enter the OAS only when the country had developed a policy towards Latin America that would permit it to operate independently of the United States when the need arose.[81] As this policy became more explicit, he intimated, Canadian contacts with the OAS should increase.

II. Trudeau's Instrumental Beliefs

1. HIS GENERAL PHILOSOPHY OF ACTION

There are three basic components of Trudeau's approach to decision-making, whether on the personal or governmental level. The first is his emphasis on realism as opposed to idealism. The first law of politics, he says, is to start from given facts, to forget 'historical might-have-beens' and 'impossible dreams' and to accentuate the feasible.[82] Just as in his personal life he says he does not try to apply 'overriding theories to all pròblems', so he told the Commonwealth Prime Ministers in 1969 that they were not philosophers committed unswervingly to the ideal but politicians whose art was that of the possible.[83] It was on the basis of this realism, which the Prime Minister often referred to as 'pragmatism', that he defended Canadian arms sales to the United States (since a ban on shipments would be a useless symbolic gesture), improved relations with the Soviet Union (although Canada may disagree with Soviet policies, the U.S.S.R. is a valuable trading partner), and the 1969 Commonwealth Prime Ministers' decision not to enforce the NIBMAR doctrine* (since the means to make it possible were not available).[84]

Mr Trudeau himself sums up his political theory in two words: 'create counterweights'.[85] In the Canadian context, multilateral alliances have often been seen as the way in which Canada can escape an uncomfortable bilateral relationship with the United States. During the debate on NORAD in 1958, for example, the Conservative government emphasized that this defence alliance with the U.S. was merely an extension of NATO, within which Canadians felt more comfortable. Mr Trudeau, however, appears to think of counterweights more in terms of trade and culture than of security. Asked by a Radio-Canada interviewer about the reason for Canada's increased contacts with the Soviet Union, Mr Trudeau replied that it was important for Canada to diversify its channels of communication because of the overpowering presence of the United States. 'Chacun sait', he continued, 'que les Canadiens se sentent passablement dominés par la présence américaine, non seulement sur le plan économique, mais sur le plan culturel, social, etc., et c'est important pour nous d'avoir d'autres

* The NIBMAR doctrine states that, for Rhodesia, there should be 'no independence before majority rule'.

interlocuteurs.'*[86] The fact that Mr Trudeau made no mention of military considerations suggests that his earlier comment to the English-language press that the danger to Canada from the U.S. was 'perhaps even [from the] military point of view' was a slip of the tongue, or at most a very minor consideration in his thinking.

It is part of Trudeau's disposition to be skeptical of traditional ideas and conventional wisdom. 'The only constant factor to be found in my thinking over the years', he explains, 'has been opposition to accepted opinions.'[87] In his early essays he chastised French Canadians for their lack of 'une philosophie positive de l'action'** and agreed with Thomas Jefferson that nothing should be unchangeable 'but the inherent and unalienable rights of man'.[88] As Peter Newman explains, Trudeau had always considered himself an 'agent of ferment', and in the Justice Department he saw an opportunity to put into practice the unconventional ideas he had developed during 'thirty years of action and reflection'. If the government was going to risk defeat, he said later in defence of his Criminal Code amendments, 'it should take the risk for being too progressive, not for failing to move.'[89] That his inclination was to change rather than maintain the status quo, or at least to subject previous policies to critical review until he was convinced of their validity, was apparent from his election statements and the way in which his government subsequently devoted itself to the issues that he had highlighted. During the 1968 campaign he said:

> Many areas of our national life are in a period of rapid evolution and will require new direction. As examples I could mention the need to reform parliament and the public administration, to revise the relations between the federal and provincial governments, to recognize and implement linguistic and other human rights, to reduce regional economic disparity, and to review our foreign policy in the light of changing international conditions.[90]

---

* 'Everyone knows that Canadians feel rather dominated by the American presence, not only economically but also culturally, socially, etc., and it is important for us to have other contacts.'

** 'A positive philosophy of action.'

2. TRUDEAU'S VIEW OF THE ROLE OF GOVERNMENT

Although a nineteenth-century liberal in his attitudes towards the rights of the individual, Trudeau believes it is the duty of governments to intervene vigorously in a wide variety of areas. Political parties, he emphasized in explaining his decision to enter political life in 1965, are not ends but means of attaining important national objectives.[91] 'The function of a state', he wrote, 'is to ensure the establishment and maintenance of a legal order that will safeguard the development of its citizens', whether in the economic, social, or cultural sphere.[92] He sees government intervention in the economy to be particularly necessary, in view of the fact that free enterprise has given rise to severe social problems. It was largely because the New Democratic Party placed more faith than the other parties in economic leadership ('dirigisme économique') and government supervision of investments ('planification des investissements') that he tended to support it in the early 1960s.[93]

It has already been shown that Mr Trudeau rejects a government based on nationalism, believing that only one imbued with rationalistic aspirations can hope to attain the goals that he sees as the *raison d'être* of a government. Such an approach involves, in the first place, a clear understanding and definition of the nation's objectives. On assuming office Mr Trudeau set a strict schedule for his government. The first three years would be spent analysing its goals and explaining them to the public, so that in the fourth year the changes necessary to attain them could be made on the basis of a carefully laid foundation. This strategy can be seen in Mr Trudeau's approach to constitutional change. Before decisions could be made concerning the division of powers between the federal and provincial governments, it was first necessary to see the general goals and values of Canadian society established in the form of a Bill of Rights.[94] In areas as diverse as welfare, housing, Indian policy, and foreign ownership of Canadian industry, task forces were formed and studies prepared to gather the basic data necessary for the determination of future goals. Nowhere did Mr Trudeau describe the general philosophy of his government so clearly as at the Liberal Party's Harrison Hot Springs conference in 1969, where he said:

> We are like the pilots of a supersonic airplane. By the time an airport comes into the pilot's field of vision, it is too late to begin the landing procedure. Such planes must be navigated by radar. A political party, in formulating policy, can act as society's radar. . . . As members of a political party we should be thinking not only of the type of goals we wish to achieve in our society, but of their relative importance, and of the best means of achieving them within a reasonable time. . . .[95]

If there was one concept that dominated the thinking of the Trudeau administration in its first year, it was the setting of priorities. When Mr Trudeau assumed office he became conscious of the extent to which Canada's financial resources, especially scarce as a result of the country's economic problems, had been committed by the actions of past governments. One of the most significant documents to cross his desk was a long-term projection of the costs of existing programs. It was clear that new programs could not be launched unless revenues were diverted from existing ones. The result was that, throughout the first three years of his administration, the Cabinet frequently spoke about making 'new money' available for programs of top priority by reducing expenditures on programs of less importance. This belief in the need to establish priorities if financial resources were to be used effectively explains many of Mr Trudeau's election comments. 'The future of the country might just escape us', he said in Regina, 'if we don't control change and stay a little ahead of it, if we don't decide wisely about our priorities.'[96] His most comprehensive explanation of the approach being followed by his government, however, was during the Throne Speech Debate in September 1968:

> One obvious limitation to government action is the available supply of resources. . . . That is why it is an essential and continuous responsibility of government to choose, to plan, and to set out priorities. . . . The balance between demands and resources can never be finally established, but in the present circumstances of competing demands and rapidly rising costs we must exercise the utmost restraint in introducing new programs which have

been replaced by more productive ones, and we must defer any which are not immediately essential.[97]

Because of its great emphasis on setting priorities, the Trudeau administration has paid far more attention to formal planning than did previous governments. It has been said that the Diefenbaker administration developed policies largely in response to the grievances of particular groups and regions, while under Prime Minister Pearson the government first adopted an impulsive 'sixty days of decision' and later tended to treat matters on an ad-hoc basis.[98] Mr Trudeau set out to reform the Canadian government's whole approach to decision-making. Formalized planning units in the Prime Minister's Office (PMO) and the Privy Council Office (PCO) were contemplated during the Pearson administration, but their establishment was postponed partly because of the need for limitations on government spending. Mr Pearson had realized that the increasing complexity and scope of governmental activity necessitated a more formal and co-ordinated approach to planning, but it was Prime Minister Trudeau, believing that such a reform was of fundamental importance and choosing to make spending cuts in other areas, who allowed the PMO and PCO to expand and to assume additional planning and co-ordinating duties. Similarly, the Cabinet Committee on Priorities and Planning was a creation of the Pearson government, but under Mr Trudeau it became far more important than it had been before.

In an attempt to improve his government's ability to plan its future actions, Prime Minister Trudeau surrounded himself with intelligent young men trained in the latest techniques of decision-making. Jim Davey, his program secretary, has been largely responsible for introducing flow charts and systems analysis into the process of policy formulation. Trudeau's chief adviser, Marc Lalonde, explained that the administration was trying to 'apply reason to broad social and economic problems' by bringing a technocratic approach to government. Lalonde likes to quote John Kenneth Galbraith's comment that 'Technology means the systematic application of scientific or other organized knowledge to practical tasks.'[99] Therefore, especially in the first two years of the Trudeau government, officials spoke frequently of the need to 'conceptualize policy-making in cybernetic terms' and to expand the Planning, Programming, and Budgeting System (PPBS). (Under this system government departments were required to establish specific objectives, defined in much greater detail than in the past, and to frame their budgetary proposals in terms of these objectives.) Whether such techniques have in fact improved the quality of policy is debatable, but they indicate that the Trudeau government attaches great importance to careful planning and the establishment of well-defined priorities. One Cabinet minister described the Trudeau administration as 'better organized to deal with its priorities' than any other government with which he was familiar, while another said it was more conscious of priorities, more analytical, and more aware of an overall strategy plan.

There is little doubt that for Mr Trudeau the most important priority, and the supreme task of his government, was national unity. One part of this problem was evidently to counter the separatist threat in Québec through policies designed to win the loyalty of the Québecois to the 'nation-state' of Canada rather than to the 'national state' of Québec. Also important was the problem of regional disparity, for in Trudeau's words, unless inequalities of opportunity were eliminated, 'the unity of the country will almost as surely be destroyed as it could be by the French-English confrontation.'[100] Trudeau and other members of the Cabinet have travelled extensively, particularly in Western Canada, in an attempt to assure Canadians outside Ontario and Québec that the government was equally concerned with their particular interests and problems.

Mr Trudeau views economic growth as one of the most important means of attaining his goal of national unity. 'An expanding economy and a fairer distribution of our national wealth', he explains, 'are fundamental to our concept of the Just Society', with the result that in its international activity Canada must search aggressively for new markets in order to expand the exports of this trade-dependent nation.[101] That economic growth is an important instrument rather than an end in itself emerges clearly from Mr Trudeau's 1965 article, 'Québec and the Constitutional Problem', in which he wrote:

> It would be a great oversimplification to adopt the attitude: social needs first, then economic. . . . In fact unless the economy is fundamentally sound, a strong, progressive social policy can be neither conceived nor applied. All social security measures, from family allowances to old age pensions, from free education to health insurance, must remain theoretical if the economic structure is incapable of bearing the cost.[102]

The result of this emphasis on domestic problems is that Mr Trudeau views foreign affairs primarily in terms of their relation to his most important national policies. During the 1968 debate on the Speech from the Throne he commented that 'One of the primary purposes of our foreign policy must be to ensure the political survival and independence of Canada.'[103] That this was undeniably Mr Trudeau's personal opinion became evident in the course of his remarkably candid discussion with reporters following his 1971 tour of the Soviet Union. Asked whether the trip had resulted primarily in direct benefits to Canada or whether it had acted as a catalyst for bringing about an improvement in the international situation, Trudeau replied with evident satisfaction that it had achieved more of the former than of the latter.[104] His government was concentrating on making Canada a better place and on fulfilling the aspirations of Canadians, he said, and this had 'some fall-out in the external field'. He saw foreign policy more in terms of the extent to which it 'helps our national policy' than as a means of improving the international environment in areas that would not be of immediate and direct importance to Canadians.

Although it might be argued that Mr Trudeau's view of Canada's national interests is broad and includes such matters as a peaceful international system, an examination of his speeches indicates that his view of both Canada's problems and its goals is much narrower in scope. Most of our national problems as Canadians, he reminded Liberal candidates in Toronto in 1968, were created not by 'the Americans, the Communists, the Fascists or by anyone else, but by us. . . .'[105] The 1968 Throne Speech reminded Canadians that it was time for them to start asking themselves about the kind of country they wanted to live in, and then proceeded to inform them that they wanted a land with a 'rising standard of living, equitably distributed among regions and individuals . . . a social security system which will underwrite the risks and hazards of modern life . . . [and] a society which has not lost sight of man's spiritual values, of his unquenchable thirst for beauty, for the pleasure of the mind and body. . . .'[106] If Canadians also wanted to contribute actively to the peace and security of the world, this was not the Prime Minister's conception of what Canada *should* be doing.

It was not long before comments began to circulate that the Prime Minister was either unknowledgeable in the field of foreign policy or unconcerned with it or both. 'In spite of long periods spent wandering around the world,' wrote columnist Leonard Beaton, 'he understands very little and does not know it'. Professor Peyton Lyon observed that 'Mr Trudeau seems never to have developed a serious interest in international affairs.'[107] Bruce Hutchison agreed that the Prime Minister was a 'confused man in foreign affairs' whose secret heart was engaged elsewhere.[108] There was some evidence to support their contention. In the book he co-authored on his travels in Communist China, Trudeau made no mention of China's foreign relations. The explanation of this omission, he said, was the fact that 'little was said to us in China on the subject.'[109] But it is difficult to imagine that anyone with even a slight interest in international affairs would not at least question his hosts on foreign-policy matters, especially when his visit occurred at the height of East-West tensions and only a few years after the dispute of 1958 in which China's attempt to annex several offshore islands in the Pacific was blocked by the American navy. Departing on a tour of the Pacific in 1970, Mr Trudeau admitted that he hoped to learn 'something about world politics' during his travels, but it soon became clear that he preferred to talk about his favourite topics—such as the virtues of pluralism and the need for dialogue between people and government—than about foreign policy. When questioned by local reporters or students on Canada's domestic affairs, he was found by Canadian reporters to be 'invariably well-briefed and cogent', but when it came to questions of substance on foreign affairs 'he seemed less sure of his ground', willing to talk only of Canada's new interest in the Pacific and then preferring to move to subjects he likes to talk about at home.[110]

During the 1969 Commonwealth Prime Ministers' Conference in London, Mr Trudeau seemed to make a real effort to learn and to ask intelligent questions. The assessment by George Bain and others was that the conference had been primarily of educational value to Trudeau who, willing to learn and conscious that he was a 'new boy', had apparently revised his earlier opinions and was inclined to judge the Commonwealth favourably.[111] Neither well informed on international affairs nor particularly interested in them when they did not directly concern what he regarded as Canada's basic national interests, Mr Trudeau was sometimes prepared to accept the views of others and to revise his own opinions on such matters. Where he seemed reluctant to compromise was on the domestic issues that he considered to be of extreme importance, and on the foreign-policy issues that related directly to these national concerns.

3. TRUDEAU'S APPROACH TO GOVERNING

In reply to critics who charged that he did not have enough political experience to be Prime Minister, Mr Trudeau replied that in a rapidly changing world 'experience isn't always very useful', and that he felt no qualms about his ability to make important decisions.[112] One of his Cabinet ministers has said that Trudeau is willing to listen at Cabinet meetings and to give everyone a chance to speak—he is a good chairman—but that final decisions are usually based on his own summary of the discussion, for 'He's very much in charge.'[113] 'There's nobody to tell me how the country should be run', Trudeau exclaimed in 1968. 'I tell *them*.'[114] There could be little doubt that the Prime Minister, unlike some of his predecessors, was prepared to intervene personally to determine a wide variety of policies.

As Minister of Justice in the Pearson government, Trudeau realized that the federal civil service had a great deal of power and at least the potential to make effective use of it, but that it lacked centralized political leadership. It was his desire to establish co-ordinated control and guidance when he became Prime Minister that led him to take such an active personal part in policy formulation that he was soon labelled a 'crypto-president'; to organize around him a group of advisers upon whom he relied so much that they became known by some disgruntled civil servants as 'the supergroup'; and to bring order and discipline to the operations of the Cabinet.

One of Mr Trudeau's first steps after the 1968 election was to reorganize and expand the Prime Minister's Office and the Privy Council Office. Unaffected by the budgetary freezes imposed on most government organizations, the two increased in size by forty per cent during the first year of Trudeau's administration.[115] According to Marc Lalonde, the Prime Minister was determined to achieve two principal objectives: to enable the government to respond more effectively to the increased demands being placed upon it, and to ensure a greater political control over the entire government apparatus.[116] It was Trudeau's belief that power had slipped in the past to civil servants and was not sufficiently in the hands of the country's elected representatives, who alone were responsible to the public. Mr Trudeau also believed that there was a need to co-ordinate more effectively the activities of various departments so that they complemented, rather than conflicted with, one another. 'In order to have this team effect', he said in 1969, 'we must make sure that every ministerial recommendation is meshed in with what is happening in the other departments ... and in order to plan we must have a strong planning control body.'[117]

The Privy Council Office was responsible for co-ordinating government planning, and its role in this field was increased by Mr Trudeau. In February 1969 he announced that it was being split into two divisions, one for operations and one for plans, in accordance with his government's desire to give 'added emphasis to planning and priorities.'[118] The increase in the planning duties of the Prime Minister's Office was largely a response to his desire to inject a greater 'political input' into policy planning. Its members—specially chosen by the Prime Minister and, unlike those of the PCO, not civil servants—are responsible for injecting Mr Trudeau's 'own input' into a few selected areas that require the personal involvement of the Prime Minister. Gordon Robertson, the head of the PCO, has summarized the differences between the two organizations in the following way: the PMO is 'partisan, politically oriented, yet operationally sensitive', while the PCO is 'non-partisan, operationally oriented yet politically sensitive.'[119] In other words both advise the Prime Minister, but the first concern of the PMO is the effect the policies it recommends will have on the Liberal Party's electoral fortunes, while the PCO thinks in terms of the effective operation of the Canadian government. There is undoubtedly some overlapping between the two, for the distinction between 'partisan' and 'political' cannot always be maintained; however, both are intended to improve the government's ability to plan effectively and to avoid as much as possible the need for ad-hoc decisions.

This noticeable expansion in the size and duties of the PMO and PCO has been cited as evidence by critics who accuse Mr Trudeau of wielding 'increasing and arbitrary power' at the expense of Cabinet, Parliament, and the civil service.[120] But Trudeau is not the first Prime Minister to recognize the importance of the PMO and PCO, for both grew in size and importance in previous administrations in response to the proliferation of government's responsibilities in the post-war period. Moreover, there are technical considerations that partly explain the rapid growth of both offices under Mr Trudeau. In the past many of their members were not officially attached to the PMO or PCO but were merely seconded from the civil service, with the result that the official size of both offices remained relatively small. This practice was altered by Mr Trudeau. (In the PMO, for example, Mr Pearson's Principal Secretary was Tom Kent, a senior civil servant; this post was not filled by someone from outside the civil service until the 1968 appointment of Marc Lalonde.) Part of the staff increase is also due to the rapid growth of service, as distinct from planning, duties; for instance, the number of letters sent to the Prime Minister has soared since Mr Trudeau took office, and all must be answered by the PMO's correspondence section (by far its largest branch). Furthermore, it is not correct to assume that the increase of the power of the Prime Minister since 1968 has necessarily decreased the important roles played by the Cabinet, Parliament, or the civil service. The responsibilities of government grow almost daily, and even when some are assumed by the Prime Minister and his assistants, the work-load of other government bodies continues to increase as well. There is no doubt that Mr Trudeau has attempted to ensure that he maintains control over the most important decisions—especially those dealing with the establishment of overall priorities, which require a great deal of interdepartmental co-ordination—and that he has assembled a large and capable staff to provide him with the best advice possible. But it is surely an exaggeration to say that he has done so with the ulterior motive of gaining 'arbitrary' power for its own sake, or to imply that he has left other arms of government virtually powerless.

One of the dangers of building up such a highly specialized body of advisers is that this might lead to a deterioration in relations between the political leaders and the civil service. This is particularly likely if the Prime Minister's advisers go beyond their role of co-ordinating the policies of several departments and begin participating in the formulation or implementation of policies for which one department is particularly responsible—as they did, for instance, in determining the NATO decision of 1969. The official government view is that relations between the Prime Minister's staff and the civil service are excellent; indeed there is little present evidence of conflict, especially since the roles of the PMO and PCO have recently been publicized in speeches by their respective heads and thereby made less mysterious and less likely to arouse suspicion. But during the first two years of the Trudeau administration, such was not always the case. Senior civil servants may not have understood the functions of the expanding PMO and PCO, and the officers of these two organizations may not have realized the dangers of becoming involved in issues that civil servants had long regarded as their own responsibility.

Some members of the Department of External Affairs resented the important role played by two former foreign-service officers: Ivan Head, then the Prime Minister's legislative assistant and later his special assistant; and Marshall Crowe, responsible until 1971 for the operations side of the Privy Council Office. The greater political responsibilities of the PMO led to Mr Head's becoming Trudeau's chief adviser in matters of foreign policy. In 1969 he made two trips to Nigeria as the Prime Minister's personal representative in an attempt to facilitate the flow of Canadian aid, and in the following year he visited Washington and Moscow in connection with Canada's Arctic activities. The important part he played in the 1969 NATO decision (outlined in

Chapter 5) also contributed to his reputation as the Prime Minister's number one foreign-policy adviser. Michael Pitfield, a close friend of Mr Trudeau's who is responsible for the planning functions of the PCO, was also thought to be influencing foreign-policy decisions. One External Affairs official, decrying what he saw as a shift of the centre of policy formulation away from his department, remarked: 'One of our most astonishing diplomatic failures was our failure to establish a link with Ivan Head.' Another complained that 'If you want to know why we aren't being listened to by this government, you need go no farther than the office of Michael Pitfield.'[121] This consternation in the ranks of senior bureaucrats was clearly not unwelcome to either the Prime Minister or his assistants. Ivan Head commented: 'I don't think it hurts the mandarins to know that the Prime Minister has people in his office with both experience and ability to challenge what comes up.'[122]

Mr Trudeau also set out to reform the working of his Cabinet. From his predecessor he inherited twenty-seven Cabinet committees whose task had been to make policy recommendations and leave the final decision to the whole Cabinet. Aware of the duplication of effort that such a procedure created, Trudeau slashed this number to nine and gave them the responsibility for making many of the final policy decisions.[123] The most important of these standing committees is the Priorities and Planning Committee, sometimes referred to as the 'Inner Cabinet', which is concerned with establishing the government's overall priorities and integrating the policies of the various departments to fit these priorities. It is chaired by the Prime Minister himself, as is the Committee on Federal-Provincial Relations (indications of the areas in which Mr Trudeau is most interested). There are four functional committees dealing with external policy, economic policy, social policy, and culture and information, as well as a statutory committee for science policy and technology. It is perhaps revealing that for the first time since its creation in 1936 the committee dealing with foreign and defence policy was chaired by a minister other than the Prime Minister (presumably the Secretary of State for External Affairs). The normal procedure is for the decisions made in these committees to be given routine approval by the full Cabinet; only if there is a division of opinion in the committee, or if the committee's decision is challenged by another minister, does the policy in question become a matter for debate in Cabinet. The intention is clearly to minimize the number of issues requiring examination by the Cabinet as a whole, for the committees speed up decision-making only when they themselves make the final decisions.

Prime Minister Trudeau has also altered the way in which Cabinet ministers participate in the formulation of policy. According to a senior civil servant, the administration has created a 'consensual' system of Cabinet decision-making in which every interested minister is given the opportunity to voice his opinion even when the issue under discussion does not come under his ministry. The system means that ministers act 'less on their own' than in the past. The extent to which a Prime Minister allows members of his Cabinet to determine foreign policy is largely a matter of individual temperament and style. It is Trudeau's style to invite the participation of as many ministers as are interested. His temperament, however, does not allow him to be influenced on issues of major importance by any but a few key ministers—most importantly Jean Marchand, Gérard Pelletier, and Donald Macdonald. Eric Kierans, the Postmaster-General, was eager to express his views on a number of issues unrelated to his own portfolio, but his departure from the Cabinet in April 1971 and his subsequent comments indicate that his influence on the Prime Minister was rarely decisive.[124] Defence Minister Cadieux was planning to leave political life and was not influential in the new administration; nor at first was Secretary of State Mitchell Sharp, who was regarded by insiders as capable and 'briefable' but (at least before 1970) without much 'pull' in Cabinet.

In a paper presented to the 1971 Commonwealth Prime Ministers' Conference at Singapore, Mr Trudeau discussed the role of the civil service in a modern government. He said there was a need for new techniques of administration to do away with the sluggishness and resistance to change of entrenched bureaucracies. 'To overcome this inertia and to redirect the momentum requires all the energy a government has, and frequently even this is not enough.'[125] Disparaging remarks about the civil service were nothing new for the Prime Minister. On February 28, 1968 he said that the government could not find answers to problems if it had to depend on the advice of bureaucrats looking for the best theoretical or abstract solution.[126] Peter Newman reports that much of Trudeau's hesitancy to run for the leadership of the Liberal Party was due to his distrust of the growing power of the inherently conservative federal bureaucracy. 'Before I make my decision', he quotes Trudeau as confiding to a few friends, 'I've got to find out whether it's really possible to do anything once you get into the prime minister's office.'[127] As early as 1951 Trudeau wrote that it was a tendency of the federal civil servant 'de se croire omniscient et omnipotent', and to bring to modern government a stifling 'fonctionarisme' that constitutes 'un danger très sérieux pour le régime de la liberté.'*[128] Mr Trudeau's disapproval of the policy-making role of the civil service may well have increased during the Pearson administration. In 1968 even R. G. Robertson, Clerk of the Privy Council, Secretary to the Cabinet, and the government's highest-ranking civil servant, was writing that

> without changes from present methods, there is a real risk of a steady reduction in the efficiency of government in coping with growing needs, together with a shift of effective decision-making from the ministers, where it ought to be, into the hands of civil servants.[129]

If Mr Trudeau was generally skeptical of civil servants, he was particularly critical of the Department of External Affairs. Other departments he viewed as excessively conservative; External he seemed to regard as largely irrelevant. In a 1969 television interview he said: 'I think the whole concept of diplomacy today . . . is a little bit outmoded.' There was a time when diplomatic dispatches were the only means of receiving information about another country, but today this information is available 'in a good newspaper'.[130] Although it could be expected that someone who had not been connected with the department (unlike Lester Pearson or Louis St Laurent) would not have

---

* 'To consider himself omniscient and omnipotent'; 'bureaucratization'; 'a very serious danger for the concept of freedom.'

absolute faith in its policies, Mr Trudeau seemed to believe that the main function of Canada's diplomatic service was to collect and dispatch information. According to Mitchell Sharp, the morale in his department had deteriorated, and many of his best men felt that 'their functions have been misunderstood', largely as a result of casual comments made by the Prime Minister.[131]

When financial problems necessitated the imposition of spending guidelines on the civil service, Mr Trudeau's views of the relative importance of the various departments became more apparent. These guidelines, Mr Trudeau announced, 'will permit the people of Canada to see what priorities we have.'[132] Policies to promote bilingualism and regional economic expansion dominated the first tier of spending priorities and were allowed to expand; international-development assistance and health and welfare were among the 'medium-growth' functions in the second tier of priorities; while military and foreign expenditures were assigned to the bottom tier and designated 'low-growth' functions. In order to remain within its fixed budget of $56 million, the Department of External Affairs was forced to cut its expenditures by approximately 12 per cent to offset the effects of inflation; seven missions were closed and 74 of the 387 Foreign Service Officers posted abroad were returned to Canada, and a number of officers were transferred to other departments, demoted, retired prematurely, and even dismissed.[133] There had never been much doubt about the nature of Mr Trudeau's personal priorities. The spending guidelines were significant as an indication of the Prime Minister's determination to put his priorities into practice.

Another result of Mr Trudeau's attitude to the civil service has been an alteration in the way policy recommendations are made to Cabinet.[134] In the past, departments tended to suggest to ministers the approach they favoured, while under Trudeau they present not recommendations but a list of all the available policy options relating to the matter under consideration. If the department has a strong preference for one point of view, this can be made obvious in its presentation. It must still, however, inform the Cabinet of the alternative courses available and provide an analysis of the pros and cons of each. Failure to do so lessens the department's credibility within Cabinet. This approach is consistent with the Trudeau administration's desire to relieve the civil service, to a greater degree than in previous administrations, of responsibility for policy formulation. If Cabinet is to have a greater role in this area it must be aware of all the policy alternatives. When these options are received from the department, they are examined by the Cabinet Secretariat and then by Cabinet committees in the light of information obtained from a variety of sources—other departments and their ministers, parliamentary committees, public opinion, and, of course, the PMO and PCO. With this multiplicity of inputs—a characteristic of the Trudeau administration—the Cabinet has succeeded in increasing political control over policy formulation.

It is a question whether Mr Trudeau is more critical of the civil service or of Parliament. He has frequently remarked that Parliament is too far removed from the people, that its operations are too slow, its deliberations often insufficiently informed, and its decisions too few.[135] Some observers, however, have criticized the Prime Minister not only for this attitude but for what they felt was a conscious attempt on his part to 'weaken and emasculate Parliament'. Walter Stewart charges that the Prime Minister 'has moved most of the effective power of Parliament' away from the House of Commons and 'into the cooler, calmer atmosphere of the East Block.'[136] As evidence he cites the rule imposed by closure setting a time-allocation for debate (Standing Order 75); the rule change that set a final date for the passage of all supply motions and thereby prevented the opposition from filibustering supply debates; and the rotation system for the attendance of Cabinet ministers at the daily question period, which was seen by the opposition to undermine its role.

The official government explanation of these reforms was that they were an attempt to speed up the business of the House and to ensure the passage of government legislation within a reasonable time period. Of all the 1968 rule changes, most were in fact approved by an all-party committee, and it was only these few that were regarded by the opposition parties as excessive. Whether even they greatly reduced the effectiveness of the House of Commons is debatable. In spite of the imposition of 'closure' on the 1971 tax-reform debate, the government made numerous changes in its bill in response to public opinion expressed by MPs on both sides of the House. Also, it is doubtful that the opposition suffers any great loss by waiting one day for a minister to be present at Question Period.

In the field of foreign policy the rule changes of the Trudeau government appear to have had even less effect on the power of Parliament, largely because its ability to influence such policies was never very great in the first place. Under Mackenzie King and John Diefenbaker, foreign-policy issues were decided primarily in the Prime Minister's office. Louis St Laurent and Lester Pearson left many of the decisions to their Secretaries of State for External Affairs, although both took an active interest in some issues. Parliament played an influential role in none of these administrations. (It was not until the time of the Pearson government that the House Committee on External Affairs and National Defence began meeting regularly.) There are several reasons for this lack of Parliamentary involvement: little interest and knowledge on the part of MPs and the electorate; a traditionally large measure of agreement on basic issues by both major political parties; a desire of Prime Ministers to keep personal control of foreign policy; and the fact that foreign policy rarely results in legislation and tends to arouse discussion in the House that is general and lacks the concrete elements that attract MPs. It would appear to be factors such as these, then, rather than any conscious attempt on the part of the Prime Minister to strip Parliament of its power, that explain why Mr Trudeau has not looked to Parliament for specific foreign-policy advice.

Though largely rejecting Parliament as a source of such advice, Mr Trudeau is very much aware of the importance, at least for political reasons, of considering the views of Liberal Members of Parliament. According to one minister, the Prime Minister heeds the views of caucus in particular, since it is highly embarrassing for a government to have differences of opinion within its ranks publicized. A 1969 study session called by the Liberal caucus to discuss ways in which it could obtain more research assistance and increased consultation on policy likely provided the impetus for subsequent attempts to keep caucus better informed of both the principles behind legislation and the way in which these principles would be implemented.

Mr Trudeau brought to his office a new concept of the relationship between government and public opinion. He frequently talked of the need to give Canadians 'a sense of full participation' in the affairs of government and to 'plug people into the decision-making process'.[137] He believes that in the future, political parties will be distinguished from one another not so much by their policies as by the methods they employ in devising these policies; hence it is important to consult the views of as many groups and individuals as possible.[138] In the 1969 Speech from the Throne, the government stated its belief in the need for 'informed public discussion before bills are drafted in their final form and before any far-reaching measures are taken.'[139] The creation of regional desks in the PMO, a rapid increase in the number of employees in the PMO's correspondence section, the publication of exploratory White Papers, and the establishment of Information Canada are ways in which the government has attempted to improve the flow of information and ideas between the people and the government.

Mr Trudeau's concept of participatory democracy seems to be based on a desire to interest and educate Canadians rather than to let their opinions determine government policy. The whole tone of his writing and speeches is directed more towards the first goal than towards the latter. 'Un Etat où les citoyens se désintéressent de la chose politique', he wrote in 1951, 'est voué à l'esclavage';*[140] freedom, he wrote on another occasion, can wither away through anarchy, 'but it can also happen through a lack of interest on the part of the people in the governing of their country.'[141] In the decision-making process, he once told a reporter from *Time*, 'people want to have some occasion to give and take, to exchange. That is the temper of today.'[142] This might explain his predilection for off-the-cuff statements, which he sees as a means of getting people used to accepting ideas 'that are put to them for purposes of discussion, or of reflection', even though they may not indicate the course of action desired by the Prime Minister.[143] (In 1969 George Bain wrote that whether Mr Trudeau's passion for debate was

* 'A State whose citizens fail to interest themselves in the political system is doomed to slavery.'

real or simulated for the purpose of creating an illusion of participation 'remains to be demonstrated'.)[144] It cannot be stated categorically that Trudeau is unaffected by public opinion, but his whole philosophy of action seems to reject the idea that governments should be directed by it. 'Modern government cannot simply react,' he told the Commonwealth Prime Ministers in a paper on the techniques of government. 'It must lead in the formulation of public opinion, give firm direction in advance of events, and act in pursuit of its objectives.'[145]

There appear to be two general occasions on which Mr Trudeau will often defer to public opinion that runs contrary to government policies. The first arises when he is not very interested in the issue at hand; the second when a policy is not one of his 'core' interests and its continued advocacy might endanger the re-election of his government. The 1969 White Paper on Indian affairs seems to be an example of the former. Faced with severe criticism from Indians, Mr Trudeau conceded that the paper had been naive in some respects and that the government was not going to force anything on anybody.[146] This was not an issue that aroused widespread public interest or one on which the government would have been greatly embarrassed by making a concession. On the other hand, the extensive changes made in the government's proposals on taxation, as originally presented in Finance Minister Benson's 1971 White Paper, seem to have been influenced by a feeling that they had aroused such widespread opposition that they could not be implemented without causing a significant decrease in the government's popularity, which was already low because of the country's economic problems.* Eric Kierans has revealed that Cabinet discussions on economic matters frequently centred on the question: 'How will this look in June 1972?', the date most frequently mentioned then for the next federal election.[147] In the tradition of Mackenzie King the Trudeau government has defended this preoccupation on grounds that the Liberals had to retain power at all costs, since they

* Government officials do say, however, that the technique of testing public opinion with 'explanatory' and 'exploratory' White Papers is a means of arriving at the 'best' decisions.

could do more than the other parties to maintain national unity, Mr Trudeau's dominant concern.

It is apparent from this analysis that Mr Trudeau has an explicit and well-developed personal philosophy. His fundamental objective is the creation of a Canadian 'nation-state' in which maximum human dignity and welfare, bilingualism and multi-culturalism, can all be realized. Instruments such as sovereignty, and in fact all aspects of foreign policy, are to be used to attain this objective. Canada's proper role is not to imitate great powers by seeking to determine world events, but consists rather in building a just society at home that will serve as an inspiration to others while at the same time permitting Canada to make a distinctive international contribution on the basis of its values. He sees no major threat to Canada in the external environment, regarding both the United States and the Soviet Union as essentially benign. He believes that the country's fundamental problems, and their solutions, are to be found within Canada.

Mr Trudeau's domestic orientation is matched by his equally firm determination to reorganize the decision-making apparatus of the Canadian government. Wary of the civil service, impatient with Parliament, and more interested in educating the public than in being influenced by it, he tends to seek advice from his personal advisers in the Privy Council Office and the Prime Minister's Office, and from a few close Cabinet friends. If he feels strongly about an issue, he will not hesitate to force it through a reluctant Cabinet, drawing back only if such action threatens to be politically disastrous. In short, the questions raised by the advent of the new administration in 1968 did not remain unanswered for long. Prime Minister Trudeau was soon identified for all to see as a leader with very definite ideas and a strong determination to put them into effect.

Notes

[1] Quoted in Donald Peacock, *Journey to Power*. Toronto: Ryerson Press, 1968, pp. 148-9.

[2] Pierre Elliott Trudeau, *Federalism and the French Canadians*. Toronto: Macmillan, 1968, p. 11.

[3] Quoted in Peter C. Newman, *The Distemper of our Times*. Toronto: McClelland and Stewart, 1968, p. 444.

[4] *Montreal Star*, December 23, 1967 (quoted in Peacock, *op. cit.*, p. 179).

[5] *Time* Magazine, Canadian Edition. June 1, 1970, p. 12.

[6] *Globe and Mail*, September 13, 1968.

[7] George Bain, 'Trend of Government', *Globe and Mail*, September 4, 1969, p. 6.

[8] *Cité Libre*, janvier 1961, p. 18.

[9] James Eayrs, 'The End of Canadian Liberalism', *Canadian Dimension*, Vol. 7, Nos. 5-6, December 1970, p. 78.

[10] *Time*, November 30, 1970, p. 7.

[11] Denis Smith, *Bleeding Hearts . . . Bleeding Country*. Edmonton: Hurtig, 1971, p. 14.

[12] Press Conference Transcript, Office of the Prime Minister, May 28, 1971.

[13] Trudeau, *Federalism and the French Canadians*, p. 175.

[14] *Ibid.*, p. 196.

[15] For a precise distinction between the 'nation-state' and the 'nationalist state' see Ramsay Cook, *The Maple Leaf Forever: Essays on Nationalism and Politics in Canada*. Toronto: Macmillan, 1971, pp. 5-6.

[16] See, for example, Trudeau, *op. cit.*, pp. 187-8.

[17] *Ibid.*, p. 185.

[18] *Ibid.*, pp. 157-8.

[19] *Ibid.*, pp. 4, 169.

[20] *Ibid.*, p. 177.

[21] *Ibid.*, p. 179.

[22] Text provided by the Office of the Prime Minister, May 18, 1971.

[23] Trudeau, *Federalism and the French Canadians*, p. 31.

[24] *Ibid.*, p. 154.

[25] Gad Horowitz, 'The Trudeau Doctrine', *Canadian Dimension*, Vol. 5, No. 5, June-July 1968, p. 9.

[26] Lester B. Pearson, *Peace in the Family of Man: The Reith Lectures, 1968*. Toronto: Oxford University Press, 1969, p. 54.

[27] Trudeau, *op. cit.*, pp. 203, 189.

[28] *Ibid.*, p. 18.

[29] Quoted in *Time*, February 14, 1969, p. 12.

[30] *Canada 70: A Summary Coast to Coast* published by the Toronto *Telegram*. Toronto: McClelland and Stewart, 1969, p. 32.

[31] See Trudeau's comments during the debate on the Speech from the Throne (*Monthly Report*, October 1969, p. 248), and in the *Globe and Mail*, April 9, 1970, p. 1.

[32] Trudeau, *Federalism and the French Canadians*, pp. 195-6.

[33] *Ibid.*, pp. 151, 158.

[34] *Ibid.*, p. 158.

[35] *Ibid.*, p. 202.

[36] See *Time*, March 30, 1970, p. 8A; and May 17, 1968, p. 14.

[37] *Globe and Mail*, October 28, 1968, p. 12.

[38] *Globe and Mail*, November 29, 1968, p. 4.

[39] Trudeau, *op. cit.*, p. 24.

[40] *Globe and Mail*, February 25, 1970, p. 1.

[41] Pierre Elliott Trudeau, 'A propos de "domination économique"', *Cité Libre*, mai 1958, p. 10.

[42] *Time*, March 30, 1970, p. 8A.

[43] *Globe and Mail*, March 4, 1970, p. B1.

[44] *Time, loc. cit.*

[45] This is John Holmes' assessment of Trudeau's visit to the Soviet Union, expressed in an interview with the author.

[46] Transcript of Press Conference, Office of the Prime Minister, May 28, 1971.

[47] Trudeau, *Federalism and the French Canadians*, p. 65.

[48] *Globe and Mail*, November 29, 1968, p. 4.

[49] *Debates*, November 12, 1968, p. 2626.

[50] Quoted in *Time*, August 30, 1968, p. 9.

[51] Transcript of the Prime Minister's Interview on Radio Canada, Office of the Prime Minister, May 20, 1971.

[52] Text provided by the Office of the Prime Minister, May 18, 1971.

[53] Transcript of Press Conference, Office of the Prime Minister, May 28, 1971.

[54] Toronto *Star*, April 27, 1968.

[55] Transcript of the Prime Minister's Press Conference in Moscow, Office of the Prime Minister, May 20, 1971.

[56] See, for example, Peyton V. Lyon, 'Quiet Diplomacy Revisited', in Stephen Clarkson, ed., *An Independent Foreign Policy for Canada?* Toronto: McClelland and Stewart, 1968, especially p. 30.

[57] *Globe and Mail*, March 2, 1968, and May 22, 1968.

[58] Television interview, quoted in Brian Shaw, *The Gospel According to St Pierre*. Richmond Hill, Ontario: Simon & Schuster of Canada, 1969, p. 23; see also the *Globe and Mail*, May 22, 1968, p. 7.

[59] Shaw, *loc. cit.*; see also the *Globe and Mail*, March 28, 1969, p. 6, for an account of Mr Trudeau's speech to the National Press Club in Washington.

[60] *Globe and Mail*, May 14, 1968; see also Shaw, *op. cit.*, p. 119.

[61] *International Canada*, February 1971, p. 29.

[62] *Globe and Mail*, June 17, 1968, p. 9. Mr Sharp said that the government was 'heading toward the target' of one per cent. ('International Development', Information Agency, Canadian International Development Agency, June 1970, p. 1.)

[63] *The Listener*. London: BBC Publications, January 9, 1969. (The interview, taped in the fall of 1968, was shown on the BBC's '24 Hours' in January of 1969.)

[64] *Globe and Mail*, June 10, 1968, p. 8.

[65] Transcript of a Press Conference at Uplands Airport, Ottawa. Office of the Prime Minister, July 29, 1968.

[66] *Le Monde*, 21 février 1970, p. 4; see also the Prime Minister's interview with the *New York Times* (quoted in the *Globe and Mail*, November 29, 1968, p. 1).

[67] *Globe and Mail*, November 29, 1968, p. 4.

[68] Quoted in Shaw, *op. cit.*, p. 128.

[69] *Ibid.*, p. 127.

[70] *Globe and Mail*, December 14, 1968, p. 2.

[71] Transcript of Remarks, Office of the Prime Minister, November 14, 1968.

[72] *Globe and Mail*, November 14, 1968, p. 6.

[73] *Globe and Mail*, February 19, 1969, p. 2.

[74] Letter to the author from John Warnock, Professor of Political Science, University of Saskatchewan, dated May 27, 1971.

[75] Pierre Elliott Trudeau, 'La Guerre! La Guerre!', *Cité Libre*, décembre 1961, p. 1.

[76] Quoted in Shaw, *op. cit.*, p. 124; see also Pierre Elliott Trudeau, 'Pearson ou l'abdication de l'esprit', *Cité Libre*, avril 1963.

[77] Transcript of the Prime Minister's Press Conference in Moscow, Office of the Prime Minister, May 20, 1971.

[78] Jacques Hébert and Pierre Elliott Trudeau, *Two Innocents in Red China*. Toronto: Oxford University Press, 1968, pp. 2, 152.

[79] *Monthly Report*, March 1968, p. 40; Shaw, *op. cit.*, p. 203.

[80] Shaw, *op. cit.*, pp. 198, 211.

[81] *Globe and Mail*, April 5, 1968, p. 8.

[82] See Horowitz, *op. cit.*, p. 9.

[83] See Peacock, *op. cit.*, p. 347; and the *Globe and Mail*, January 11, 1969, p. 3.

[84] *Monthly Report*, February 1968, p. 31; transcript of the Prime Minister's Press Conference aboard the Nuclear Icebreaker *Lenin*, Office of the Prime Minister, May 25, 1971; and the *Globe and Mail*, January 13, 1969, p. 8.

[85] Trudeau, *Federalism and the French Canadians*, p. xxiii.

[86] Transcript of a Radio-Canada Interview from Moscow, Office of the Prime Minister, May 20, 1971.

[87] Trudeau, *Federalism and the French Canadians*, p. xix.

[88] Pierre Elliott Trudeau, 'Politique fonctionnelle', *Cité Libre*, juin 1950, p. 21; see also Trudeau, *Federalism and the French Canadians*, p. 53.

[89] Newman, *op. cit.*, p. 443; *Globe and Mail*, January 24, 1968, p. 2.

[90] Quoted in Peacock, *op. cit.*, p. 328.

[91] Pierre Elliott Trudeau, 'Pelletier et Trudeau s'expliquent', *Cité Libre*, octobre 1965, pp. 3-4; see also Trudeau, 'Reflexions sur la politique du Canada français', *Cité Libre*, décembre 1952, p. 60.

[92] Trudeau, *Federalism and the French Canadians*, p. 21.

[93] Pierre Élliott Trudeau, 'A l'ouest rien de nouveau', *Cité Libre*, février 1961; see also his articles 'A propos de "domination économique"', *Cité Libre*, mai 1958, pp. 13, 15; and 'Un Manifeste Démocratique', *Cité Libre*, octobre 1958, p. 21.

[94] For a detailed examination of Mr Trudeau's philosophy of governing, see Bruce C. Doern, 'Recent Changes in the Philosophy of Policy-making in Canada', *Canadian Journal of Political Science*, Vol. IV, No. 2, June 1971, p. 245.

[95] *Ibid.*, p. 248.

[96] *Globe and Mail*, June 12, 1968, p. 6.

[97] *Debates*, September 16, 1968, p. 65.

[98] See Doern, *op. cit.*, on many of the points in this section.

[99] *Time*, October 31, 1969, p. 13.

[100] *Time*, March 30, 1970, p. 6; see also *Time*, September 13, 1968, p. 16.

[101] Peacock, *op. cit.*, pp. 335-6.

[102] Trudeau, *Federalism and the French Canadians*, pp. 25-6.

[103] *Debates*, September 16, 1968, p. 66.

[104] Transcript of Interview, Office of the Prime Minister, May 28, 1971.

[105] Quoted in John D. Harbron, *This is Trudeau*. Don Mills: Longmans, 1968, p. 2.

[106] *Debates*, September 16, 1968, pp. 63-4.

[107] Quoted in James Eayrs, 'Dilettante in Power', *Saturday Night*, April 1971, p. 12; Peyton V. Lyon, 'A Review of the Review', *Journal of Canadian Studies*, May 1970.

[108] Bruce Hutchison, 'Why Canada should not divorce NATO', *Globe and Mail*, February 20, 1969, p. 7.

[109] Hébert and Trudeau, *op. cit.*, p. 150.

[110] *Globe and Mail*, May 16, 1970, p. 11; and May 23, 1970, p. 7.

[111] *Globe and Mail*, January 13, 1969, p. 7; and January 14, 1969, p. 1; *Time*, January 24, 1969, p. 14.

[112] *Globe and Mail*, November 29, 1968, p. 4.

[113] *Time*, May 10, 1968; see also Eric Kierans' description of the Trudeau administration in *Maclean's*, July 1971.

[114] *Maclean's*, September 1968, p. 8.

[115] *Globe and Mail*, February 3, 1970, p. 7.

[116] Marc Lalonde, 'The Changing Role of the Prime Minister's Office'. A paper presented to the 23rd annual meeting of the Institute of Public Administration of Canada, September 8, 1971, p. 22.

[117] *Ibid.*, p. 23.

[118] *Globe and Mail*, February 3, 1970, p. 7.

[119] Gordon Robertson, 'The Changing Role of the Privy Council Office'. A paper presented to the 23rd annual meeting of the Institute of Public Administration of Canada, September 8, 1971, p. 20.

[120] Walter Stewart, *Shrug: Trudeau in Power*. Toronto: New Press, 1971, p. 175.

[121] *Maclean's*, December 1969, p. 41; October 1969, p. 44.

[122] *Globe and Mail*, January 15, 1969, p. 9.

[123] For an excellent description of the organization of Cabinet committees in the Trudeau administration, see Fred Schindeler, 'The Prime Minister and the Cabinet: History and Development', in Thomas Hockin, ed., *Apex of Power: The Prime Minister and Political Leadership in Canada*. Toronto: Prentice-Hall, 1971; and Gordon Robertson, 'The Changing Role of the Privy Council Office', a paper presented to the 23rd annual meeting of the Institute of Public Administration of Canada, September 8, 1971.

[124] See Walter Stewart, 'Baby, It Was Cold Inside', *Maclean's*, July 1971.

[125] Ottawa *Citizen*, January 21, 1971, p. 15.

[126] Quoted in Peacock, *op. cit.*, p. 255.

[127] Newman, *op. cit.*, p. 447.

[128] Pierre Elliott Trudeau, 'Politique fonctionnelle II', *Cité Libre*, février 1951, pp. 24, 26.

[129] R. G. Robertson, in *Canadian Public Administration*, Vol. XI, No. 3, Fall 1968, p. 276.

[130] *Maclean's*, December 1969, p. 35.

[131] *Globe and Mail*, March 17, 1970, p. 11.

[132] *Time*, August 22, 1969, p. 11.

[133] See Lyon, 'A Review of the Review'.

[134] This paragraph is based primarily on interviews with a Cabinet minister in the Trudeau government and with a senior civil servant.

[135] *Globe and Mail*, September 13, 1968; see also *Debates*, December 10, 1968, p. 3787.

[136] Stewart, *Shrug: Trudeau in Power*, pp. 145–6.

[137] Peacock, *op. cit.*, p. 337; *Maclean's*, September 1968, p. 8.

[138] Anthony Westell and Geoffrey Stevens, 'What made Trudeau decide to run?' *Globe and Mail*, February 17, 1968; see also the press release of Trudeau's speech to the Liberal conference at Harrison Hot Springs, November 21, 1969.

[139] *Debates*, October 23, 1969, p. 3.

[140] Trudeau, 'Politique fonctionnelle II' *Cité Libre*, février 1951, p. 28.

[141] Shaw, *op. cit.*, p. 126.

[142] *Time*, November 22, 1968, pp. 20–1.

[143] *Loc. cit.*

[144] George Bain, 'What's the Purpose?' *Globe and Mail*, June 23, 1969, p. 6; see also Bain, 'The Essence of the Style', June 19, 1970, p. 6.

[145] Ottawa *Citizen*, January 21, 1971, p. 15.

[146] *Globe and Mail*, June 19, 1970, p. 6.

[147] *Maclean's*, July 1971, p. 63.

4

The Decision to Review

On May 29, 1968, Prime Minister Trudeau announced that his government was planning a 'thorough and comprehensive review' of Canada's foreign policy. Since the Robertson review had been completed just a few months earlier, the inference was that the new administration regarded this first study as unsatisfactory. Far from being a mere announcement of a review that would result in future decisions, the Prime Minister's statement indicated that a number of concrete decisions had already been made concerning the future direction of Canadian foreign policy. It announced the government's intention to establish diplomatic relations with Communist China, to increase Canada's contacts with Latin America and the countries of the Pacific rim, and to give a higher priority to international development assistance and the projection abroad of Canada's bilingual character. The statement was also significant because many of the final policy decisions made in 1969 and 1970—such as a new relationship with Europe and a shift of emphasis in the United Nations, as well as the emphasis on national interests—were all contained in it at least by implication.[1]

In explaining its reasons for undertaking the new review, the government made much of changes in the external environment. Canada's post-war record in international affairs was described as 'brilliant' in many respects under the leadership of Lester Pearson, and it was stressed that re-assessment had become necessary 'not because of the inadequacies of the past but because of the changing nature of Canada and of the world around us.' These changes included the emergence of the Third World and the recovery of Western Europe, which meant that Canada's relative power had also changed drastically. With this assessment few could disagree. Somewhat more controversial was the emphasis on détente as the trend of the present and future in East-West relations, and the statement that 'It is no longer true to say that the Communist world is monolithically and implacably hostile to us.' There followed a discussion of Canadian defence policy—an indication that it would be influenced by this perception of the external environment. 'We shall take a hard look', the announcement said, '. . . at our military role in NATO and determine whether our present military commitment is still appropriate to the present situation in Europe.' Since the European situation had already been described as greatly changed, and in view of a later statement that Canada's military stake in Europe had declined, this was a very clear indication that the government was not satisfied with Canada's existing role in NATO.

In spite of the changes in the international environment (discussed in Chapter 2), the Pearson government had decided against altering Canada's military contribution to NATO or downplaying Canada's role as a mediator. Although the external changes indicated that a shift in Canadian foreign policy was possible, and perhaps even desirable, they by no means made such an alteration inevitable or essential. The importance for foreign policy of these external changes depended primarily on the way in which they were perceived and interpreted by the decision-makers. The interpretation of the officials in the Departments of External Affairs and National Defence, presented in the Robertson Report and apparently accepted by Mr Pearson and Mr Martin, had been that the external environment imposed no need for major changes in Canada's foreign policy, at least for the time being.

If the international situation did not necessitate sweeping changes, could the same be said of the internal environment? From a military point of view, pressures for change were present but again not compelling. The presence of two units of the Canadian Armed Forces in Europe definitely impeded the goal, set forth in the 1964 Defence White Paper, of achieving as great a degree of multiple-tasking as possible. This situation, however, had existed for several years without causing insoluble logistics or training problems, and the Robertson Report had not regarded it as a serious handicap to the efficiency of Canada's armed forces.

As for NORAD, the May 29 announcement stated that Canada's role in this organization would be reviewed 'in the light of the technological advances of modern weaponry and of our fundamental opposition to the proliferation of nuclear weapons.' From a military point of view, however, the continued use of nuclear weapons was clearly desirable. Few contested the fact that they would be much more effective than conventional weapons in destroying attacking bombers and in reducing the danger to Canadian territory because of their greater 'kill capacity' and their ability to 'cook' enemy warheads.[2] Nor did their possession by the CAF represent a proliferation of nuclear weapons, for Canada could not use them independently. The warheads remained firmly under the American 'two-key' system and could be used only in the event of military action involving both the United States and Canada. Opposition to nuclear weapons was largely a moral issue and depended primarily on individual perceptions and values.

There were excellent military reasons for at least reviewing Canada's NORAD role, however, in light of the possibility that anti-bomber defences were irrelevant in the missile age. Canada's existing weapons systems for continental defence were expected to be obsolescent by the early 1970s, and it was only logical that the government should begin thinking about whether it would be in Canada's best interests to replace its obsolete weapons and aircraft at that time or to withdraw from participation in anti-bomber defence. The decision announced in the 1964 Defence White Paper not to provide new equipment for Canada's NORAD forces, the prospect that existing equipment would soon be obsolete, and doubts about the military value of anti-bomber defence, made it almost inevitable that the government would take a close look at Canada's role in NORAD.

From a strictly economic point of view, the necessity for changes in defence or foreign policy does not appear to have been overwhelming. Of the economic problems facing the country there could be little doubt. Nevertheless there was no compelling reason why limitations on government spending, which were obviously desirable, should lead to changes in Canada's defence policy. It has been shown that Canada's per-capita defence expenditures were among the lowest in the world. The Robertson Report had indicated that no savings could be expected if a mobile force were created in Canada to replace the country's two units in Europe. This had been clearly understood by Mr Pearson, who, in spite of the financial difficulties facing his administration, had not thought of a Canadian withdrawal from Europe as a means of reducing the defence budget. Financial considerations of this kind 'didn't bother me very much', he remarked later, for he knew that 'even if we got out of NATO completely we wouldn't have saved very much.'[3]

During most of the 1960s it had been deemed politically unwise, whatever the economic state of the nation, to increase defence spending beyond a certain level. When the defence budget was frozen at $1.8 billion in June 1969, some decision-makers may have begun to doubt whether Canada could fulfil its NATO commitments without exceeding this limit. If the decision-making élite had consulted senior civil servants, however, it would probably have become apparent to them that, as one knowledgeable official remarked later, 'The government could have even cut the defence budget in half and maintained the same number of troops in Europe if it had wanted to.'

In Chapter 2 it was shown that little pressure for change appeared to come from the Canadian public. All available public-opinion polls indicate that there was no public resistance to the foreign policy inherited by the Trudeau régime, and one of Trudeau's cabinet ministers has confirmed that the government perceived no widespread pressure for change. With the exception of the issue of nuclear weapons, there seems to be no justification for Professor Garth Stevenson's comment that 'public opinion in those years was marked by a growing moral distaste for nuclear weapons, a growing conviction that Canada's military expenditures were wasteful and irrelevant . . . and a growing suspicion that Canada's close alliance with the United States was becoming incompatible with its desire to play a distinctive, useful, and altruistic role in international politics.'[4] The public approved of Canada's alliance commitments and support of peacekeeping, and voiced mild objections only to Canada's reliance on nuclear weapons.

Within the Liberal Party there seemed to be no desire for new departures in foreign policy, with the exception of recognition of Communist China. Even on NATO there was no clearly discernable trend of thought. Only from the New Democratic Party and the academic community was there any substantial criticism of Canada's existing foreign policy. The majority of academic commentators appeared to be critical of Canada's role in NATO, its addiction to quiet diplomacy, and its general relationship with the United States, preferring instead a more active role in the Third World and the United Nations. Like the New Democratic Party, they stressed the issue of Canadian-American relations and the need for a greater contribution to international development.

It is extremely difficult to determine precisely what influence, if any, these various forces had on the government's decision to review foreign policy. As James Rosenau has written, 'We have only a scanty knowledge of how external opinions enter and shape the deliberations of officials,' and can do little more than 'observe behaviour and infer therefrom which influences are operative.'[5] Even more pessimistic is James Eayrs, who writes that such questions 'are surely to be answered only by Mr Trudeau himself.'[6]

The Prime Minister's statement of May 29 reflected some but by no means all of the articulated opposition to Canada's existing foreign policy. The decisions to review the country's NATO role with a critical eye; to improve political and economic relations with Latin America by dispatching a ministerial mission; to take a 'new interest in Pacific affairs generally'; to increase Canada's foreign aid, particularly towards francophone countries; and to involve outsiders, especially those 'with expert knowledge in the universities and elsewhere', in the search for new approaches and policies—all these decisions were in keeping with the general trend of academic and Parliamentary criticism. Much less in tune with it, however, was the government's attitude to Canadian-American relations. Although hostility towards the United States was the basis of most of the academic criticism of NATO, NORAD, the Defence Production Sharing Agreement, quiet diplomacy, and economic continentalism, and it was commonly considered that Canada had not established diplomatic relations with Communist China or diversified its relations beyond the North Atlantic because of American pressures, the reference to the United States in the May 29 statement was particularly mild. Canada, it said, had a 'major aim of maintaining mutual confidence and respect in our relations with the United States' and, far from being faced with the task of opposing American interference on all fronts, had rather 'to sort out the dilemmas which that complex relation poses for us so as to widen the area of mutual benefit without diminishing our Canadian identity and sovereign independence.' The government's failure to undertake a serious review of Canadian-American relations was a clear indication that it intended to make foreign-policy decisions on the basis of factors other than criticism from the attentive public.

It was also significant that, in describing the primary goal of Canadian foreign policy, the May 29 announcement spoke of far narrower national interests than most of the critics favoured. Canada's 'paramount interest', according to the document, was 'to ensure the political survival of Canada as a federal and bilingual sovereign state', which meant strengthening Canadian unity as a 'basically North American country', reflecting in its foreign relations Canada's 'cultural diversity' and bilingualism, and developing procedures so that Canada's external relations could take into account 'the interests of provincial governments in matters of provincial jurisdiction.' Both the Parliamentary and academic critics had urged a more active international role for Canada on the grounds that the country had an obligation to contribute to world peace and security. However, the announcement took a more modest approach to Canada's international potential. Realism, it said, should be the 'operative word' in Canada's definition of its international aims, and Canada should not exaggerate the extent of its influence upon the course of world events; our need 'is not so much to go crusading abroad as to mobilize at home our aspirations, energies and resources' behind external policies that 'we know to be within our resources'. The announcement emphasized that the approach 'will be pragmatic and realistic—above all, to see that our policies in the future accord with our national needs and resources.'

In short, the May 29 statement differed with most of the academic and Parliamentary critics on Canadian-American relations, on the fundamental goals towards which Canada's foreign policy should be directed, and on the extent to which Canada could expect to influence the international environment through its foreign policy. It emphasized the need for improvements in Canada's development assistance but nowhere indicated that any increases in aid would be accomplished by diverting resources from the defence budget, as Escott Reid had proposed. Jack Granatstein and others who hoped for a more active Canadian role in the peacekeeping ventures of the United Nations had cause for concern. Canada's contribution to the United Nations, which Mr Pearson was not alone in associating with support of peacekeeping ventures, was said in the announcement to be in need of 'some shift of emphasis'. This seemed to imply that Canada's peacekeeping efforts would be somewhat de-emphasized, despite the subsequent affirmation that there would be 'no slackening of our broad policy of support' for the United Nations. It was primarily because of its peacekeeping activities that people had begun to think of Canada as having a 'middle-power role', but in the announcement of the review the government questioned whether the 'conceptions and role-casting' of the past were relevant to present conditions.

Although the academic critics of Canadian foreign policy do not appear to have provided the decisive input for the government's decision to conduct a policy review, their role was at least marginally important. It was their ideas that were publicized by the press, and they filtered into other sectors of the attentive public, particularly Parliament. According to a senior official, it was Stephen Clarkson's *An Independent Foreign Policy for Canada?* that had made the Department aware of an 'unfortunate communications gap' between External Affairs and the academics. This official also stated that the foreign-policy review conducted by Norman Robertson in 1967-8 concentrated on those subjects that had aroused most discussion and criticism among the academics, implying that they had influenced both the decision to have the review and the issues it examined. (This could not have been the only consideration affecting the Robertson undertaking, however, for it has already been shown that Mr Pearson was displeased with many aspects of Canada's foreign policy and had been one of the major advocates of the review.) There were indications that External Affairs had attempted to improve its relations with the academic community in the establishment in 1967 of the Academic Relations Section within the Department, in External's willingness to invite academics to lecture to its officers and to offer its own speakers in return, in the holding of policy conferences with selected officers and academics, and in the Department's intention to hire academics to do contract research and to allow them greater access to its files.[7] When the Policy Analysis Group was established in 1969, its terms of reference included the instruction to keep in touch with the academic community. According to Professor Denis Stairs, the fact that the Department of External Affairs made such a concerted effort to appease academics provided 'at least circumstantial evidence that the foreign policy community tends to regard the university group as its principal source of anguish.'[8]

Denis Stairs also suggests a reason why Canadian academics acquire an influence greater than their numbers alone would warrant. Foreign-policy makers tend to be susceptible to general academic criticism of existing policies because they are themselves intellectually oriented and are not averse to adopting the ideas of academics—'the attitudes of the latter may be particularly important to the self-esteem of the former.'[9] Jack Granatstein believes that the very limited size of the Canadian academic community facilitates contacts between academics and policy-makers.[10] Since there are only a few Canadian academics who specialize in foreign policy, much less Canadian foreign policy, they tend to be reasonably well known by decision-makers. It can be surmised that a small number of well-articulated points of view will be better known to policy-makers than would the differing views of a much larger Canadian academic community. At the Conservatives' 1967 Montmorency Conference, Jack Granatstein and Thomas Hockin of York University, neither one a practising Tory, came very close to convincing the delegates to adopt a 'revisionist' foreign policy; and, although he had never met Dalton Camp, Granatstein was asked to play a part in shaping Camp's ideas for his Montmorency speech.[11]

It is virtually impossible to determine the extent of the influence of the academic community on the decision to review Canada's foreign policy. Academic criticism may have reinforced key decision-makers' own prejudices and discontent with existing policy. In the absence of concrete evidence that academics provided a decisive influence, it seems unwise to go beyond Denis Stairs' observation that if academic criticism played a role it was in confirming the impression of decision-makers that there was a 'general malaise' in the state of Canadian foreign policy and in encouraging them to alter this situation.

There are at least four reasons for concluding that the decisive influence on the decision to conduct a review, and on the direction the review would take, came from the Cabinet, and particularly from Mr Trudeau and his personal advisers. In the first place there is the likelihood that a new government such as Mr Trudeau's would be disinclined to accept in its entirety the foreign policy it had inherited from Mr Pearson. James Eayrs surmised that it was 'the normal inclination of a new prime minister succeeding someone of the same party to want to differentiate the product from the past.'[12] Lester Pearson himself agrees that it was only normal for a new administration to wish to project a new image and to show the Canadian public that it would not be dazzled by 'other Prime Ministers, Nobel Prizes, etc.'[13] Mr Trudeau had to do something in the field of foreign affairs, Professor John Warnock writes, 'to show that he was different from the previous Liberal leadership',[14] while an official in the Privy Council Office concurs that the review indicated the desire of a new government 'to establish its own personality'. Initiatives in foreign policy had been one of the characteristics of the Pearson government, at least in the public mind, and if the Trudeau administration was to demonstrate that it was more than a carbon copy of its predecessor, it was only natural that foreign policy would be one area towards which it would direct its attention.*

---

* This interpretation has been contested by one of Mr Trudeau's top advisers, who insists that it was not a case of 'change for the sake of change' but rather a realization by the Prime Minister that some changes were necessary and desirable.

Second, the decision to review foreign policy was probably based on much more than 'the normal inclination' of any new Prime Minister. Mr Trudeau had won the leadership of the Liberal Party in April 1968 at least in part because of his 'swinger' image and the expectations of change, however vague and undefined, that were associated with his style. Since it was this image that he intended to project in the election campaign (which lasted from April 23 until June 25), it was understandable that in May the government should announce that existing policy would be reviewed, that several specific changes would be made, and that still others would probably be forthcoming upon completion of the review. The Prime Minister's tendency to criticize Canada's NATO policy during the course of the election campaign was interpreted by Anthony Westell, then of the *Globe and Mail*, not as new thinking on the part of Mr Trudeau 'so much as evidence that he was with it, progressive, and open to new ideas.'[15] There could be no doubt that it was the Prime Minister's intention to subject existing policy of all kinds to review, in keeping with his desire for substantial reforms as well as his desire to project a politically appealing image. After a year in office he described the purpose of his government as one of attempting 'to redefine our policies in all spheres.' We have done it, he said, 'in the cultural, in the constitutional, in the trade spheres', and we are 'doing it in the area of our foreign policy and of our defence policy.'[16]

A third indication that it was primarily the Prime Minister and his Cabinet who desired the review lies in a policy-making characteristic of the previous administration. Under Lester Pearson the Cabinet was seldom involved in foreign- or defence-policy discussions. 'Only rarely are matters discussed in detail,' commented one of Mr Pearson's ministers; the unification of the Armed Forces, for example, was discussed in detail on only two occasions, both times in connection with approval of the 1964 Defence White Paper.[17] Former Cabinet minister Judy Lamarsh spoke more bluntly in her memoirs. 'If I may generalize', she wrote, 'a Cabinet is usually told little about military policy . . . [and] the same holds for foreign policy. These two vital areas of responsibility are left in the hands of the Prime Minister and the responsible minister (and no inquiries are invited, thank you).'[18] Paul

Martin believed that foreign policy should be determined directly between himself and Mr Pearson since they were the two members of the Cabinet most concerned and with the greatest experience in the field.[19] Several ministers became particularly hostile towards Martin's tendency to keep issues from going to Cabinet and, when he did bring them to Cabinet, to present them in technical terms that discouraged discussion. It is understandable, therefore, that ministers such as Trudeau, Gérard Pelletier, and Donald Macdonald, whose views had not been sought in the making of foreign policy, would wish to take part in its formulation in the new administration. Had their ideas been incorporated into foreign policy in the Pearson government, it is less likely that they would have felt as great a need to conduct an in-depth review as they did when they assumed office in 1968. Since their views on such issues as relations with Communist China and Latin America had not even been discussed, they must have welcomed the belated opportunity to examine such questions in detail. Although Mr Pearson believes that, had the Robertson Report been published, the Trudeau government would probably not have felt the need to review foreign policy,[20] it seems that the members of the new administration were as critical of the manner in which previous foreign policy had been formulated as they were of its substance and articulation. Above all, they wanted an opportunity to express their own views and to have the relevance and potentiality of their opinions considered.

The final and most persuasive indication of the Prime Minister's influence on the decision to conduct a foreign-policy review is the fact that there is a far greater correlation between the May 29 announcement and Mr Trudeau's personal philosophy than between the announcement and the stated views of any other possible sources of influence. The document's interpretation of the external environment—a trend towards détente and a decrease in Canada's relative power because of the rise of Europe and the Third World—was consistent with Mr Trudeau's own view of the world, as were the new approaches that it announced. The decisions to emphasize economic, cultural, and social relations with Europe at the expense of military ties, to explore new avenues in Latin America and the Pacific, to accord a higher priority to aid, and to recognize the government of

Communist China as soon as possible—all are policies that Mr Trudeau was on record as favouring well before May 1968. That the announcement did not adopt a hostile attitude to the United States and indicated that Canada's military role in NATO would be examined with a critical eye were very much in keeping with Mr Trudeau's own inclinations. The announcement implied that Canada's participation in NORAD was in some ways inappropriate—a more critical line than Mr Trudeau himself appears to have favoured at that time—but this is the only exception to what is generally an extremely close correlation between the May 29 announcement and Mr Trudeau's own views. It is also significant that the survival of Canada as a federal and bilingual state—the very goal that was at the top of Mr Trudeau's personal list of priorities—was given as the first concern of Canadian foreign policy. Justification of foreign policy in terms of national interests other than peace and security was a major departure (at least in articulation) from the approach of the Pearson administration.

Although some of the specific issues mentioned in the May 29 statement have already been discussed, little attention has yet been paid to its dominant theme. On practically every page there is some reference to the need for a more realistic approach to Canada's goals and capabilities on the international scene. On page 1 the 'conceptions and role-casting' of the past are questioned; on page 2 a call is made for 'realism in how we see ourselves', since 'we shall do more good by doing well what we know to be within our resources'; and on page 3 it is stated that Canada must adopt a 'pragmatic and realistic' approach so that its policies 'accord with our national needs and resources'. On page 5 Canadians are told that their need 'is not so much to go crusading abroad as to mobilize at home our aspirations, energies and resources', and on page 6 the need for endeavours that lie 'within our national resources' is stressed. The statement concludes on page 7 with an appeal for a foreign policy that is 'pragmatic, realistic and which contributes effectively both to Canada's political survival and independence and to a more secure, progressive, free and just world society.'

By emphasizing a new 'realistic' approach to foreign policy in its May 29 announcement the government clearly indicated that some changes were in the offing. The announcement was saying that foreign policy should be based on factors other than a desire to be altruistic or to achieve prestige for Canada—the somewhat grandiose ambitions that had resulted from the 1956 Suez crisis, which led to the myth that Canada could play a middle-power role in acting as a world peacekeeper. Two clear indications that it was primarily this rhetoric that the Trudeau government was attacking emerged from testimony before the Commons' Standing Committee on External Affairs after the review was completed. Asked to specify causes of the 'public disenchantment' that the government claimed had existed, Geoffrey Murray of the Department of External Affairs pointed to the 'expectations built up either from outside (or within) the government' that Canada would be able to accomplish a great deal more than was in fact possible.[21] An even more revealing comment made before this committee came from Mitchell Sharp, who explained the government's attitude in this way:

> A growing body of Canadian opinion was questioning Canada's position on specific foreign policy issues. The government was concerned about the focus of the criticism being expressed, with its concentration on issues primarily involving other powers and their policies and interests and its preoccupation with Canada's role, rather than with the furtherance of national aims and interests.[22]

This was likely the government's thinking, for the emphasis on national interests in both the statement of May 29, 1968 and the 1970 foreign-policy papers themselves was very much in keeping with Mr Sharp's comment. What is particularly significant about his remark is the suggestion that the critics of Canadian foreign policy were just as preoccupied with an unrealistic international role for Canada as the Canadian public and some members of previous Canadian governments. By suggesting that Canada could play a greater role in UN peacekeeping if it withdrew at least in part from its military alliances (as Jack Granatstein suggested), or that it could have a 'second golden decade' by playing the role of aid-giver *par excellence* (as Escott Reid proposed), the critics were succumbing, in the government's view, to the same temptations to acquire glory and prestige for Canada that the Prime Minister considered to be the major flaw in existing Canadian foreign policy. Therefore, if the decision to review Canada's policies and to base them on more 'practical' considerations was largely influenced by the government's dislike of the rhetoric about Canada's international role, the decisive influence could not have come from the academic and Parliamentary critics, for they were advocating precisely a more active role—one designed to enhance Canadian prestige and self-respect—to which the government objected.

During the period of the review only three prominent people advocated ideas whose general thrust was similar to those on which the May 29 announcement, the 1969 NATO decision, and the 1970 foreign-policy papers were all based. In his Montmorency speech Dalton Camp called for a foreign policy based on national interests and a concentration on foreign aid rather than on NATO, NORAD, or the UN. The government ultimately rejected his call for a virtually total withdrawal from NATO and NORAD, but the fact remains that Camp was one of the first of the post-war foreign-policy critics to speak of Canada's distinctive national interests. Similarly Professor James Eayrs, while supporting some increase in foreign aid, placed much more emphasis on the desirability of a dramatic cut in defence expenditure and on the need to pay more attention to domestic problems. 'Our thing', he said, 'is to concentrate upon matters at home,' an approach that he described as reflecting a healthy 'mood of introversion'.[23] It is known that Mr Trudeau met Professor Eayrs at least twice to discuss foreign policy, and there is speculation that much of Eayrs' hostility towards diplomats, and towards the Canadian Department of External Affairs in particular, rubbed off on the Prime Minister, or at least reinforced his own feelings.

The third advocate of the 'national-interest' approach was Prime Minister Trudeau, whose instrumental beliefs include the idea that it is the function of government to build a national consensus by pursuing policies designed to further the basic aspirations of its citizens. He clearly considers foreign policy important primarily to the extent that it contributes to such goals as national unity, economic growth, and the creation of a just society in Canada. Given this central preoccupation, there could have been two decisive influences on the basic decision concerning the future direction of Canadian foreign policy. One was that of Mr Camp or Professor Eayrs. Whether or not Mr Trudeau was convinced by the arguments of either of these men is a question that remains to be answered conclusively. Although asked by the author how much influence he felt his views had had on the Prime Minister, and how much contact he had had with Mr Trudeau before and during the policy review, Professor Eayrs ignored both questions in his brief written reply, saying that only the Prime Minister could know what the decisive factors were. One of Mr Trudeau's closest advisers subsequently remarked that Eayrs was being 'overly modest'—that his influence on the review was 'zero, absolutely zero'.

In view of the striking similarity between almost all aspects of the statement of May 29 and Mr Trudeau's personal beliefs, it is more likely that it was the Prime Minister who was the guiding light and who provided the decisive input for the foreign-policy review. It was primarily his decision, based on his interpretation of the internal and external environments, to conduct the review in the first place, and it was his views, influenced only marginally by outside advice, that determined its direction.

Notes

[1] Pierre Elliott Trudeau, 'Canada and the World', *Statements and Speeches*. No. 68/17, May 29, 1968.

[2] See Jon B. McLin, *Canada's Changing Defense Policy, 1957-1963: The Problems of a Middle Power in Alliance*. Toronto: Copp Clark, 1967, pp. 131-2.

[3] Interview with Lester B. Pearson.

[4] Garth Stevenson, 'For a Real Review'. *Current Comment*, Ottawa: School of International Affairs, Carleton University, 1970, p. 15.

[5] James N. Rosenau, *Public Opinion and Foreign Policy*. New York: Random House, 1961, pp. 4, 11.

[6] Letter to the author, May 24, 1971.

[7] See Denis Stairs, 'Public and Policy-Makers', *International Journal*, Winter 1970–1, p. 247.

[8] Letter to the author, May 21, 1971.

[9] *Loc. cit.*

[10] Letter to the author, June 25, 1971.

[11] *Loc. cit.*

[12] Letter to the author.

[13] Interview with Lester B. Pearson.

[14] Letter to the author, May 27, 1971.

[15] *Globe and Mail*, October 4, 1968, p. 7.

[16] Pierre Elliott Trudeau, 'The Relation of Defence Policy to Foreign Policy', *Statements and Speeches*. No. 69/8, April 12, 1969, p. 6.

[17] See Roddick Byers, 'Executive Leadership and Influence: Parliamentary Perceptions of Canadian Defence Policy', in Thomas A. Hockin, ed., *Apex of Power: The Prime Minister and Political Leadership in Canada*. Toronto: Prentice Hall, 1971, pp. 178–9.

[18] Judy Lamarsh, *Memoirs of a Bird in a Guilded Cage*. Toronto: McClelland and Stewart, 1968, p. 31.

[19] See Peter C. Dobell, 'Canada and NATO'. *Orbis*, Vol. XIII, Spring 1969, p. 318.

[20] Interview with Lester B. Pearson.

[21] *Minutes of Proceedings and Evidence of the Standing Committee on External Affairs and National Defence*, November 24, 1970, p. 9.

[22] *Ibid.*, October 23, 1970, p. 7.

[23] *Ibid.*, February 6, 1969.

5

The NATO Decision

In spite of Prime Minister Trudeau's frequently expressed desire to ensure that Canada's defence policy flowed out of its foreign policy, the decision to revise Canada's military contribution to NATO and to set new defence priorities preceded by fourteen months the publication in 1970 of the government's papers outlining its new approach to foreign policy. Because of the exigencies of fiscal planning, the Cabinet needed to know as quickly as possible the size of the defence budget for the fiscal year 1969-70: only after a thorough review of defence policy could the government decide whether this budget should be reduced, increased, or frozen. Secondly, the annual review of NATO by all its members was approaching, when Canada and the other member-countries would be required to make firm military commitments for one year and tentative forecasts for the next five years. Mr Trudeau acknowledged that the need to meet this deadline (April 10, 1969) had influenced the order in which the components of Canada's external policy had been reviewed, saying: 'It is more difficult, and not easier, for us to have to make a decision on NATO before we have made a decision on other aspects of our foreign and defence policy.'[1] Finally, it can be surmised that the defence review was given priority because NATO was the issue that seemed to arouse the greatest interest among critics of Canadian foreign policy, and because it was one of the areas in which Mr Trudeau himself appeared critical of existing policy.

For the proponents of a new Canadian foreign policy, NATO had become the symbol of the detested status quo—a military alliance dominated by the United States, a power bloc that lessened Canada's credibility in the Third World and as a peacekeeper, and a bottomless pit into which were thrown resources that could be put to better use in foreign aid. The advocates of existing Canadian foreign policy, on the other hand, saw NATO as a symbol of all that was laudable in Canada's approach to international affairs—its concern with contributing to the stability of Europe, the area in which world peace was most immediately threatened; its emphasis on gaining influence with its NATO allies, particularly the United States, and using it to encourage diplomatic imagination and military caution; and its search for counterweights to offset Canada's dependence on the U.S.

There were six courses of action open to the government:

1. Adopt a policy of non-alignment, which would mean withdrawal from both NATO and NORAD.
2. Withdraw from NATO but remain in NORAD.
3. Remain in NATO but withdraw all forces from Europe.
4. Remain in NATO but reduce the number of troops in Europe.
5. Remain in NATO with present force strength.
6. Remain in NATO and increase the size of the force in Europe.

The NATO issue involved far more than military considerations, for it went to the very basis of Canada's philosophy of foreign policy. This may explain why, for the first time ever, the Canadian government made a conscious and serious attempt to involve Parliament, academics, and the public in the formulation of foreign and defence policy.

I. The NATO Review Process

One innovation of the NATO review process was the government's decision to look beyond the civil service for policy proposals. Mr Trudeau aroused much speculation when he said in the House:

> The policy decisions of this government are based on advice not only from civil servants but from all the areas which are available to us. This government is not taking the position that it must necessarily be guided only by what is decided by the civil servants. We are ministers who are responsible to the Canadian people and we are seeking advice from all possible sources.[2]

'May I ask the Prime Minister, then,' said John Diefenbaker, 'why he is getting this information outside of cabinet circles and outside the Department of External Affairs, and why he does not tell us who are these anonymities who give advice to the Canadian government about what it ought to do?' Mr Trudeau refused to satisfy the Opposition's curiosity about his advisers. In reply to a question from Gordon Fairweather, a Conservative MP, he confirmed that Lester Pearson was not one of these sources, but he would not comment further.[3]

Another innovation that emerged in the course of the NATO review was the Prime Minister's encouragement of his Cabinet ministers to express in public their own differing views on the NATO issue. Questioned in Parliament on the obvious differences between ideas expressed by Léo Cadieux and Eric Kierans, Mr Trudeau said they were offering 'suggestions for thinking' to the Canadian people and that their ideas were purely 'exploratory'.[4] Neither of them, he insisted, was presenting the views of the government, for the government had not yet decided its policy with respect to NATO. Mr Trudeau may have been testing public opinion by allowing an open debate to see how far the government could safely venture in changing existing policy. It is more probable, however, that he was trying to educate the public and to interest Canadians in foreign and defence policy, since this would be more consistent with his philosophy (see Chapter 3). Whatever his intention, the enunciation of differing views by Cabinet ministers served to stimulate public interest in the foreign-policy review, although it also increased the confusion of Opposition MPs and others who wanted a clear indication of the government's thinking.

1. ACADEMIC VIEWS

Mr Trudeau and his ministers made a concerted effort to familiarize themselves with the views of Canadian academics. The Prime Minister discussed foreign and defence policy with them on at least two occasions. One of these meetings, in Toronto on the day after the 1968 Grey Cup game, was described by James Eayrs, a participant, as less than enlightening. 'I would like to believe', Eayrs wrote of Trudeau, that 'he was just fatigued from a late night rather than just bored as he appeared to be.'[5] Another was a dinner party at 24 Sussex Drive with a group of academics suggested by John Holmes at Mr Trudeau's request. (He had asked for as wide a spectrum of views as possible.) It was Mr Holmes' impression that the Prime Minister listened carefully and asked penetrating questions.[6] According to other participants, the Prime Minister appeared to listen with special attention and interest to James Eayrs.

Not long afterwards other ministers began to follow Mr Trudeau's lead. Mr Sharp met a group in Toronto in the fall of 1968. At that meeting James Eayrs reports that Mr Sharp appeared to have already made up his mind that Canada would remain in NATO and the tenor of the conversation was that the academics 'tried to persuade Sharp that if the government was reviewing foreign policy some changes in policy should result and it would not be enough to stand pat. Recognition of Red China was urged on Sharp as the easiest new departure he could make in foreign policy.'[7] In March 1969 John Holmes was again asked—this time by Donald Macdonald—to suggest a group of academics with whom he and other interested ministers could discuss foreign and defence policy. Mr Holmes suggested Stephen Clarkson, David Cox, Jack Granatstein, Franklyn Griffiths, Lewis Hertzman, and Robert Spencer, who along with Holmes met six Cabinet ministers at the Park Plaza Hotel in Toronto. (The fact that neither Mitchell Sharp nor Léo Cadieux was invited to attend appears to be because both had previously met with academics, whereas the ministers who participated in the Park Plaza meeting had not.) The main impression of those present was that a very wide measure of disagreement existed among the ministers. While Eric Kierans, Donald Macdonald, and James Richardson seemed to favour significant changes in Canada's NATO policy, Paul Hellyer, Jean-Luc Pépin, and Otto Lang apparently advocated more of a status-quo approach.

On December 3, 1968, Peter Newman wrote in the Ottawa *Journal* that he had identified ten people 'involved' in the foreign-policy review who had met in September with Mr Sharp and two senior officials.[8] However, Mr Sharp told the House the next day that these people merely came together to select several academics who could meet later with the government officials and make their views on foreign policy known to them. This meeting, Mr Sharp said, would take place in Hull on the weekend of January 3-5, 1969. He also expressed the hope that the academics would in due course write about the seminar in order to foster wider public discussion and debate.[9]

The large number of university professors and high-ranking government officials at the Hull seminar indicated the ambitiousness of this attempt to engage the academic community in a serious discussion of policy. Invitations had been forwarded to a wide range of interested academics, and David Cox, Thomas Hockin, Gilles Lalande, Trevor Lloyd, Frank Marzari, Louis Sabourin, H. G. Skilling, Hugh Thorburn, and R. A. Spencer were able to attend. Also invited were John Holmes, the Director General of the Canadian Institute of International Affairs, which had arranged the meeting; Peter C. Dobell of the Parliamentary Centre for Foreign Affairs and Foreign Trade; and Roy Mathews of the Private Planning Association of Canada. Leading the government representation were two deputy ministers: Marcel Cadieux of External Affairs and Maurice Schwarzmann of Industry, Trade and Commerce. The delegation from the Department of External Affairs included Ambassador Paul Tremblay, one of the co-chairmen of the government's Task Force on Europe; Ross Campbell, Canada's NATO representative in Brussels; and J. G. H. Halstead of the European Division; as well as several others. The Department of National Defence was represented by Lt.-Gen. W. A. B. Anderson; the Department of Defence Production by John Killick; the Department of Manpower and Immigration by J. R. Cross and R. J. Curry; the Department of Finance by R. Y. Grey and G. Howarth; the Treasury Board by H. G. de Puyjalon; and the Bank of Canada by R. W. Lawson, the Deputy Governor. Also present were three members of the Privy Council Office: J. R. Whitehead, H. H. Wright, and G. H. Dewhirst.[10]

To stimulate discussion, the government distributed six background papers covering such topics as Canada's relations with Eastern Europe, Canadian-European economic relations, Europe and national unity, and Europe as a counterweight to the United States. It was the paper dealing with Canada's defence relations with Europe, however, that dominated the discussions. It soon became clear that the academics had come to talk about NATO.

Although the seminar was closed to the public, it is possible to assess the discussions from comments made by those present. While the Executive-Director of the Canadian Institute of International Affairs later remarked that the talks had been frank and that there had been no real conflict of ideas between the academics and government officials, not everyone shared his assessment. According to one of the government officials who attended the session, it became very much a confrontation between academics and bureaucrats that resulted in a hardening of positions on both sides. Thomas Hockin of York University, presenting the academics' side, said that the two groups had spoken frankly but that it was a 'dialogue of the deaf', since 'each side speaks a different language with different premises and different preoccupations.' But according to another observer Canada's NATO representative, Ross Campbell, gave what he himself and other government officials thought was an extremely persuasive defence of the case for NATO. The academics did not raise any strenuous objections and the officials concluded that the government had won its case. What Mr Campbell and his colleagues did not realize was that most of the academics had remained relatively silent only because they regarded the government's presentation to be so preposterous, and the views of its officials so fixed, that discussion would have been meaningless. The academics apparently felt that Ross Campbell had talked too much and had treated them with condescension, so that his lengthy defence of NATO proved counter-productive. Before long there was a general consensus that, as Mitchell Sharp later observed, the attempt to create a dialogue at Hull 'was perhaps little more than a lesson in how *not* to do it.'[11] Nevertheless that seminar was a valuable learning experience. Although a dialogue had not been created, government officials at least were made aware of some of the academics' views and, as a government spokesman said, would have to come up with convincing counterarguments if they expected their own views to win respect.[12] The meetings on other aspects of foreign policy that were later held between officials and academics, businessmen, and other members of the attentive public proved more rewarding.

2. THE PARLIAMENTARY COMMITTEE REPORT

In the first three months of 1969 the Commons' Standing Committee on External Affairs and National Defence undertook an extensive examination of Canada's NATO policy. Hearings were held twice weekly and reported in considerable detail by newspapers such as the Toronto *Globe and Mail*, an indication of the general enthusiasm and interest that surrounded the NATO debate.

For one of the first times in the history of this Parliamentary Committee, attendance was regular and the members took a real interest in its work. In November 1968 the Prime Minister had assured the House that evidence before the Committee would be considered 'very important' by the government, and in December Mitchell Sharp told the Committee that the government would 'take into account views which were expressed in the committee both by witnesses and by members of the committee.'[13] The rules changes of December 1968, which promised a greater role for Parliamentary committees by increasing the number of matters assigned to them for study, also contributed to the unprecedented atmosphere of optimism among MPs on both sides of the House. Many felt that the Committee, formerly considered to be an investigative but not a policy-forming body, would be able to influence the government's eventual decision. Indeed, Chairman Ian Wahn announced at the beginning of the first hearing that the aim of the Committee's study was to hear from experts and to stimulate debate in the hope of influencing the current review of defence and foreign policies.[14]

From the outset the steering committee worked on the principle that the Committee should be exposed to as wide a variety of opinions as possible in order to arrive at the most favourable NATO policy for Canada.[15] This deliberate search for people who would challenge existing views was highly unusual, but it was in keeping with the government's own predilection for exposing itself to all possible sources of advice. As one Committee member later remarked in the House: 'Name it and we heard about it in that committee.'[16]

Professor James Eayrs of the University of Toronto was the first well-known critic of Canadian defence policy to appear before the Committee. After explaining the various functions of military forces, he concluded that Canada was 'overspending on each and every purpose for which its military establishment is maintained', and that it could without difficulty pare a full $1 billion from its present defence budget. This, he said, could be accomplished by abandoning Canada's anti-bomber defences for the protection of North America, which would create a gap that the United States would be compelled to fill in its own interests, and by withdrawing from the defence of Western Europe through NATO, which he described as 'an illusory search for influence and international prestige.' By taking this 'free ride', Eayrs said, financial resources would become available for such worthy international ventures as a Canadian development and assistance corps, though he placed more emphasis on domestic goals for Canada's revenues and armed forces. Where the Canadian Armed Forces had a real role to play, he suggested, was in the surveillance of Canada's territorial waters, since this was the one military function that could not be entrusted to a foreign country.[17]

For three of the witnesses the only way in which Canada could play an active and constructive role in international affairs was as a completely non-aligned country. A complete withdrawal from NATO and NORAD, said Michael Brecher of McGill, would create 'a distinct image in the external world of an autonomous Canadian identity', while the resulting decrease in the defence budget would provide more resources for foreign aid and peacekeeping, as well as for the alleviation of financial problems within Canada. Kenneth McNaught of the University of Toronto presented very much the same argument in support of a role of military non-alignment for Canada. The money freed from the defence budget could be used to expand the country's foreign-aid program and alleviate poverty within Canada. The main difference between this view and that of John Warnock of the University of Saskatchewan lay in the bitter anti-Americanism of the latter. By participating in NATO and NORAD, he said, Canada had served as an 'extension of the American military system' and been hampered in its peacekeeping activities by its identification with the United States.[18]

Two other witnesses maintained that Canada could play a constructive role without withdrawing completely from its military alliances. Jack Granatstein of York University believed that peacekeeping should be the primary function of the Canadian Armed Forces. He noted that participation in NATO had not hampered Canada's role as a peacekeeper in the past; what was needed now was the withdrawal of Canada's forces from Europe and the establishment in Canada of a mobile force that, in addition to fulfilling any peacekeeping obligations, could also play a useful role in NATO in case of war. Stephen Clarkson of Toronto believed that Canada's 'very considerable international responsibility' lay primarily in the field of foreign aid, and that within ten years the present budgetary allocations for military and aid spending should be reversed. 'I am not against being in clubs,' Clarkson said, 'but I am very much in favour of one's defining one's role in a club, one's membership, in a creative fashion appropriate to the conditions of the time.' Like Granatstein he favoured the creation of 'an extremely mobile peacekeeping force' based in Canada.[19]

There are several indications that the testimony of these critics failed to convince many of the members of the Committee—most of whom, according to Douglas Harkness, became 'rather fed up' with these academics because of their apparent self-righteousness, arrogance, and ivory-tower idealism.[20] The 'free ride' of James Eayrs was considered intolerable for a country with any self-respect, while many realized that the Granatstein-Clarkson concept of a mobile force might involve even higher military expenditures in the future. The anti-Americanism that was implicit in the proposals of most of the advocates of non-alignment and explicit in the views of John Warnock repelled almost all of the Committee members. Ian Wahn later remarked that if there was one factor that discredited these critics in the eyes of the Parliamentarians, it was their anti-Americanism. Douglas Harkness also noted that the politically conscious Members of Parliament realized that the Canadian public would never accept a foreign policy based on hostility towards the United States, nor would it favour withdrawal from NATO and NORAD, or even a massive increase in foreign aid. For all these reasons the academic critics seem to have had little influence on the Committee members.

To balance the testimony of these academic critics, the Committee heard from eight witnesses who were in varying degrees generally sympathetic to Canadian participation in military alliances. John Gellner of *The Commentator*, Theo Sommer of *Die Zeit*, and Professor Adam Yarmolinski of Harvard all emphasized that NATO continued to perform an important military function, since it was in Europe that they perceived the greatest danger to world peace and security. They agreed that Canada's military contribution was primarily symbolic but still very important, and that any Canadian withdrawal of its forces might trigger a chain reaction of other withdrawals on the part of Holland, Denmark, Norway, and perhaps even the United States.[21]

The only Canadian academic who vigorously defended Canadian participation in NATO was Albert Legault of Laval. He did this on the grounds that Canada's contribution to NATO was not based on a need for national security (since its territory was not in danger) but rather constituted a 'profession of faith' in an alliance that was important for the defence of Western Europe. The prime objective of Canadian foreign and defence policy, he said, had always been to escape the American political orbit, and Canada's NATO contribution furthered that goal by confirming 'the awareness of a national unity through the prism of international accomplishments. . . . ' Finally, he repeated the familiar argument that only with a military contribution could Canada hope to be fully consulted and gain influence within the alliance.[22]

The Committee also heard from two members of Canada's military establishment. On February 4, Major-General Michael Dare presented a strictly factual description of the existing roles and capabilities of the Canadian Armed Forces. However, it was the testimony of General Charles Foulkes, former Chairman of the Joint Chiefs of Staff Committee, that seems to have particularly intrigued the Committee members. General Dare was prevented by his position from offering his personal views, but General Foulkes, who was then a university professor, was able to give not only impressive factual information but his own opinions as well. Although he believed that a Canadian military presence in Europe was still desirable, General Foulkes considered the present commitment to have 'rather dubious' validity. He described the nuclear-strike capacity of the alliance as one 'of doubtful and diminishing value under today's strategy', and advocated the handing over of the 'wasteful' ground role to Britain or Germany. Canada, he said, should reorganize its contribution as a mobile formation based in Europe, for this would best suit Canadian aptitudes and would also provide the necessary flexibility to meet UN peacekeeping roles. General Foulkes went on to shock the Committee members by revealing, for perhaps the first time publicly, that Canada's claim to ownership of the Arctic islands was not beyond dispute and that he had been informed recently that some American maps showed these Arctic islands as 'disputed territory'. Thus, he said, as the Arctic became more important economically, the necessity for 'surveillance, control, and policing' would increase. His final argument against a posture of unarmed neutrality for Canada consisted of the warning that there was no guarantee that Canada would escape the civil disorders that had plagued other countries, and that it would be unwise to ignore the need for the means of controlling any such outbreaks of violence.[23]

Finally both David Golden, former Deputy Minister of the Department of Defence Production, and Dr O. M. Solandt, former Chairman of the Defence Research Board, offered a defence of Canada's armed forces that stressed their role in NORAD rather than in NATO.[24] Both argued at length that it was in Canada's best interests to co-operate with the United States in the defence of the North American continent. Only if resources permitted, however, should Canada participate in other military ventures, for NATO—unlike NORAD, which maintains forces in Canada and the United States in defence of North America—was not viewed as contributing directly to the country's territorial security. Their reluctance to support wholeheartedly Canadian participation in NATO was evident in Dr Solandt's comment that 'If I had to make the decision, I would say let us stay in, but if a government decided on balance that they were going to pull out I would not say that the government was completely wrong.'

The arguments of these witnesses against a state of non-alignment or unarmed neutrality for Canada seem to have been favourably received by the Committee members and to have accorded with their own sympathies. The practical and realistic tenor of these arguments seemed preferable to the idealism of many of the academic critics. But if these witnesses had shown clearly the desirability of Canada's remaining in NATO, they may also have contributed to the feeling that Canada's military role was in need of adjustment. The contentions that it was in North America rather than in Europe that Canada faced its main security threat, that Canada's NATO contribution was of doubtful military importance, that (according to no less an authority than General Foulkes) the nature of Canada's military contribution should be revised, that there was a great need for Canada's armed forces for northern surveillance and internal security, and that NATO was important but secondary to NORAD—all these points implied that changes should be made in the nature of Canada's existing contribution to NATO.

The Committee began a tour of Europe early in March as the final stage of its deliberations.[25] In London, Alistair Buchan of the Institute of Strategic Studies pointed to recent increases in the Soviet defence budget as proof of the continuing need for NATO, an argument repeated in Brussels by Canada's NATO ambassador, Ross Campbell, and by Pierre Harmel, the Belgian Minister of Foreign Affairs. In Germany the Committee was told that Canada's forces in NATO were making a valuable contribution to peace. In Geneva, Canada's UN representative, George Ignatieff, said that Canadian participation in NATO gave the country a greater voice in disarmament discussions, and in Stockholm Canadian Ambassador Arthur Andrew informed the Committee that Sweden based its position of neutrality on two considerations: its territory was not strategically important and it was prepared to pay a high military bill in order to defend itself if necessary. He intimated that neither condition existed in Canada. The only exception to this procession of NATO supporters was General Gallois of France, who told the Committee in Paris that NATO 'makes no sense at all', since it is a military system based on traditional rather than nuclear weapons. The general attitude of the Committee members to this statement was expressed by Marcel Prud'homme, who told General Gallois that his testimony had left him 'completely dumbfounded'. Another critical Committee member asked the General: 'Have you considered that your decision could bring about a world war? Or was your thought merely France's sovereignty?'

There appears to be little doubt that this two-week exposure to European views helped convince most members of the Committee who were still undecided that there was a need for Canada to remain in NATO and continue its military activity in Europe. Two meetings were particularly influential in this regard. The first was a private session with the German Defence Minister, Helmut Schmidt, who, despite his socialist affiliation, emphasized the value of NATO as an instrument of détente. The other was a meeting with members of the Swedish Committee on Foreign Affairs, who, although representatives of a neutral country, all asked that Canada remain in Europe. These encounters may have done little to dispel doubts that the nature of Canada's military contribution was in some ways inappropriate, but they convincingly refuted the view that Canada should withdraw totally from membership in NATO and military involvement in Europe. It can also be assumed that these arguments carried some weight in Cabinet.

By mid-March the Committee members had developed clearly formed opinions. Among the most passionate and articulate supporters of NATO were Douglas Harkness, Norman Cafik, and Perry Ryan, who were instrumental in convincing most of the other Committee members of the need for Canada to remain in Europe. Only two Liberal members opposed this view. One was the Committee Chairman, Ian Wahn, who was inclined to favour a complete withdrawal from NATO. Realizing, however, that neither the government nor the Committee would ever accept such a proposal, he instead stressed the need for a complete military withdrawal from Europe. The other opponent was Warren Allmand, who wanted Canada to play a significant political role in NATO but to withdraw all its forces from Europe. He issued his own minority report to this effect. The possibility of determined opposition to NATO from the NDP was lessened by the difference of opinion that existed among its three Committee members. Although David Lewis's inclination was toward a complete withdrawal from NATO, the party's defence spokesman, Andrew Brewin, wanted only a military withdrawal from Europe, while Harold Winch believed that some Canadian troops should be left in Europe.

Since the influence of the chairman in the drafting of committee reports is often decisive, the fact that Ian Wahn was not able to convince the other members of his views suggests that a strong consensus had developed in favour of maintaining Canadian forces in Europe. Mr Wahn drew up a preliminary report that reflected his own views, as is customary.[26] Since the Cabinet deadline was rapidly approaching, he prepared this draft during the Committee's European trip and showed it for the first time to the other members during the weekend plane trip from Geneva to Ottawa on March 23. When the Committee met officially on Monday, March 24, his draft was attacked by almost every member. It was rejected entirely, and the steering committee set out to prepare a new report. It began with the recommendations, which were completed by 10 p.m. that evening. At this point the steering committee contacted the Parliamentary Centre for Foreign Affairs and Foreign Trade and asked its director, Peter C. Dobell, who had worked closely with the Committee throughout its NATO study, to produce the body of the report. Mr Dobell summarized the facts and the opinions of the members and organized them in a manner that would indicate the reasoning followed by the Committee in arriving at its recommendations. Within twenty-four hours he had submitted the report—his text, plus the recommendations of the steering committee—to the Committee for its approval. Ian Wahn immediately proposed that the Committee submit a report consisting of only one paragraph—a recommendation that Canada remain in NATO, but that the Committee had had insufficient time to consider what its military role should be. His suggestion gained no support, however, and it was left to David Lewis to propose that the text submitted by Peter Dobell should form the basis of the report. Mr Lewis's motion was accepted and the Dobell draft, with some amendments, was released as the Committee's Final Report to the House on March 25.

The Report contained five recommendations. First, it stated that

Canada should remain a member of NATO because the organization was necessary for the security of both Europe and Canada, because membership did not impair Canada's effectiveness in peacekeeping or in the Third World, and because considerations of both geography and cost made non-alignment unfeasible. Secondly, Canada should maintain troops in Europe, for the Committee rejected the notion that Canada could take a 'free ride' without losing freedom both of action and influence; it also discounted the idea that defence expenditures were disproportionately high. It saw no advantage to be gained from basing this force commitment in Canada and suggested that a Canadian withdrawal might 'possibly' bring about other withdrawals of NATO members. Both the third and fourth recommendations, however, pointed in the direction of change. Canada should continue its present military roles in Europe until the equipment for its Air Division and Mechanized Brigade became obsolete in 1972, and a prompt review of possible future military roles should be undertaken so that new defence policies would be available for the post-1972 period. (The Report stated that the Committee did not have enough information to recommend what these future roles should be.) The final recommendation was an uncontroversial statement that Canada should in future emphasize the political functions of NATO and encourage it to seek détente and balanced force reductions with the Warsaw Pact countries.

3. STAFFEUR

At the same time as the NATO debate was stimulating the interest of Canadian academics and Parliamentarians, the civil-service departments involved in foreign activities were carrying on their own review of Canada's relations with Europe.[27] The Prime Minister's statement of May 29, 1968, had revealed the government's intention to establish an interdepartmental Special Task Force on Relations with Europe, which would soon be known by the code name STAFFEUR. While its defence policy was being reviewed, the government wanted to reassess Canada's relations with Europe in the political and economic fields, which 'are inevitably intermingled with our defence commitments'.[28] The Special Task Force, therefore, was intended to investigate

Canadian-European relations in their totality, with one aspect of this review dealing with NATO. As the Secretary of State for External Affairs explained, STAFFEUR was one of the new government's first steps in breaking down the broad subject of foreign policy into areas for intensive study.

The Task Force began its work in the summer of 1968 under the chairmanship of Ambassadors Robert Ford and Paul Tremblay. Although the Department of External Affairs supplied the secretariat and STAFFEUR was to report to the government through Mr Sharp, the Force's twenty-five to thirty-five members were chosen from several departments. By the beginning of 1969, STAFFEUR had completed its study and submitted to the government a four-hundred-page report analysing Canada's past and present relations with the countries of Eastern and Western Europe. The report examined such matters as Europe's role in counteracting the influence on Canada of the United States and in promoting Canadian unity, Canadian-European defence and economic relations, and Canada's general relations with Eastern Europe. As for NATO, the Task Force concluded that Canada should continue to station troops in Europe since it was in Canada's economic and political, as well as military, interests to be actively involved on the continent.

4. THE EXTERNAL-DEFENCE REPORT

While STAFFEUR was examining Canada's overall relations with Europe, the Departments of External Affairs and National Defence were conducting a joint study of a more specialized nature. Their report, known as the External-Defence Report and classified as 'Secret, For Canadian Eyes Only', considered the problems and costs of maintaining and replacing military equipment, the international obligations to which Canada was committed, and analysed all possible options ranging from neutrality to increased support of NATO. The External-Defence Report reached conclusions that were almost identical to STAFFEUR's recommendations about NATO: maintain Canada's existing NATO forces, at least for the time being. The two reports differed in form, however. The External-Defence Report consisted mainly of little more than a set of options, while STAFFEUR adopted a more prescriptive approach and made definite policy recommendations. Nevertheless, since neither External Affairs nor National Defence were prepared to see their traditional policy of support for NATO rejected, the External-Defence Report clearly implied in its listing of options that a continuation of military activities in Europe was desirable.

5. THE PMO/PCO

Dissatisfied with the STAFFEUR and External-Defence reports, still awaiting the report of the Parliamentary Committee, and with the April 10 deadline rapidly approaching, Mr Trudeau decided in late March to turn to his own advisers. The Prime Minister asked Ivan Head to take a fresh look at the whole question of Canada's military policy in the hope that he would be able to develop a satisfactory solution to what had become a much more difficult and controversial issue than Mr Trudeau had expected. Head chaired a small committee that examined both general and specific questions dealing with military policy. Working with him were senior civil servants who served as 'resource people', answering any detailed questions that he raised in the course of his study. By March 29 Head had completed his special report, entitled 'Canadian Defence Policy—a Study' but referred to by a few knowledgeable insiders as the 'non-group report' (a somewhat caustic allusion to the large bureaucratic and parliamentary committees that had prepared the other NATO studies). The document was prepared with the utmost secrecy: neither Mitchell Sharp nor Léo Cadieux apparently even knew of its existence until it was distributed to Cabinet ministers only hours before the March 29 Cabinet meeting.[29] It apparently contained the recommendations that Canada remain in NATO, retain in Europe approximately 3,000 men out of its existing 9,800-man contingent, and abandon its nuclear-strike role.[30]

II. The Government's Decision

Throughout the review process Mr Trudeau consistently refused to speculate about its outcome or take any action that might prejudge its results. In a CBC interview in January 1969 the Prime Minister said he did not know what the NATO review would lead to: 'This is why we're having the review.'[31] Not until February 1969 did he even indicate when the review would be completed. The deadline, he told the House, had been March 15, since a decision was required before the meeting of NATO foreign ministers in Washington on April 10.[32] However, since the Commons' Committee had begun its work at such a late date that its ability to submit a report by the middle of March was doubtful, the government was prepared to delay its decision in order to include this report in its deliberations. As a result the Cabinet did not meet to decide on Canada's defence policy with respect to NATO until the weekend of March 29-30, and it continued its discussions into the next week. On Tuesday, April 1, the Prime Minister told the House that he hoped, but could not guarantee, that a statement would be made the following day. It was not, and on Wednesday a disappointed House of Commons rose for the Easter recess without having had an opportunity to hear or debate the government's NATO decision. This prompted an outburst from NDP leader David Lewis: 'I say the only reason he is not making the statement today is that he has no respect for the House of Commons and for Parliament and wishes to make the statement outside.'[33] It was, in fact, the very next day, April 3, that the Prime Minister announced the government's decision, and the delay seems clearly attributable to a serious division of opinion that existed within Cabinet rather than to any desire on the part of Mr Trudeau to by-pass Parliament.

There are three documents that must be examined in an attempt to explain either the content of the NATO decision or its rationale. The first is the Prime Minister's statement of April 3; the second the transcript of his subsequent press conference; and the third a speech given by Mr Trudeau in Calgary on April 12. The general tenor and philosophy of the arguments are so consistent in all three statements that to facilitate analysis they can be examined almost as one.[34]

The Prime Minister's April 3 statement began with the announcement of the government's rejection of a non-aligned or neutral role for Canada. One of the most important reasons for staying in NATO, Mr Trudeau explained, was Canada's desire to play a political role and to orient NATO towards seeking détente and arms reduction with the East.[35] He said Canada shared the same values as the other NATO members; if he did not feel that Canada could have some influence in the policies that further Canada's interests, he would have recommended total withdrawal. But, although it would remain a member of NATO, Canada had decided to 'bring about a planned and phased reduction of the size of the Canadian forces in Europe.' Mr Trudeau refused to divulge the size of this reduction, saying only that it would be decided 'in consultation with Canada's allies', and that it would constitute the second phase of the NATO review. (The decision of April 3 was the conclusion of the first phase.) The withdrawal, the Prime Minister noted, was purely unilateral, occasioned not by any desire for a reciprocal reduction in Warsaw Pact forces or to weaken NATO, but rather by Canada's belief that there were better uses for its armed forces in Canada than in Europe.[36] As for NORAD, the Prime Minister announced that Canada intended to continue to co-operate with the United States in the defence of North America, although the details of this joint defence effort had still to be discussed with the Americans.

As Mr Trudeau himself observed, what had been decided was not so much the details of Canadian defence policy as the government's new 'philosophy of defence'.[37] The most significant part of the April 3 statement was the announcement of the government's new defence priorities, based on the concentric-circle principle that money would be provided for low-priority activities only after those of high priority had been adequately financed. These priorities, which defined the future roles of the Canadian Armed Forces, consisted of:

(a) the surveillance of our own territory and coast-lines—i.e., the protection of our sovereignty;
(b) the defence of North America in co-operation with United States forces;
(c) the fulfilment of such NATO commitments as may be agreed upon;
(d) the performance of such international peacekeeping roles as we may, from time to time, assume.

The reasoning behind the government's decision to downgrade Canada's NATO role became clear in Calgary on April 12 when the

Prime Minister delivered a speech entitled 'The Relation of Defence Policy to Foreign Policy'. Its theme was that NATO, a military organization, had in the past determined Canada's defence policy, which had in turn determined the country's foreign policy. We had 'no foreign policy of any importance except that which flowed from NATO,' Mr Trudeau said, and 'this is a false perspective for any country.' What the government was attempting to do, he explained, was to 'stand the pyramid on its base' instead of its head—'to review our foreign policy and to have a defence policy flow from that, and from the defence policy to decide which alliances we want to belong to, and how our defences should be deployed.' And that, the Prime Minister concluded, 'is why we gave a series of four priorities.' Not until the government had presented its foreign policy to the country would it decide on its defence policy 'in a final way'. Since the NATO ministerial meeting had obliged the government to announce its defence philosophy before it could complete its White Paper on Foreign Policy, Mr Trudeau was able to announce only in general terms the foreign policy upon which his government had based its NATO decision. But he said that the aims of Canada's foreign policy were 'to serve our national interests and to express our national identity abroad.' This, it seems, is the explanation for the government's emphasis on sovereignty as Canada's first defence priority. 'When we place sovereignty at the head of the priorities,' Mr Trudeau explained at his press conference on April 3, 'it is because we believe this is essentially the role of a foreign policy and of a defence policy.' It was far from clear, however, what he meant when he talked of sovereignty. In his April 3 statement he equated it with 'the surveillance of our own territory and coast-lines'; during the press conference he expanded his definition to include 'assistance to the civil power', protection of our 'territorial waters', and the Gaullist line that the country should provide as large a part of its own protection as possible rather than 'having the Americans do it for us'. Then in Calgary he said simply that the government's first priority was the protection of Canadian sovereignty 'in all the dimensions that it means'. Although no one knew how far the government intended to carry its determination to defend Canadian sovereignty, the decision to emphasize sovereignty appears to have been inspired by the belief that defence policy had to be based on national interests that were more North American-oriented than were contributions to world peace and security through participation in NATO. Mr Trudeau explained that the redefinition of the roles of the Canadian Armed Forces that this implied was intended to reassure the CAF personnel, and 'especially' to convince the public, that there was a valid role for armed forces in Canada.

There were many questions that remained unanswered, however. How quickly would the NATO cuts take place? Would the withdrawal of forces from Europe be total? Would Canada's nuclear role be maintained? What would be the future size and role of the naval forces? Would the new priorities result in a reduction or increase in the defence budget? Some of these questions were dealt with in statements made by Defence Minister Cadieux on June 23 and September 19, 1969, but for the answers to other more tactical questions it was necessary to await the 1971 White Paper on Defence.

The government made it clear from the outset that the decision to reduce Canada's forces in Europe was not negotiable, and that only the size of the reduction would be a matter for discussion with Canada's allies. When Mr Cadieux attended the May meeting of the NATO Defence Planning Committee in Brussels, he informed the ministers of Canada's intention to reduce the size of its forces in Europe. As had been the case during the April meeting in Washington, the withdrawals were criticized by other NATO members—particularly the British and West Germans—as 'highly inadvisable' and likely to be 'infectious'. The other NATO members were so opposed to a Canadian cut-back that the European Defence Ministers, with American encouragement, met in caucus to decide in advance the arguments they would use. When Mr Cadieux arrived in Brussels he was met with a well-co-ordinated stream of criticism that American Ambassador Harlan Cleveland later described as 'the toughest talk I have ever heard in an international meeting'.[38] British Defence Minister Denis Healey delivered a particularly scathing attack on Canada, accusing it of 'passing the buck to the rest of us', a comment that was leaked to the press.[39] In the House a few days later Mr Cadieux admitted that Canada's proposals had not been well received, but claimed that the principal objection concerned Canada's failure to conform exactly to prescribed procedures of consultation.[40] This, Mr Cadieux said, Canada had agreed to do, and during the summer months there were several lengthy exchanges of notes between the Department of National Defence and NATO headquarters. Reliable sources indicate that the government had originally been thinking of a two-thirds reduction in the size of Canada's forces in Europe, but on September 19 Mr Cadieux announced that only half the forces would in fact be withdrawn. Although reluctant at the time to say that the government had compromised, the Defence Minister admitted three months later in the House that, as a result of consultation with our allies, 'we had modified considerably our original plan.'[41]

Mr Cadieux also announced in September that the remaining 5,000-man force in Europe would be organized by the autumn of 1970 into a land and air force located in the same area that would replace the separate brigade group and air divisions. Canada would also disengage gradually from all nuclear activities in Europe, dropping the 'Honest John' nuclear role in 1970 and the nuclear-strike role for the air force in 1972. By 1972 and after the country would be maintaining in Europe a conventionally armed land and air element of approximately the same size (5,000 troops).[42] However, Mr Cadieux did not explain how this decision, which seemed final, was consistent with the government's earlier promises that final defence commitments would not be made until the foreign-policy review had been submitted to the country.

One of the problems with a compromise solution that neither totally withdrew nor fully maintained Canada's forces in Europe, as the government soon discovered, was that it satisfied virtually none of the critics of Canadian defence policy. Among the Parliamentarians, for example, the government's decision of April 3 was interpreted in a variety of ways. For T. C. Douglas and the NDP, the government had committed itself to no real changes, since Canada was remaining in NATO and saying only that 'at some indeterminate time there will be, possibly, some indeterminate reduction of Canada's forces in Europe'. Douglas Harkness, on the other hand, concluded that 'the Prime Minister intends to end our military contributions as quickly as possible'.[43] Mr Cadieux's September 19 announcement resolved some of the confusion, however, and interest in the NATO question rapidly declined. The government's new defence priorities also drew criticism on the grounds that they represented a swing toward 'isolationism and continentalism' (according to Robert Stanfield) and ignored the vital role of the United Nations in contributing to world peace (according to Andrew Brewin). Only the Créditiste Party agreed with the government's emphasis on national interests, which it defined even more narrowly than Mr Trudeau seemed inclined to do. Charity begins at home, said Créditiste leader Réal Caouette, and Canada should concentrate on solving its own economic problems rather than on worrying about such remote concerns as European security or international development assistance.[44]

III. Assessment of Influences

1. THE EXTERNAL ENVIRONMENT

In Chapter 4 it was shown that changes in the external environment—the movement towards détente and an increase in the strength of Western Europe—made a decrease in Canada's military contribution to NATO possible but not inevitable. However, during the course of the NATO review in Canada (between May 1968 and April 1969), there occurred two important events in the external environment that might have discouraged any decision to withdraw Canadian forces from Europe. One was the decision of the NATO ministers in Reykjavik in June 1968 to press for mutual and balanced force reductions (MBFR) with the Warsaw Pact countries, a move based on the understanding that no NATO member would take unilateral action that would reduce the overall military capability of NATO and thereby weaken the credibility of the MBFR approach. Although Mr Trudeau stressed in his press conference of April 3, 1969 that Canada was merely redeploying its forces and was not reducing the strength of NATO, the Canadian decision to withdraw some of its troops from Western Europe without gaining in return the withdrawal of some Soviet forces from neighbouring states in Eastern Europe was clearly against the spirit, if not the letter, of the Reykjavik communiqué. The second major international event was the Soviet-led invasion of Czechoslovakia in the fall of 1968, which greatly increased East-West tensions. The fear and uncertainty that it created in the West remained for some months, and there was talk in NATO of the need to maintain and possibly increase the strength of its forces.

If the Canadian government's decision to reduce its forces in NATO was not dictated by external events, it was also not affected by the advice of Canada's NATO allies. At a 1969 Sussex Drive dinner party for a selected group of academics, Mr Trudeau revealed that during his trip to the Commonwealth Prime Ministers' Conference in London in January, the British had vigorously pressed their belief that Canada should continue its existing NATO commitments. British Defence Minister Denis Healey, on a visit to Canada that same year, had stressed that economic difficulties would make it extremely difficult for Britain to fill any gap caused by a Canadian withdrawal from Europe.[45] Germany, the other NATO country that would be required to supply more troops if Canada departed, also applied pressure, arguing that it did not want to appear to dominate the alliance. That this particular influence did not affect Mr Trudeau is indicated by his refusal to delay a skiing holiday by one day in April 1969 in order to discuss foreign affairs with the visiting West German Foreign Minister, Willy Brandt.[46] The United States, the one country that might conceivably have altered Canada's decision had it chosen to apply extreme pressure, did not. According to Mr Trudeau: 'We were not made to feel that if we were nice on the military and strategic problems that they would be nice on other bilateral questions.'[47] In fact the comments made to Mr Trudeau by American officials such as presidential-adviser Henry Kissinger may well have counteracted the advice from other quarters. When he said that atomic weapons would never be used in Europe, Mr Kissinger appeared to be directly contradicting the statements of such NATO supporters as Léo Cadieux, who had stressed that Canadian participation in NATO was necessary to maintain the nuclear balance in Europe.[48] The warnings of NATO members concerning the effect on other countries of a Canadian withdrawal also failed to influence Mr Trudeau, who told reporters at the National Press Club in Washington that

> We may be excused, I hope, if we fail to take too seriously the suggestion of some of our friends from time to time that our acts or our failure to act in this or that way will have profound international consequences or will lead to widespread undesirable results.[49]

The only 'external' influence on Mr Trudeau's thinking about NATO seems to have been the Italian Minister of Foreign Affairs, Pietro Nenni, with whom Mr Trudeau talked during his brief visit to Rome in January 1969. Mr Nenni emphasized that there was a vital political role for NATO in the promotion of détente and arms reductions, and that Canada should therefore remain in the organization. This point had been made many times before by Canadian supporters of NATO, but it seemed to have more effect when it was expressed by an intellectual socialist who, as Mr Trudeau said, was 'hardly a cold warrior'. At the Sussex Drive dinner party mentioned earlier the Prime Minister confirmed that Mr Nenni had influenced his thinking about NATO.

2. ECONOMIC CAPABILITY

The part played by financial and military considerations on the NATO decision is particularly difficult to determine. Mr Cadieux said in the House that finances had definitely been considered and that he had told the NATO Defence Planning Committee in Brussels that Canada's NATO decision 'was occasioned, in part, by a requirement for budgetary restraints on all Canadian government departments.'[50] But he did not reveal how important these restraints were compared to other factors. No mention was made of financial difficulties in the Prime Minister's statement of April 3, in spite of the fact that the country's economic problems might have been one of the most effective arguments the government could have used to defend its controversial cutbacks. In his press conference of April 3, Mr Trudeau did not mention financial questions and said only that considerations of Canada's foreign-exchange situation had not influenced the government. In reply to another question, Mr Trudeau said that a decision on whether the government was spending too much money on defence would be made later. ('C'est une décision que tous les gouvernements sont obligés de prendre, et que nous prendrons.')* More suggestive were his frequent references in Calgary to the size of the defence budget ('That's a lot of money') and to 'the tendency on the part of all Canadians' to want to transfer money from this area into more 'worthwhile' activities. However, the Prime Minister refused to say whether he agreed with critics who said that Canada was spending too much on defence. 'Perhaps and perhaps not' was his less-than-enlightening conclusion. If financial considerations played an important part in the government's decision, it was not apparent from the Prime Minister's comments.

One thing was clear, however: the government did decide to freeze the dollar value of the Canadian defence budget for at least the next few years and those who shaped Canada's defence policy would have to keep this limitation very much in mind. Mr Cadieux told the House on June 23, 1969, that the goal of his department was to achieve the transition to a new defence posture 'within a defence budget which will be maintained for the next three years at its current dollar level.'[51] In a time of severe inflation this meant that cuts had to be made in some commitments, but it did not necessarily dictate an immediate cut in Canada's NATO contribution, since in the short run the withdrawal of some or even all of its troops from Europe would effect a relatively minor saving.** By 1972 new equipment costing $300 to $400 million would be needed for the NATO forces. So it is only in the long run that financial considerations were likely to have any impact on the NATO decision. It is significant that both the STAF-

* 'That is a decision that all governments must make, and one that we will make.'

** It should be noted, however, that financial considerations dictated *some* of the tactical changes associated with the new defence posture. For example, the brigade group and the air division in Germany were replaced with a co-located land-and-air element under one headquarters; this was seen as a step towards removing the incompatibilities between the Canadian- and European-based forces and thereby reducing defence costs. (Cadieux, *Debates*, April 24, 1969, p.7927.) The need to decrease defence costs by increasing the 'multiple-tasking' capabilities of the Canadian Armed Forces was another important consideration in the NATO decision, but senior officials admit that it was certainly not the major one.

FEUR and External-Defence reports agreed that Canadian participation in NATO would probably have to be curtailed by 1972, since not even the NATO supporters in the government and civil service were willing to spend the sums required to purchase the new equipment.[52]

But while the freeze in the Canadian defence budget meant that financial considerations would have some bearing on overall defence policy in the long run, it did not dictate which immediate priorities the government was obliged to adopt. If the government had decided that instability in Europe constituted a direct and serious threat to Canadian security and that NATO should therefore be the country's first defence priority, money could have been diverted from other military roles that were perceived to be less vital. Instead, a deliberate decision was made to emphasize military roles in North America. As Defence Minister Donald Macdonald stated in a 1971 interview, defence of the Canadian North requires long-range surveillance aircraft, and 'unless the government backs away from the expensive new roles implied in its 1969 statement, the defence budget and the manpower ceiling may begin to rise again.'[53] That financial considerations alone were not enough to determine Canadian policy was also indicated by a statement made in May 1969 by Mitchell Sharp:

> The Government does not share the view of those who would leave the entire burden for North American bomber defence to the United States. This might keep the cost to Canada at a minimum, but it would run counter to the aim of maintaining national identity and independence.[54]

Once Canada's main national interest was defined as 'national identity and independence' rather than peace and security, it was inevitable that NATO would be accorded a lower priority in Canada's defence policy than formerly. It was this new 'philosophy of defence' (to use Mr Trudeau's expression of April 3), not financial considerations, that determined the money that would be made available for Canada's various military roles and the priorities given to them.

3. THE ACADEMIC CRITICS

There is no indication that the views of Canadian academics played a significant role in determining the government's NATO decision. The academic commentators had talked on the one hand of complete withdrawal from at least military participation in Europe and on the other of maintaining fully Canada's existing commitments. There had been virtually no advocacy of the kind of halfway measures announced on April 3 by Mr Trudeau. In that statement he firmly rejected the policy of non-alignment for Canada that Brecher, McNaught, and Warnock had advocated. As early as September of the previous year, Mitchell Sharp was saying publicly that the government had never seriously considered the possibility of total withdrawal from NATO. 'No one has suggested we should withdraw from NATO,' he said; 'this has never been the question.'[55] Whatever the reasons for this repudiation of neutralism, it shows that the government rejected the proposals of the most radical academic critics of existing NATO policy. Jack Granatstein's views fared equally poorly, as peacekeeping was relegated to the government's last defence priority. The April 3 decision did not even imply the transfer of resources from defence to foreign aid, which Escott Reid and Stephen Clarkson had consistently advocated. This does not mean, of course, that the academics had *no* influence. Several of them, James Eayrs in particular, may have convinced the key decision-makers that some policy changes were necessary. All that can be stated with certainty is that other influences were relatively more important.

4. THE STAFFEUR AND EXTERNAL-DEFENCE REPORTS

One of the reasons why the NATO decision is so significant is that it was the first clear indication that the role of the civil service in foreign- and defence-policy formulation had changed drastically. During the St Laurent and Pearson administrations, the Departments of External Affairs and National Defence had with few exceptions been able to convince the government to accept the policies they advocated. A senior official, describing the ease with which approval for Canadian voting in the United Nations was obtained, noted: 'All it took was a phone call [from the department] to the Minister. He would call the Prime Minister and we could have our decision in minutes.'

If senior civil servants expected that this approach would be continued in the Trudeau administration, their hopes were dashed when the Cabinet rejected the NATO recommendations of both the STAFFEUR and External-Defence reports. One major Cabinet criticism of both was that they took for granted the effectiveness of the existing weapons of Canada's NATO contingent without offering the detailed proof that already-skeptical ministers demanded. The view expressed in the reports that Canada's CF-104 Starfighters provided an effective second-strike capability was typical of the kind of civil-service reasoning that the Cabinet regarded as faulty. Convinced that the presence of Soviet missile bases only three hundred miles away made it unlikely that the aircraft would ever get off the ground in the event of war, Cabinet soon came to the conclusion that the civil service's NATO recommendations were based not only on a lack of imagination but also on faulty judgement.

Both External Affairs and National Defence seemed to reflect the traditional conservatism of established bureaucracy at a time when the key decision-makers, particularly the Prime Minister, were looking for more innovative and creative approaches. James Eayrs has written that 'All bureaucracy's conservative, but the conservatism of diplomatic bureaucracy is in a class by itself.'[56] Dean Acheson, Henry Kissinger, and Karl Deutsch all agree that the bureaucratic routine makes men cautious rather than imaginative; they are so oriented towards policy implementation that they rarely have time to subject existing policy to severe scrutiny or to think of radically new departures.[57] This was certainly the case in Canada. Mr Pearson has observed that, during the years of his association with External Affairs, the department was so small and its activities were expanding so rapidly that the emphasis had to be on activity not policy review. Discussion of underlying principles occurred only in passing, in speeches by the Secretary of State for External Affairs; if the department had a theoretician, it was Escott Reid. The absence until 1969 of a Canadian equivalent of the State Department's Policy Planning Staff indicates what James Eayrs has called the 'general skepticism in which the planning of Canadian foreign policy has been held by governments and bureaucracy alike.'[58]

There was another factor, related to a civil-service department's specialized frame of reference, that hampered its ability to come up with the kind of policy proposals and analyses for which the government was looking during the NATO debate. Even NATO's severest critics were prepared to admit that there were some advantages to be gained by keeping Canadian troops in Europe, but they argued that these benefits were outweighed by other costs. Because of its limited orientation, however, the Department of National Defence was incapable of weighing non-military costs against what were clearly military benefits. It could not, for example, answer a question such as 'Are the benefits of NATO participation worth the amount of money being spent?' Nor could the department reasonably be expected to define its goals in terms other than peace and security, the purpose for which it had originally been established. It could determine whether non-military costs outweighed military advantages by working closely with other departments, but the many problems involved in inter-departmental consultation have not yet been adequately solved.* Only the country's political leaders can determine the overall priorities and philosophy that will guide the whole government apparatus and in terms of which each department must formulate its policies. During the NATO review communication between the Cabinet and the civil service was clearly inadequate. Perhaps because of Mr Trudeau's distrust of bureaucracies, and especially of External Affairs,[59] senior civil servants were never made adequately aware of the kind of things the country's political leaders wanted to do and the priorities that governed their thinking. The result was that the policies recommended by External Affairs and National Defence were both too unimaginative and too foreign to the government's guiding philosophy to be accepted by the Trudeau Cabinet.**

5. THE PARLIAMENTARY COMMITTEE'S REPORT

In so far as the Report of the Parliamentary Committee had any

* The approach used during the foreign-policy review—the creation of large interdepartmental task forces—was abandoned during the preparation of the 1971 Defence White Paper in favour of a small group of key officials who reported directly to the Minister of National Defence.

** The responsibility for this breakdown in communications was not solely the fault of Cabinet, however. (See Chapter 6, pp. 177-8.)

influence at all on the NATO decision, it was mainly an indirect one, through the Liberal caucus. The role of caucus is often underestimated because of the secrecy surrounding its deliberations. The degree to which the caucus of a party in power can influence policy depends on a variety of factors, particularly the strength and attitude of the Prime Minister. Although there have been complaints from Liberal backbenchers that they have been ignored, Mr Trudeau seems much more receptive to the views of caucus than he does to the House of Commons in general (see Chapter 3). The 1969 reforms of the Liberal caucus, requiring Cabinet to submit its legislative plans to caucus at least one month in advance of presentation in the House and to inform caucus of ministerial proposals in Cabinet committees, indicates a tendency on the part of the Trudeau government to take into consideration the collective views of its MPs.

The hearings for the Parliamentary Committee Report on NATO produced a group of MPs who were in general much better informed than the majority of the members of Cabinet. Debate in caucus on the NATO issue was particularly intense, and the Liberal members who favoured continuing Canada's role in Europe presented their arguments very forcefully and effectively. One Liberal MP observed that the great weight of opinion in the party was in favour of continuing a strong relationship with NATO, 'and this cannot be ignored.' Another Liberal member, Norman Cafik, predicted that if the government decided on the immediate withdrawal of troops from Europe, 'it would split the party wide open.'

Though many of the recommendations of the Parliamentary Committee resembled those of the STAFFEUR and External-Defence reports, they may have had slightly more impact on Cabinet than either of the civil-service documents, and more than even some of the Committee members realized. The Parliamentary Committee report was tabled just three days before the weekend in March when the ministers began their final deliberations, and this is cited by many as proof that it could not have had a decisive influence on Cabinet. David Anderson (L—Esquimalt-Saanich) insists that there was no way such a report could have been worked into a final decision in only a few days. (He notes that there is usually a period of ten days from the time an issue is first examined closely in cabinet committees until it goes to the full Cabinet, so that questions arising from a report can be checked and examined in detail.) However, this opinion overlooks the fact that the Committee made no recommendations of a kind that would have required detailed study—future equipment purchases or military roles, for example. It expressed views of a general nature, with which Cabinet was familiar, having already gone over the same arguments many times. The Committee Report could therefore have exerted *some* influence on the final decision. 'It did tip the balance slightly in favour of staying,' according to one minister.*

Both Ian Wahn and Douglas Harkness, the leaders of the pro- and anti-NATO factions within the Committee, are convinced that the Committee report exercised a moderating influence on the government, which originally intended to go much further. That this was so, while the two civil-service documents, expressing very much the same opinions, appear to have had little influence, can be explained by political considerations. One of Trudeau's ministers has observed that it is highly embarrassing for a government if there is an obvious discrepancy between its policies and the views of its MPs. The challenge facing a government is to work first of all towards a consensus within its own party; if the majority of MPs are firmly opposed to a policy, the government is usually inclined to moderate it. Faced with a near-consensus in favour of NATO in caucus, the government may well have been persuaded to alter any original intentions towards complete military withdrawal in Europe.

It is interesting that, according to inside sources, the Committee's Report was slightly more conservative than the real consensus of the majority of the Committee members. Most of the Liberal and NDP members of the Parliamentary Committee, as well as some of the Conservatives, favoured a reduction in Canada's existing NATO commitment in Europe even *before* 1972. Because the first draft of the

* According to Ian Wahn, the hearings of the Committee were followed with a great deal of interest by officials in the PMO. The announcement of defence priorities on April 3, 1969, was so similar to the arguments advanced by General Foulkes at the Committee hearings (see page 131), that the government through its PMO advisers may have paid particular attention to his testimony.

Report, prepared by Chairman Ian Wahn, had been so extreme in both tone and content, there was a hardening and polarization of opinion within the Committee: members who had favoured a modest military cutback in Europe became proponents of maintaining the 'status quo until 1972', in reaction against Wahn's proposal for a complete military withdrawal. Within the Liberal caucus, on the other hand, many of the same Committee members pressed for a partial reduction of the kind announced on April 3—an indication that the views expressed within caucus may have had more influence on the government than the actual Committee Report.

The Parliamentary Committee may have had *some* influence, both direct and indirect, on the NATO decision, but it was certainly not a decisive or an all-encompassing one. Asked whether the government had decided to continue its military contribution to NATO until the heavy equipment became obsolete, the Prime Minister replied: 'We are not saying that. I believe that is something along the lines the Parliamentary Committee is suggesting, but this is not what we are saying.'[60] The announcement of September 19, 1969, that Canada intended to maintain forces in Europe in the post-1972 period, was a further indication that the government had not based its NATO decision on the Committee's suggestion (as Mr Trudeau apparently interpreted its recommendations) that Canada consider withdrawal from Europe after 1972.

It should be emphasized that the decision to reduce Canada's military contribution to NATO was only one part of the announcement of April 3. The basis of this NATO decision was the government's newly articulated defence philosophy that military policy had to flow from foreign policy, which was to be determined by basic national interests such as national unity and identity. Although, for the sake of convenience, the April 3 decision is often referred to as the 'NATO decision', many other considerations were involved. Asked to explain the main reason for the government's delay in arriving at a decision, the Prime Minister told a reporter:

> La principale, c'est que nous avons voulu étudier tous les aspects de cette question. Nous n'avons pas voulu prendre une décision

> uniquement sur l'OTAN, comme si c'était une chose dans le vide, abstraite. Nous avons voulu insérer notre décision sur l'OTAN dans le contexte de nos forces militaires, de notre rôle, de notre philosophie de la défense dans tous les domaines. C'est pourquoi nous parlons également du NORAD; nous parlons également des forces du maintien de la paix, nous parlons également de la protection de la souveraineté canadienne. Alors, ce sont tous ces aspects-là qui ont pris du temps, et qui ne sont pas les aspects qui ont été étudiés par le comité parlementaire, qui lui n'a regardé que le problème de l'OTAN. Nous, on a voulu couvrir l'ensemble.[61]*

It was these broader considerations that determined that NATO would be accorded a lower priority in the government's defence policy. The Parliamentary Committee, however, had examined only the question of NATO, and made no attempt to relate it to any other foreign- or defence-policy considerations. This is probably the best evidence available that the advice of the Committee was not of major importance. It may well have contributed to the final decision not to withdraw completely Canada's military forces from Europe, but it could not have influenced the more fundamental ordering of overall priorities upon which the decision to decrease Canadian participation in NATO was based. For the key influence, therefore, it is necessary to look elsewhere.

6. THE CABINET

Another possible source of influence was Mr Trudeau's Cabinet colleagues. Although theoretically first among equals, the Prime Minister

---

* 'The main reason was that we wanted to study all the aspects of this question. We didn't want to make a decision only on NATO, as if it were an abstract, isolated issue. We wanted to insert our decision on NATO into the context of our overall military forces, our role, and our defence philosophy. That is why we are also talking about NORAD; we are also talking about forces to maintain peace, we are also talking about the protection of Canada's sovereignty. So, all these aspects took time; they were not the aspects that the Parliamentary Committee studied, for it looked only at the problem of NATO. *We* wanted to cover everything.'

cannot automatically be credited with the decisive influence on any one issue, for his position of primacy depends on his relationship with his ministers. Mr Pearson's approach, for example, was in most cases to let his ministers take the initiative in policy discussions and to intervene personally only if there were an otherwise unresolvable difference of opinion. A recent study of the unification of the Canadian Armed Forces shows that it was mainly the influence of the Minister of National Defence that affected the final decision.[62]

We have seen in Chapter 3 that Mr Trudeau's 'collegiate approach' emphasizes the participation of all interested ministers but tends to place greater importance on the ideas of Marchand, Pelletier, and perhaps Macdonald, even on issues that do not lie within the scope of their departments. It is known that Mr Macdonald submitted a report of his own when Cabinet was debating the NATO issue, although it is not clear whether it recommended complete withdrawal from NATO or a complete military withdrawal from Europe (this seems more likely).[63] On the other hand the pro-NATO approach of Mitchell Sharp, Léo Cadieux, and the majority of the other ministers—the 'status quo at least until 1972'—was also rejected. The views closest to the eventual April 3 decision may well have been those of Jean Marchand and Gérard Pelletier, but even they appear to have leaned more in the direction of a complete military withdrawal than towards a partial reduction.

On the first day of the Commons debate on the government's new NATO policy, which took place on April 23 and 24, Mr Trudeau delivered a speech that stressed a Canadian foreign and defence policy that was as active and internationally inclined as his earlier statements had been domestically oriented.[64] Gone was the emphasis on sovereignty as the prime goal of Canadian defence policy. Instead he stressed that Canada was continuing to participate in collective-security arrangements that were necessary for the peace and security of the world. He said that Canada was on the threshold of a new international role, one that would be characterized by participation in international peacekeeping forces, by a search for détente, by contributions toward arms limitation and disarmament, and by assistance to developing countries. Mr Sharp told the House the following day that the

Prime Minister's statement 'makes it very clear that Canada is broadening its horizons in every direction and is intent on playing a still more active role in world affairs.'[65] The Prime Minister's principal foreign-affairs adviser, Ivan Head, was even more emphatic, suggesting that Mr Trudeau's speech might well rank as one of the most internationalist statements ever made by a head of government while still in power.

The international orientation of this April 23 speech expressed such a different tone from the Prime Minister's statement of April 3 that it is tempting to speculate about the motives that prompted it. According to one of the Prime Minister's senior advisers, the Department of External Affairs had submitted a draft speech for the Prime Minister's consideration, as is the custom. Mr Trudeau rejected this text, however, and requested the PMO and Ivan Head to prepare his speech.* On the basis of this official account, it appears that the Prime Minister decided to have his own officials do the drafting because he wanted them to express his belief that a de-emphasis of NATO did not mean that his government was not interested in constructive international activity—that there were other ways of achieving security than through support of collective-security organizations. (Increased foreign aid and active participation in social and legal issues before the United Nations were given as two examples.) In addition, there is little doubt that the Prime Minister realized that his statement of April 3 had aroused concern in Cabinet, among some segments of the articulate public, and among Canada's allies. It was therefore wise, for both political and diplomatic reasons, to offer assurance that Canada would continue to play an active role in NATO. As James Eayrs wrote later, the Prime Minister's April 23 statement was designed 'to reconcile contending Cabinet factions, to allay public apprehension and to reduce anguish among allies.'[66]

* Although Ivan Head was the principal author of Mr Trudeau's April 23 speech, insiders report that very significant changes were made in it at the insistence of Mitchell Sharp and Léo Cadieux, who wanted to ensure that the government left no doubt about the sincerity of Canada's commitment to NATO. The fact that the Prime Minister permitted several major alterations in Ivan Head's original text is clear proof that Mr Trudeau was willing to compromise on the NATO issue in the face of a strong difference of opinion within his cabinet.

It is difficult to assess the extent of the division in Cabinet over the NATO issue, but the fact that the decision was so long in coming indicates that it was considerable. The Prime Minister's April 23 speech was in part an attempt to repair this breach. It can also be assumed that he realized before April 3 that it would have been extremely difficult (as well as politically unwise) to ignore completely the 'pro-NATO' views of the majority of his ministers. The decision to leave a token force in Europe appears to have been inspired at least in part by the need to reconcile through a compromise solution the varying views of members of Cabinet.

7. TRUDEAU AND THE PMO/PCO

It has been shown that the decisive influence in the April 3 decision was not provided by the external environment, considerations of a military or economic nature, academic or Parliamentary criticism, the civil service, the Parliamentary Committee, or individual ministers. Nor is there any indication that the Canadian public played a major role or was even very interested in the debate. So far only the political necessity for a Cabinet consensus seems to have had much importance, but this had to do with only one part of Canada's new defence posture —the extent of its contribution in Europe. The decision to reduce Canada's NATO commitment was clearly based on the overall philosophy of defence that relegated NATO to a comparatively low priority. Nowhere is there any indication that this basic philosophy was determined by the need for a Cabinet consensus. The pressures that led to the formation of this new defence philosophy clearly came from sources or considerations that have not yet been examined.

The only influences that remain to be studied are those of the Prime Minister and his personal advisers in the PMO and PCO. It will be remembered that Ivan Head's special report, 'Canadian Defence Policy —A Study', which Mr Trudeau commissioned, recommended that Canada remain in NATO, retain some 3,000 men in Europe, and abandon its nuclear-strike role. The first suggestion was repeated in Mr Trudeau's statement of April 3, the second was altered slightly after consultation with Canada's NATO allies, and the last became government policy when the country's new defence posture was announced on September 19. Indeed large extracts from this Study appeared in the Prime Minister's April 3 statement, were paraphrased by Mr Trudeau in his press conference of the same day, and were found in his Calgary speech. (One of Ivan Head's conclusions was that since Canada's CF-104s in Europe used too much fuel to be effective over long distances and were very vulnerable to surprise attack, they would be perceived by the Warsaw Pact countries as a first-strike attack force. In his Calgary speech Mr Trudeau spoke in remarkably similar terms. 'Is our squadron of CF-104s', he asked, 'the right kind of contribution? Will it be used only as a second strike? Are the 104s soft targets? And are not the Soviets entitled to ask themselves, "They are soft targets, they are on the ground, we know where the airfields are. Isn't it likely that they might be used to attack us first?"') Whether Mr Trudeau directly influenced the 'non-group report' or merely accepted its recommendations is almost impossible to determine; it is difficult to separate the two 'inputs' since they are in most cases almost identical. Ivan Head and his associates would not have been asked by Mr Trudeau to prepare this report had he not been aware that their views largely coincided with his, nor would he have been willing to urge its acceptance upon Cabinet had he not agreed with it. The Prime Minister had confidence in Head and trusted him to find a workable solution to the problem of NATO, but at the same time both must have shared the conviction that Canada's existing contribution was inappropriate and undesirable.

Although Mr Trudeau accepted the recommendations of the Study largely because he realized the political need for a compromise position,* it was very much his decision to do this. In other words, political factors precluded a total Canadian withdrawal from Europe, but it was Mr Trudeau who decided that this withdrawal would nevertheless be substantial. According to one official, the Prime Minister made it clear to Cabinet that it was the recommendations of the

* A senior adviser to the Prime Minister rejects the idea that the 'non-group report' was a compromise solution, saying that it was the 'right decision'. Nevertheless, it seems that Mr Trudeau originally desired even greater cuts in Canada's NATO contribution and would have achieved them had he not encountered such stiff opposition in Cabinet.

'non-group report' that were to be presented in Washington on April 10, and that substantial alterations were unlikely. One of the Cabinet members similarly relates that the majority of ministers, opposed to the decision to withdraw Canadian troops from Europe, gave in to prime-ministerial pressure. Mr Trudeau's ability to impose his wishes on Cabinet was, he speculated, due both to tradition within the Liberal Party and to Mr Trudeau's vote-getting ability. Less than a year after the election that brought them to power, and with 'Trudeaumania' still gripping the Canadian public, the Cabinet ministers might well have been reluctant to stand up to Mr Trudeau over an issue that interested only a small number of informed Canadians. Furthermore, there are indications that the Prime Minister believed a substantial withdrawal was necessary in order to make an impact on the Canadian public. One Cabinet minister revealed in private conversation that Canada could easily have persuaded its NATO allies to accept a quiet, delayed cutback, but that some of his Cabinet colleagues insisted on a demonstrative cut for domestic purposes. Mr Trudeau may well have felt that only by publicizing the NATO decision could he make Canadians aware that foreign and defence policy should be directed towards more immediate and important national interests than a search for peace and security through NATO.

Another reason that the Prime Minister was able to reach a Cabinet consensus based on the 'non-group report' stems from the fact that it presented new and compelling ideas that many ministers had not previously considered. According to one official, the realization that Canada's air element in Europe was likely to be perceived by the Soviet Union as a provocative first-strike force sent ministers 'climbing the wall' in surprise. The logic of the arguments presented in the Study and defended by the Prime Minister may have convinced some ministers of the need to alter Canada's contribution to NATO.

One of the best indications of the Prime Minister's decisive role in the NATO review—whether it was direct or indirect—is the striking similarity between the 1969 defence-policy decisions and his personal beliefs. His lack of hostility to the Soviet Union helps explain why Canada could reduce its NATO commitment only half a year after the Soviet-led invasion of Czechoslovakia, while his belief that Canada's natural alliance is with the United States was reflected in the high priority given to NORAD. If, as Mr Trudeau desired, Canada was to adopt a more modest international role and to be selective in its ventures, a partial withdrawal from Europe was very much in order. His long-standing antipathy to nuclear weapons is seen in the government's decision to phase out Canada's nuclear-strike role in Europe. From the point of view of Mr Trudeau's instrumental beliefs, a reduction in Canada's NATO commitment was consistent with his general philosophy of action and his predilection for challenging conventional ideas. His conception of the role of government—one of using foreign policy to promote national unity and identity—is reflected in the philosophy of defence that he articulated in Calgary. Finally, Mr Trudeau's reliance on his own views and those of his personal advisers rather than those of senior civil servants in determining the NATO decision was entirely in keeping with his approach to governing and his belief in centralizing decision-making power in the Prime Minister's office.

The one major contradiction between Mr Trudeau's personal beliefs and the defence-policy decisions concerns the matter of sovereignty, which was so central to the April 3 decision and has so often been opposed by Mr Trudeau. It must be remembered, however, that for the Prime Minister, while sovereignty is undesirable if it is used as the justification for the independence of an ethnic group, or if it becomes such an obsession that it gives rise to excessive nationalism, it is an important means to be used judiciously in promoting a strong central government and a healthy national identity.[67]

A defence policy based on considerations of sovereignty was such a novelty on the Canadian scene that there was some concern that the government might be intending to regard it as an end in itself and as something that had to be defended in its entirety. It seems to have been partly this fear that inspired observers such as Peyton Lyon to question whether the government could ever develop a convincing rationale for defence based on the concept of national sovereignty.[68] The government's reluctance to specify what it meant by this new emphasis greatly contributed to such fears.* When the long-awaited 1971 De-

* See pages 140-1.

fence White Paper was published, however, it became apparent that the Cabinet had been thinking in far different terms. 'Sovereignty' was an important concept of the paper, but it was defined with precision, and the idea that Canada's sovereignty had to be defended in its entirety was rejected. What the government meant by 'sovereignty' was jurisdiction and internal security—the idea that any national government had to be capable of surveillance and control activities over its own land, territorial waters, and airspace. The first real indication that sovereignty was not viewed as an end in itself but rather as a means came in April 1970, when Canada asserted jurisdiction over its off-shore waters; this was done for the specific and limited purpose of establishing pollution and fishing control. It soon became apparent that the government was also thinking in terms of asserting its jurisdiction in the Arctic for purposes of pollution control and economic growth. Government officials implied that the emphasis on sovereignty was designed to remind Canadians that they should be more moderate and realistic in their conception of Canada's international role, and think less in terms of 'crusading'.

The importance of the second aspect of sovereignty—internal security—became particularly apparent after the FLQ crisis in 1970, but the government was conscious of the need for more emphasis in this direction as early as April 1969. In both his April 3 statement and his press conference, Mr Trudeau made it clear that his government considered support of the civil authority as one of the prime functions of the Canadian Armed Forces. And insiders report that during part of 1969, aid to the civil authority was the first priority within the Department of National Defence. After the FLQ crisis, Mr Trudeau implied that considerations of internal security had been very much in the government's mind when the new defence priorities were being determined. One result of our more realistic approach, he said, 'was the decision taken 20 months ago to re-align our military forces to make sure that they would be available for the defence of Canadian sovereignty and as an aid to civil authorities. That decision has been proven correct in recent weeks.'[69]

The only area, then, in which Mr Trudeau appears to have altered his original views during the NATO review was over the extent of the withdrawal of Canadian forces from Europe. His own opinion seems to have been that Canada should remain in NATO in order to increase Canada's political, economic, and cultural relations with Europe, but that it should terminate its military activity in Europe, concentrating instead on the North American security alliance. During the NATO review, however, he constantly emphasized that these were purely his personal inclinations and not government policy. He was keeping an open mind about the extent of Canada's NATO involvements. Peter Dobell wrote that for the Prime Minister, 'the policy review is a process of discovery, in which he is constantly testing his evolving views against the views of his colleagues, his advisers and the informed public.'[70] Clearly Mr Trudeau listened to other views, while keeping in mind the need for a Cabinet consensus. It seems inaccurate to imply, as James Eayrs did,* that he was unwilling to depart from his preconceived ideas to even the slightest degree.

It would be much fairer to say that he was prepared to give and take on minor tactical questions, but that it was his influence that determined the basic philosophy on which the April 3 decision was based. As Peyton Lyon writes: 'Exposure to more facts, and the arguments of the officials, may have tempered some of Mr Trudeau's earlier intentions. However, the basic approach, and even more its rationalization, still bear the clear imprint of the determined ex-professor who became prime minister of Canada in April 1968.'[71]

The compromise reflected in deciding to withdraw one half instead of two thirds of Canada's forces from Europe was, after all, of little importance compared to the decision that the country would henceforth concentrate its military efforts in Canada. The idea that defence policy should be determined by a foreign policy that was based on such national interests as the promotion of a Canadian identity explains why sovereignty became the country's first defence priority, a decision that seems to have no other source than the Prime Minister.

---

* Professor Eayrs, in an article in *Saturday Night*, seemed to discount the sincerity of Mr Trudeau's desire for advice from all possible circles. His tendency to encourage conflicting points of view, Eayrs says, 'was unnerving while it lasted, but it was not to be taken seriously, just another aspect of the Trudeau manner.' (James Eayrs, 'Dilettante in Power', *Saturday Night*, April 1971, p. 13.)

And the most notable change in foreign policy—the decision to relegate peacekeeping to last place in the new list of priorities, which was a conscious attempt to focus the attention of Canadians on more important national objectives than an idealistic search for international glory—seems clearly inspired by Mr Trudeau.

What happened in April of 1969 was that the Prime Minister took from the civil service the initiative in formulating the basic principles and objectives towards which defence policy was to be directed. While tactical decisions might still originate in the civil service, it was in the Prime Minister's Office that the overall strategic decisions were being made.

Notes

[1] *Globe and Mail*, April 4, 1969, p. 2.

[2] *Debates*, November 14, 1968, p. 2720.

[3] *Debates*, November 25, 1968, p. 3132.

[4] *Debates*, February 4, 1969, p. 5109; see also November 25, 1968, p. 3129, and November 26, 1968, p. 3188; see also the *Globe and Mail*, January 13, 1969, p. 1.

[5] *Canadian Annual Review, 1968*, p. 222.

[6] Interview with John Holmes.

[7] *Canadian Annual Review, 1968*, pp. 221-2.

[8] *Monthly Report*, December 1968, p. 140.

[9] *Loc. cit.*; see also *Globe and Mail*, January 4, 1969, p. 3.

[10] See the *Globe and Mail*, January 4, 1969, p. 3, for a list of those who were originally invited. Not all were able to attend however. Most of the persons who actually participated are listed on page 125.

[11] Mitchell Sharp, 'Canadian Foreign Policy and the Third World', University of Toronto, September 18, 1970, p. 2 (statement released by the Office of the Secretary of State for External Affairs).

[12] *Globe and Mail*, January 6, 1969, p. 8.

[13] *Debates*, November 22, 1968, p. 3068; January 28, 1969, p. 790.

[14] *Globe and Mail*, January 29, 1969, p. 3.

[15] *Minutes of Proceedings and Evidence* (hereafter referred to as *Minutes*), January 21, 1969, p. 722.

[16] *Debates*, April 24, 1969, p. 7910 (N. A. Cafik).

[17] *Minutes*, February 6, 1969 (see especially pp. 911, 922, and 924).

[18] *Minutes*, February 13, 1969, pp. 952, 954-6 (Brecher); February 18, 1969, pp. 1018-20 (McNaught); February 25, 1969, pp. 1051, 1078-9 (Warnock).

[19] *Minutes*, March 4, 1969, p. 1146 (Granatstein); March 6, 1969, pp. 1165-71, pp. 1189-91 (Clarkson).

[20] Much of the following assessment of the influence of the witnesses on the Committee members is based on interviews with members of the Commons' Committee on External Affairs and National Defence.

[21] *Minutes*, January 21, 1969, p. 763; February 27, 1969, pp. 1108-10; February 5, 1969, p. 864.

[22] *Minutes*, February 27, 1969, pp. 1101-14, 1085.

[23] *Minutes*, February 12, 1969, pp. 943-4.

[24] *Minutes*, February 20, 1969, pp. 1029, 1030, 1048; January 28, 1969, pp. 768-71.

[25] *Minutes (Members of the Committee Travelling in Europe)*, No. 50, March 8-22, 1969, pp. 1824; 1925, 30, 31, 37; 1783; 1791, 1809; 1834; 1847, 1853-7.

[26] This account of the evolution of the Committee's report is based on an interview with a senior official who asked that his identity not be revealed.

[27] See Albert Legault, *Le Devoir*, 25 novembre, 1969, pp. 1 and 6 for the most complete account available of this review.

[28] Mitchell Sharp, 'Canada's Relations with Europe'. *Statements and Speeches*. No. 69/1, January 3, 1969.

[29] This account of the PMO report is based partly on Albert Legault's article (*op. cit.*, p. 6) and also on interviews with senior government officials.

[30] See Peyton V. Lyon, 'A Review of the Review', p. 38, for a brief account of the original proposals for a force reduction. For the most part, the contents of this document are a matter of speculation; some government officials are aware of its general contents, but few appear to have actually seen the report.

[31] Brian Shaw, ed., *The Gospel According to St Pierre*. Richmond Hill, Ontario: Simon & Schuster, 1969, p. 199.

[32] *Debates*, February 21, 1969, pp. 5801-2.

[33] *Debates*, April 2, 1969, pp. 7417.

[34] Pierre Elliott Trudeau, 'A Defence Policy for Canada', *Statements and Speeches*. No. 69/7, April 3, 1969; *Transcript of Press Conference*, Office of the Prime Minister, April 3, 1969 (hereafter referred to as *Press Conference, April 3*); Pierre Elliott Trudeau, 'The Relation of Defence Policy to Foreign Policy', *Statements and Speeches*. No. 69/8, April 12, 1969.

[35] *Press Conference, April 3*, pp. 7-8.

[36] *Ibid.*, p. 3.

[37] *Ibid.*, p. 9.

[38] Harlan Cleveland, *NATO: The Transatlantic Bargain*. New York: Harper & Row, 1970, p. 128.

[39] *Globe and Mail*, May 30, 1969, p. 1; *Monthly Report*, May 1969, pp. 138-9.

[40] *Debates*, June 2, 1969, p. 9327; June 3, 1969, p. 9382.

[41] *Debates*, December 8, 1969, p. 1681.

[42] Léo Cadieux, 'Canada Adopts a New Defence Posture', *Statements and Speeches*. No. 69/15, September 19, 1969.

[43] *Debates*, April 23, 1969, p. 7876 (Douglas); April 26, 1969, p. 7908 (Harkness).

[44] *Debates*, April 23, 1969, p. 7875 (Stanfield); April 23, 1969, p. 7890 (Brewin); April 23, 1969, p. 7883 (Caouette).

[45] Legault, *Le Devoir*, 26 novembre, 1969, p. 5; see also *Globe and Mail*, January 7, 1969, p. 4, for an account of Mr Wilson's attempt to influence Mr Trudeau.

[46] See Peyton V. Lyon, 'A Review of the Review', p. 36.

[47] *Time*, April 4, 1969, p. 13.

[48] Legault, *Le Devoir*, 25 novembre, 1969, p. 6.

[49] *Globe and Mail*, March 28, 1969, p. 6.

[50] *Debates*, December 8, 1969, p. 1681.

[51] *Debates*, June 23, 1969, p. 10518.

[52] See Legault, *loc. cit*. The real question, he writes, was only one of *when* there would be a new definition of Canada's NATO role.

[53] John Burns, 'Defence Gets an Advocate in Macdonald', *Globe and Mail*, February 1, 1971, pp. 1, 6.

[54] *Debates*, May 8, 1969, p. 1429.

[55] *Monthly Report*, September 1968, p. 93.

[56] James Eayrs, *Fate and Will in Foreign Policy*. Toronto: CBC Publications, 1967, p. 50.

[57] Acheson (quoted in Eayrs, *op. cit.*, p. 57); Kissinger (quoted in Rosenau, *International Politics and Foreign Policy*, p. 264); Deutsch (*The Analysis of International Relations*, p. 94).

[58] James Eayrs, *The Art of the Possible: Government and Foreign Policy in Canada*. Toronto: University of Toronto Press, 1961, p. 157.

[59] *Maclean's*, December 1969, p. 42. This distrust appears to have become particularly acute during the Biafran controversy. 'Biafra was our Bay of Pigs', according to one diplomat, for Mr Trudeau's acceptance of External's advice that there was nothing Canada could or should do about Biafra proved very embarrassing for the government.

[60] *Press Conference, April 3*, p. 2.

[61] *Ibid.*, p. 3.

[62] Roddick Byers, 'Executive Leadership and Influence: Parliamentary Perceptions of Canadian Defence Policy', in Hockin, *op. cit.*, p. 171.

[63] Albert Legault mentions the existence of this report, but was apparently unaware of its contents (Legault, *loc. cit.*).

[64] *Debates*, April 23, 1969, pp. 7866–70.

[65] *Debates*, April 24, 1969, p. 7905.

[66] James Eayrs, 'NATO Policy tries to Reconcile the Cabinet and our Allies', Toronto *Star*, April 27, 1969.

[67] See Chapter 3, section 1.

[68] Peyton V. Lyon, 'Sovereignty: Does it Deserve to be our First Defence Priority?' *The Commentator*, May 1971.

[69] *International Canada*, November 1970, p. 254.

[70] Peter C. Dobell, 'Canada and NATO', *Orbis*, Vol. XII, Spring 1969, p. 323.

[71] Lyon, 'A Review of the Review'.

6

The Foreign-Policy Papers

On June 25, 1970, twenty-five months after the inception of the review of defence and foreign policy, the Canadian government published the results of this re-examination. Although it had earlier spoken of producing a 'white paper', what emerged were six separate booklets with the overall title *Foreign Policy for Canadians*, which came to be known as the foreign-policy papers.[1] There could be little doubt that their publication was a considerable relief to the government, which had been subjected to questioning about the date of their appearance for nearly a year. In January 1969 Mr Trudeau expressed the hope that the review would be concluded 'during the current year'.[2] By May, however, Mitchell Sharp was forced to admit in the House that 'the production of the white paper is becoming a much more complicated question than we had originally estimated' and would say only that it would be published 'as soon as possible'.[3]

The policy papers consisted of one general booklet, setting out the 'conceptual framework' that was to serve as the basis for future foreign policy, and five sector papers dealing with Canada's external activities in Europe, Latin America, the Pacific, the United Nations, and in the field of international development assistance. The general booklet, which subsequently became the subject of a nine-month study conducted by the Commons' External Affairs Committee, stated that Canada's foreign policy should not be based on a desire to play the role of a 'helpful fixer'. The theme of this booklet was that foreign policy is the extension abroad of national policies, and that it should be designed to attain Canada's specific national interests rather than simply to react to external events. The foreign-policy pattern in the 1970s, according to this paper, would place particular attention on three national 'themes': economic growth, social justice, and quality of life. The themes of peace and security, sovereignty and independence, and a harmonious natural environment were placed in the government's second tier of priorities.

The five sector papers dealt in more detail with specific foreign-policy issues. The booklets on Europe, Latin America, and the Pacific set out some of the ways in which Canada hoped to increase its political, cultural, and above all economic relations with these countries. The United Nations paper described the areas in which Canada expected to concentrate its UN efforts (primarily social, technological, and legal matters, although the country's continued support for peace-keeping was affirmed), and the International Development booklet set out the ways in which Canada intended to increase both the quantity and quality of its foreign aid.

At the time of their publication it was not immediately realized that the policy papers contained little that was actually new. The basis of the conceptual framework—the idea that foreign policy was the extension abroad of national policies—could be found in Mr Trudeau's announcement of May 29, 1968 that Canada's paramount interest was to ensure its political survival as a federal and bilingual sovereign state, and in his 1969 Calgary comment that the aim of Canada's foreign policy was to serve its national interest and express its national identity abroad. Mr Trudeau's May 1968 statement also announced his government's intention to institute the very policies that were contained in the five sector papers: the broadening of Canada's relations with Third World countries, an increase in foreign aid, and an altered role in Europe and in the United Nations. The Commons Committee on External Affairs and National Defence accurately observed that these 'were decisions taken either before or during the process of review,' and 'it cannot therefore be argued that these new policies were a product of the review.'[4] The sector papers were concerned more with the ways and means of putting these decisions into effect than with the development of new policies. They dealt with tactical decisions rather than with strategic ones.

I. The Sector Papers

The foreign-policy review began with the establishment of the Special Task Force on Relations with Europe (STAFFEUR), which examined not only the NATO issue but also all aspects of Canadian-European relations. Since it was the first part of the re-examination of Canada's foreign policy, the European review established the general approach that was followed in the other sector reviews. The creation of interdepartmental task forces, which consulted on occasion with academics and other members of the attentive public, was the procedure followed in the review of Canadian policy in the Pacific and Latin America as well as in Europe.

1. EUROPE

In the booklet dealing with Europe, no major decisions or announcements could be found that differed from already-established or previously announced policy. The 1969 NATO decision remained unchanged, and Mr Trudeau's 1968 emphasis on increased political, economic, and cultural ties with Europe formed a central part of the document. 'The present emphasis on Western Europe will be maintained,' the booklet said, 'in order to serve the basic objectives of national unity and national identity.'[5] High priority was to be given to cultural relations with francophone countries, particularly France, in order to satisfy the needs of Canada's bilingual society. Another major justification for increased relations with Europe—whether in the political, economic, technological, or social sphere—was the need to orient Canadian external policy towards countries other than the United States. Europe was described as one of the most promising areas in which Canada could diversify its contacts and develop 'at least some measure of countervailing influence.'[6] In short, there is nothing in the European booklet that contradicts, and much that confirms, the conclusion that it was Mr Trudeau who determined what future Canadian-European relations would be—although he was certainly not the first person to think of Europe as a counterweight to the United States.

2. LATIN AMERICA

The Latin American review began when the Ministers of External Affairs, Trade and Commerce, and Energy, Mines and Resources, the Secretary of State, and the Minister Without Portfolio in charge of the Wheat Board—accompanied by thirty senior civil servants—toured Latin America in October 1968. The only document that resulted directly from this trip was a preliminary report urging that closer Canadian-Latin American links be forged through increased trade, greater development assistance, and new political and cultural initiatives.[7] An interdepartmental task force emerged from this mission and in March 1969 took part in a CIIA-sponsored seminar. The participants included officials from the Brazilian Light and Power Company, the DeHavilland Aircraft Company of Canada, the Association of Universities and Colleges of Canada, the Toronto *Telegram*, the Victoria *Daily Times*, and CUSO, in addition to nine professors.

But again, nothing that was done by the ministerial mission, the task force, or the seminar participants appears to have altered the course announced in Mr Trudeau's statement of May 29, 1968. The Latin American booklet, which the task force prepared, contained little more than a list of the ways in which Canada could increase its political, economic, and cultural relations with the continent—precisely the general approach upon which the Prime Minister had already decided. One of the few policy decisions contained in the booklet was the announcement that, at least for the time being, Canada would not join the Organization of American States. Membership, the government concluded, could limit Canada's freedom of action at a time when OAS members were interested in closer relations with Canada whether or not Canada joined the organization.[8] Mr Trudeau was on record as favouring Canadian membership in the OAS, but he had attached the qualification that Canada must first develop a policy towards Latin America that was independent of that of the United States. It is not known with complete certainty whether the OAS decision was contrary to his wishes or accorded with them. The government's subsequent announcement that it intended to seek 'observer' status within the organization seems to be an indication that it leaned towards eventual membership in the OAS, in accordance with Mr Trudeau's own wishes.

3. THE UNITED NATIONS

The third sector review dealt with the United Nations and differed substantially in nature from the others. Whereas in most cases task forces representing as many as ten or fifteen interested departments were created, the United Nations booklet was prepared almost exclusively by the Department of External Affairs, with only a slight contribution from Health and Welfare and Labour. The basis of the document was a study prepared by Canada's former Ambassador to the UN, Mr George Ignatieff, that accepted the principle that Canada had an obligation to work actively in the United Nations and suggested areas in which Canada should concentrate its attention.[9]

It is difficult to determine the extent to which the UN recommendations of this sector paper reflect the views of the Department of External Affairs itself. Those concerning social and economic development, arms limitation, satellite systems, the seabed, human rights, the codification of international law, and the improved functioning of the United Nations seem to involve the kind of tactical decisions that the Trudeau government is willing to leave to the civil service, although most of these are themes the Prime Minister likes to see stressed. The desire to project Canada as a bilingual country within the UN, on the other hand, seems to be based on the government's basic philosophy, but it is also an attitude fully shared by many External Affairs officials. The one section of this paper in which it is clear that the civil-service influence was not dominant concerns Canadian policy in South Africa. The decision to continue commercial relations in order to increase Canada's economic growth rather than end all trade in the interests of social justice was made in Cabinet. The Department of External Affairs dealt primarily with the options available to Canada in its relations with South Africa and, in accordance with Mr Trudeau's wishes, made no policy recommendations. The similarity between the South African decision and Mr Trudeau's refusal to suspend arms sales to the United States on the grounds that this would constitute a useless symbolic gesture suggests that he personally favoured, and probably helped determine, this decision.

Implicit in the UN study was the belief that Canada was moving towards a less political role in the United Nations, just as the Ignatieff document recognized the need for an emphasis on such issues as economic development, international air and sea law, and environmental problems. Lester Pearson thought this shift was 'related to the withdrawal of the UN itself from political initiatives towards social and economic problems',[10] but it may also have been in response to guidance from the Prime Minister's Office. In his statement of May 29, 1968, Mr Trudeau had mentioned the need for 'some shift of emphasis' in Canada's UN activity, and it seems probable that he was thinking in precisely those terms that came to be presented in the third sector review. When Mr Trudeau sat as a member of the Canadian delegation to the United Nations in 1965, he became disillusioned with what he considered to be the Canadian government's search for unrealistic political initiatives in an attempt to win public support at home. The decision to emphasize 'non-political' activities was therefore very much in keeping with his own inclinations.

4. INTERNATIONAL DEVELOPMENT

The international-development study, which took place at the same time as the UN review, was conducted primarily by the Canadian International Development Agency, and involved the departments of Industry, Trade and Commerce, Finance, and Manpower and Immigration. Again, the decisions announced in the 1970 booklet—a steady increase in the amount of aid, less aid tied to purchases in Canada and more channelled through multilateral institutions, the creation of an International Development Research Centre, and increased encouragement of aid from the private sector—were basically the tactical decisions needed to put into effect Mr Trudeau's announcement of policy in May 1968 when he stated the government's intention to improve its foreign-aid program.

The justification for an increase and improvement in aid is particularly interesting. Such programs should be given priority, the booklet stated, since Canada believes in the importance of the welfare of the individual and Canadians 'could not create a truly just society within Canada if we were not prepared to play our part in the creation of a more just world society'; furthermore, such efforts would increase international support for Canadian interests and policies.[11] The emphasis on individual rights, the term 'just society', and the relating of international activities to national interests are, of course, associated with Trudeau and suggest that his influence on the review was considerable. However, this does not necessarily mean that the Prime Minister imposed his ideas on the civil servants who drafted the booklet. It is more likely that in this instance they formulated their arguments in terms they knew would be well received by the Prime Minister.

Nowhere in this document is there even the implied suggestion that this increase in foreign aid was to be made possible by cutting the defence budget, which many academic and Parliamentary critics of Canadian foreign policy had advocated. The closest the Prime Minister ever came to a direct refutation of their proposal was his 1970 comment to a Singapore audience that, while Canada intended to increase its aid to the countries of the Pacific region, 'The partial withdrawal of Canadian forces from the European theatre of NATO has not been made with an intention of shifting our strength to the Pacific area' but rather to meet Canada's first priority, 'which is the defence of Canadian sovereignty and our role in the defence of the North American continent.'[12] On an earlier occasion, in December 1969, he said that there would be an increase in the absolute amount of Canadian aid, but that this would not reach the objective of one per cent of the country's GNP.[13] He explained that the financial problems facing the country precluded such a massive increase in aid at that time. Even in this context Mr Trudeau expressed no interest in the prospect of channelling funds from defence to aid—another indication that the critics of Canada's aid program had not been heeded closely when the government formulated its aid policy.

5. THE PACIFIC

The re-examination of Canada's relations with the countries of the

Pacific was the last stage of the foreign-policy review undertaken by the government. The first and most significant aspect of this fifth sector review was the decision to negotiate with the Peking government for the establishment of diplomatic relations with the People's Republic of China. 'More than any other issue of foreign policy,' John Holmes wrote in 1970, 'relations with China have become, in the public eye, the criterion of Canada's independence in international affairs.' As early as 1964 a Gallup poll reported that 51% of the Canadian public favoured recognition of China while only 33% disapproved—a considerable change from a 1959 poll in which 32% of the public approved and 44% opposed such a move. Demands for recognition of China, which many Canadians believed was being prevented solely by American pressure, were increasing as public displeasure with American policy in Viet Nam increased.[14] According to a senior External Affairs official, the failure to establish diplomatic relations with China had long been a source of frustration to many members of the department. When to this was added the hostility of the majority of countries to UN membership for China, the Pearson government decided in 1966 that Canada should approach China through bilateral rather than multilateral activities.[15] The Cultural Revolution, however, delayed any such attempts, but it was clear that changes in both the external and internal environment were becoming favourable to eventual recognition.

If the decision to seek diplomatic relations with China was not a difficult one for the Trudeau government, it at least required a conscious effort. Though opposition within Canada was declining, there was little public pressure in favour of recognition, and certainly none that the government could not have resisted with ease. Polls conducted in the early 1960s indicate that the Canadian public favoured recognizing Communist China only if ties could be maintained with Taiwan, another sign that there was no great public pressure influencing the government's decision to recognize Peking at the expense of Taipei.[16] Even the desire for action within External Affairs had been stilled, at least temporarily, by the troubling Cultural Revolution. Clearly it was very much the initiative of Mr Trudeau that led to the opening of negotiations with the Chinese. While the trend towards diplomatic relations had begun in the Pearson administration, a senior official in the Pacific and Far Eastern section of the Department of External Affairs commented that actual negotiations might not have begun for several years had it not been for the direct intervention of Mr Trudeau. The same official continued: 'I think that he decided on his own that he was going to push this [matter of improving relations with China] as far as he could.'

In February 1969 Mitchell Sharp announced the government's decision to contact the Chinese government with the proposal that talks concerning diplomatic relations between the two countries be held in the near future. He admitted that it would probably not be possible to recognize two governments of China, implying that Canada had accepted the necessity of ending diplomatic relations with the government of Nationalist China.[17] The actual decision made by the Cabinet was contained in a two-paragraph memorandum sent to the Department of External Affairs. It stated the government's desire to establish diplomatic relations and contained only two specific directives. One said what the government was prepared to do—support the Chinese bid for representation in the United Nations; the other what it was not prepared to do—affirm that Taiwan was an integral part of mainland China. The only other instruction that ever came from Cabinet was that the Canadian negotiators should also avoid stating that Taiwan was *not* part of China. Apart from these directives, the Department of External Affairs was given almost complete freedom in seeking means by which satisfactory terms for recognition could be obtained. Its efforts were successful, for the announcement of the establishment of diplomatic relations in October 1970 contained the qualification that Canada merely 'took note of' the Chinese claim to Taiwan, thereby satisfying the second of the Cabinet conditions. The now-familiar pattern of the civil service implementing strategic decisions made by Cabinet, which were influenced primarily by the Prime Minister, had been repeated.

Since diplomatic relations with China had not been established when the Pacific sector paper was published, it contained little of a specific nature. A few months earlier in Singapore, Mr Trudeau accurately predicted: 'I don't think there is going to be any dramatic realignment or dramatic announcement of new policies.'[18] The paper contained little more than Canada's stated intention to increase its relations, particularly those of an economic nature, with the countries of the Pacific rim. The underlying theme was expressed in the title of the second chapter: 'Canada as a Pacific Power'. Increased contacts with this region were seen to be necessary for the evolution of Canada 'as a unique and independent national community in North America.'[19] Nowhere has Mr Trudeau expressed his attitude towards the Pacific region as frankly as he did in an interview with *Le Monde*, in which he stated: 'Si nous voulons empêcher certaines aliénations dans l'ouest du pays, il faut que notre politique à l'égard des nations du Pacifique soit plus vigoureuse.'*[20] This was also the view expressed in the sector paper, which noted that the Pacific world was particularly important for the economy of Western Canada. 'Of the 54 principal Canadian commodities selling in Japan,' the booklet stated, 'no fewer than 48 are primarily of Western Canadian origin. China as a market for the wheat of Western Canada is another, and indeed uniquely important, case in point.'[21]

As had been the case with the other sector papers, the Pacific booklet reflected Mr Trudeau's belief that Canada's external activities should be directed towards its basic national interests of national unity and identity.

II. The General Paper**

By the summer of 1969 the sector reviews were well advanced and the process of submitting them to the Cabinet Committee on External Policy and Defence had begun. The Department of External Affairs, whose influence on the sector papers had been greater than that of the other departments, expected that these five studies would form the

* 'If we want to prevent a certain alienation in the west of the country, our policy with respect to the nations of the Pacific must be more vigorous.'

** This account is based largely on interviews with several senior government officials who, since the information they provided often dealt with confidential Cabinet deliberations, cannot be identified.

basis of the forthcoming White Paper on foreign policy. However, the reaction of Cabinet to them came as a great shock to the civil-service departments involved. The review, it said, was proving inadequate, for it was not going deeply enough into the basic assumptions underlying foreign policy. Ministerial reaction to the STAFFEUR report, for example, had been: 'What about basic assumptions, basic aims and objectives?' When the international-aid study reached Cabinet level, the question immediately raised was: 'Where does this fit into the total picture of foreign policy?' The arrival of the other sector papers provoked similar comments, and before long Cabinet decided that something far different was needed. The result was a Cabinet request that External Affairs produce a general paper that would deal with ultimate purposes and not merely with current strategies. Furthermore, Cabinet also decided that the total review would be published, which necessitated the deletion of a great deal of classified information that had been included in the sector papers in order to influence policy.

Coming only a few months after the government had ignored its NATO recommendations, this latest rejection convinced External Affairs that the Trudeau government was determined to formulate its own foreign policy. The NATO decision and the Prime Minister's disparaging remarks about the Department had already given rise to frustration and discontent, and in addition a generation gap was developing: morale sagged as criticism of senior departmental officers by junior officers became more apparent. Though it is probable that only the most senior officials were aware of Cabinet's rejection of their approach to the foreign-policy review, this induced a further traumatic effect on the Department. Words such as 'turmoil' and 'confusion' are used frequently by officials to describe the mood of External Affairs at this time. Confidence had broken down between the Cabinet and External Affairs, and a barrier had developed between what one official calls the 'established bureaucracy' and the 'new bureaucracy' of the Prime Minister's personal advisers. The basic problem as far as policy was concerned was that the department simply did not know precisely what the government wanted or meant by a 'conceptual framework'. Looking back, officials now believe that this breakdown in communication was due in part to an age difference between the senior civil servants and the younger ministers, whose exclusion from foreign-policy formulation in the Pearson government had made them impatient to exercise a dominant influence. There was also a 'psychological problem' within the department, for the majority of its senior officers had become so accustomed to the traditional post-war approach to policy formulation, based on agreement between the Secretary of State for External Affairs and the Prime Minister, that they found it difficult to adjust to the new approach apparently desired by the Trudeau administration. Years of conditioning precluded an easy acceptance by the civil service of the predominating influence of the new government.

'There is perhaps no more unpleasant condition for a professional civil servant,' Professor Denis Stairs has observed, 'than one in which his views go apparently unheeded—even ignored—by his political superiors.' Faced with this situation, the Department of External Affairs became 'extremely intense, if not obsessive'[22] in trying to re-establish its credibility and influence. If the Prime Minister was determined to have a conceptual framework, the Department concluded, then it would have to produce a good one that would re-establish its prestige in the eyes of the Cabinet. The first step towards this goal was the establishment in the fall of 1969, of a Policy Analysis Group (PAG), whose function was officially described as assisting 'in the development and analysis of major policy alternatives', in keeping with the emphasis being given to "objective analysis" in the formulation of new policies.[23] Like the American Policy Planning Staff, the PAG was to be an attempt to relieve senior officers from the day-to-day task of policy implementation and allow them to think of foreign affairs in terms of long-range goals and objectives. As a first step in the process of independent policy planning, the PAG attempted to develop a conceptual approach to foreign policy that would meet the Prime Minister's specific demands.

In accordance with the government's wishes, then, basic principles and national aims were first on the PAG agenda. After considerable discussion, six basic concepts emerged—the six policy themes that form the basis of the general paper published in 1970. It was not enough, however, merely to identify these themes; a framework into which they could be inserted was necessary both to facilitate analysis and to appeal to the Prime Minister's predilection for capsulized information. Since there were six themes, the idea of a hexagon gradually emerged. Each theme was allotted one side of the hexagon, so that none of the six assumed priority over any other; this visual presentation enabled ministers to see readily interrelationships among the six themes, and showed them that, in particular cases, conflicts of interest among these themes could arise, which could be resolved only by a deliberate choice by the government.

As the Cabinet was under Mr Trudeau's leadership, the contents of the general paper were formulated by External Affairs with Mr Trudeau very much in mind. While the Policy Analysis Group was instrumental in suggesting the framework that would be used, the general paper was actually assembled by one official, Geoffrey S. Murray. Recalled to Ottawa from London in August 1969, Mr Murray was given the title of Special Assistant to the Under-Secretary of State and the responsibility of 'co-ordinating' the policy review. He began by reading everything Mr Trudeau had ever written or stated publicly on foreign-policy questions, including some of his *Cité Libre* articles and at least a hundred speeches the Prime Minister made between April 1968 and mid-1969. His next step was to summarize Trudeau's ideas, which he included in a draft memorandum on policy that he circulated to the heads of divisions within External Affairs in order to solicit their opinions and comments. Not all reacted well to what a few considered to be an overly subservient approach to the Prime Minister. One head of division reportedly suggested sardonically that they should request Ambassador Arthur Andrew, then negotiating with the Chinese over recognition, to find out from them how they extracted a foreign policy from the sayings of *their* Chairman. Nevertheless most officials were of the opinion that Mr Murray's approach was in no way demeaning and that the department's duty was to develop the kind of policy framework that the Prime Minister was seeking.

The striking similarity between the contents of the general paper and Mr Trudeau's stated philosophy was described by one official as not coincidental but 'purely intentional'. The paper represented, according to another, the efforts of the department 'to approach the

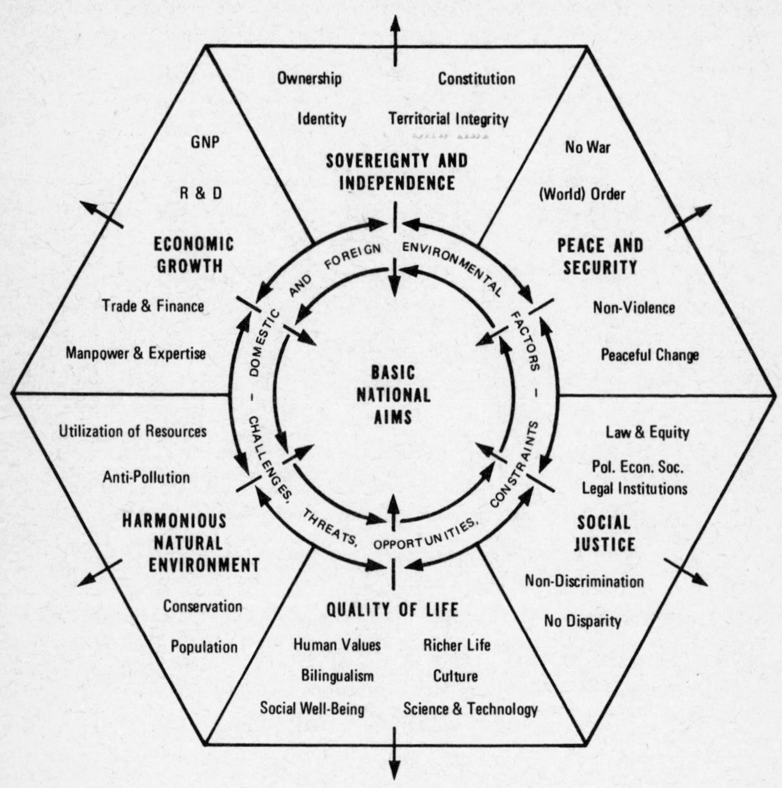

THE FOREIGN-POLICY HEXAGON*

In each segment the 'key words' in small print indicate the kind of policy questions that may arise, though not always under the same theme necessarily.

The straight arrows indicate the relationship between basic national aims and external functions. The one-way arrows in the inner circle indicate the ever-changing environmental factors: the two-way arrows in the outer circle signify the interrelationships among the policy themes.

---

* Canada. House of Commons. The Standing Committee on External Affairs and National Defence. *Fourth Report respecting 'Foreign Policy for Canadians'*. June 1971, p. 48.

review from the way the Prime Minister was approaching foreign policy.' He defended this approach on the grounds that 'it is only right that the politicians, who are responsible to the electorate, have the final say in policy.'

Since Cabinet had already seen the sector papers in the summer of 1969, its deliberations that fall and early in 1970 centred on the general paper. It was examined in the vital Cabinet Committee on Priorities and Planning, chaired by Mr Trudeau. At these meetings External Affairs officials made presentations in which they used the hexagon as a framework for describing alternative approaches to foreign-policy issues. An advantage of this diagram was that it permitted issues to be shown in the brief and readily understandable terms that were most useful for ministers with crowded schedules and perhaps only a passing interest in external affairs. The department had learned from its experience over the NATO decision that what Cabinet wanted was not recommendations but an analysis of the various alternatives available. Its officials therefore used the hexagon to show the six themes that could be emphasized, leaving it to Cabinet to decide which priorities it preferred. It was at Cabinet level that the decision was made to place greater emphasis than in the past on the three themes of economic growth, social justice, and quality of life. The basis of this decision, according to a well-placed source, was Cabinet's belief that the country's most important concerns were 'inflation, jobs, and national unity'. As the Cabinet perceived no immediate threat to national security, peace and security were relegated to the second tier of priorities.

Once Cabinet's deliberations were concluded, officials in the External Affairs Department set out to rewrite the general paper in a way that would express the priorities decided upon by the government. It was necessary to insert in the final chapter a new section entitled 'Policy Patterns', setting out the two tiers of priorities that became a central part of the booklet. The five sector papers had also to be revised in order to reflect the theoretical framework of the general paper. In some places the changes were very significant. We have seen that it was the Cabinet's decision to emphasize economic growth: this determined the government's policy on trade with South Africa that was announced in the UN booklet. In other places the changes were very minor, consisting of the addition of a few lines or paragraphs here and there that justified policy in terms of the priorities announced in the general paper. In the European booklet, for example, a section was added to explain how Europe was the 'only area outside North America where the major themes of Canadian policy converge.' A similar section in the Pacific paper concluded that strengthened relations with the Pacific would 'serve the broad objectives of Economic Growth, Social Justice and Quality of Life.' By the middle of May the Cabinet had approved the redrafted general and sector papers and a relieved Mr Sharp was soon able to inform the House that 'The period of gestation is over now and we are only waiting for delivery from the Queen's Printer.'[24]

When the foreign-policy papers were tabled in the House on June 25, the similarity between their views and those of Mr Trudeau could hardly be overlooked. Many of his ideas, observed the Toronto *Globe and Mail*, 'are reflected in the white paper despite all the special reports by foreign-service officers and by high-powered academic task forces.'[25] In a similar vein a *Montreal Star* reporter commented that the white paper 'is a perfect reflection of the Prime Minister and his government, both in its virtues and in its deficiencies.'[26]

The theme of the general paper was that both foreign and domestic policies were determined by, and should be used to promote, the same national aims. Foreign policy, in the booklet's key sentence, 'is the extension abroad of national policies.'[27]

The reason for this new emphasis is found in Mr Trudeau's perceptions of Canada's most immediate problems. Since national unity had long been his prime preoccupation, it was not surprising that the general paper expressed a concern that 'the survival of Canada as a nation is being challenged internally by divisive forces,' and that foreign policies designed to strengthen national unity were therefore in order. That the promotion of national unity was in fact the basis of the government's decision to emphasize national interests has been confirmed by Geoffrey Murray. Testifying before the Commons' Committee on External Affairs, he said:

> People have often said to me, 'this book is not concerned at all with national unity.' My answer to that is that, basically, this is a

> foreign policy which gets its main motivation from an attempt to support and develop national unity.[28]

Peter Dobell had recognized in 1969 that, given these domestic problems and Mr Trudeau's concern with them, a more inward-looking foreign policy would be the logical result. 'Inevitably,' he wrote, 'when national energy is focused inward, a nation's external relations assume a lower priority; foreign policy tends to be seen more in terms of its domestic implications and impact.'[29] National unity and the general well-being of Canadians were of highest priority to Mr Trudeau, and his new foreign-policy philosophy was designed with these goals very much in mind.

One of the most controversial of the general paper's statements was that 'the foreign policy pattern for the seventies should be based on a ranking of six policy themes which gives highest priorities to Economic Growth, Social Justice and Quality of Life policies.'[30] The last two themes reflect Mr Trudeau's personal belief in the importance of the welfare and comfort of the individual. The two terms appear frequently in his speeches and must have been perceived by those who drafted the general paper as being central to Trudeau's thought.

Although the three themes are grouped together as deserving of highest priority, there appeared to be little doubt that extra emphasis had been placed on economic growth. The booklet noted the priority the government attached to policies designed to promote economic growth, and in a press conference Mr Sharp stated flatly that 'The priorities are clearly set out. Economic growth takes precedence.'[31] Although Mr Murray later denied that economic growth had been ranked higher than the other two themes in the first tier of priorities,[32] the decision to continue trade relations with South Africa seemed to prove that, in case of conflict, economic growth had priority over considerations of social justice. Of the four main challenges to Canadian interests that were perceived by the government, three were purely economic in nature: trade protectionism in the policies of foreign governments or regional groups; other developments abroad, including excessive inflation or deflation seriously affecting Canada's economy; and the effect on Canadian identity and independence of American activities in the field of multinational corporations and international trade unions. The fourth challenge, in which economic considerations were present but not decisive, was ideological conflict and/or violent disturbances abroad, 'which are not only important in themselves but can also be detrimental to trade and investment abroad and to unity and security at home.'[33]

When announcing in January 1970 the appointment of A. E. Ritchie, an economist, as Under-Secretary of State for External Affairs, Mr Trudeau said that this was in keeping with his government's desire to emphasize the 'trade and commerce' aspect of External Affairs rather than the 'political and metaphysical'.[34] The emphasis of the policy papers on economic growth is consistent with Trudeau's view of economic growth as a means rather than an end in itself, for a key element in his thinking is the role a strong economy can play in the attainment of his objectives of national unity and individual dignity. To enlarge Canada's activity in such areas as development assistance, disarmament negotiations, the promotion of détente, and peacekeeping, 'it will be essential', the booklet noted, 'to maintain the strength of Canada's economy.' But Mitchell Sharp indignantly rejected the charge that emphasis upon economic growth was a 'self-seeking fast-buck philosophy' when he appeared before the Commons' External Affairs Committee:

> There has been a tendency on the part of some observers at home and abroad to identify these themes as national objectives and to lose sight of the fact that they are the means of achieving national aims. Economic growth, for example, is not an end in itself, but is fundamental to achievement of the national aims—unity, independence, prosperity, distinct identity.[35]

The relegation of peace and security to the second tier of priorities, like the emphasis on economic growth, were decisions arrived at in Cabinet. People outside the Cabinet had little, if any, influence on these decisions, for the attentive public, most of the academic and Parliamentary critics, and most External Affairs officials did not desire a de-emphasis in Canada's concern with policies designed to promote peace and security. Few seemed to agree with the government's contention that in the 1970s the most serious challenges to Canada would be trade protectionism, economic instability abroad, or civil war in the Western world, although there may have been considerably more support for the concern expressed in the booklet about the effect on Canada of American economic penetration. Most of the academic and Parliamentary critics considered Canada's role to be primarily the promotion of peace and security, although they differed about whether it should be done through increased foreign aid or support of the United Nations. Within External Affairs and National Defence, NATO and NORAD were still regarded as necessary for world stability. Mr Trudeau was one of the few Canadians who appeared to think that peace and security were no longer being threatened, and that there were more important areas in which Canada's foreign-policy efforts should be concentrated.

Although the government's emphasis on sovereignty in the NATO review had puzzled observers because of its apparent divergence from Mr Trudeau's own views, his ideas are very clearly reflected in the treatment of sovereignty expressed in the foreign-policy papers. The idea that 'Canada will continue secure as an independent political identity' was described as one of the country's three basic national aims.[36] It has been seen that Mr Trudeau has long believed that only in a nation-state such as Canada are the basic goals of cultural dualism and ethnic pluralism likely to be attained: this is why Canada must resist any loss of sovereignty or independence to the United States. Far from being inconsistent with Mr Trudeau's basic philosophy, this concept of Canadian sovereignty is central to it.

In the conceptual framework presented in the general paper, however, where sovereignty and independence were discussed as 'themes' rather than 'basic national aims', they appeared in the government's second tier of priorities on the grounds that the need to emphasize them depended primarily on the extent to which they were challenged. That they were clearly means to be used rather than ends in themselves—a vital part of Mr Trudeau's approach to sovereignty—is indicated by the statement that 'The key to Canada's continuing freedom to develop according to its own perceptions will be the judicious use of Canadian sovereignty whenever Canada's aims and interests are placed in jeopardy. . . .'[37] Four aspects of sovereignty and independence were emphasized: territorial integrity, constitutional authority, national identity, and freedom of action. The last three are to be found frequently in Trudeau's writing and speeches, an indication that the way in which the general paper treated sovereignty and independence was greatly influenced by the Prime Minister's personal views.

On the other hand, emphasis on territorial integrity appears rarely, if ever, in Mr Trudeau's pre-1968 thought, and pressure for its inclusion in the policy papers may well have come from other sources. Public interest in sovereignty, particularly in the Arctic, had been aroused in 1969 by the prospect of large petroleum discoveries in the Canadian North and by American attempts to exploit these findings, dramatized by the two voyages of the *Manhattan* in 1969. That same year large oil spills were caused by the sinking of two ships, the *Torrey Canyon* and the *Arrow* (the latter off Canada's east coast), and the Canadian public was awakened to the danger of massive pollution of the territorial waters and coasts of Canada—at a time when pollution of all kinds was becoming a major issue throughout the country. The extent of public concern was revealed when the Commons' Standing Committee on Indian Affairs and Northern Development recommended that Canada should immediately declare its sovereignty over all the waters of its Arctic Archipelago, since 'the safeguards and pollution controls necessary to protect Canada's Arctic environment and ecology will neither be possible nor enforceable without an effective exercise of Canadian control' over these waters.[38] The unanimous support in Parliament for the government's two bills passed in April 1970 extending Canada's territorial waters and areas of jurisdiction indicated the mood of the Canadian public. The government did not merely respond to this pressure; it was almost certainly formulating an active policy in reaction to Canada's disappointing failure to achieve international support at a 1969 Brussels conference for measures designed to prevent marine pollution resulting from the sinking of ships. Nevertheless there was considerable pressure on the government to increase and exercise its jurisdiction over Canada's off-shore waters, and the inclusion of 'territorial integrity' in the 1970 foreign-policy papers may well have been in response to this demand.

As was to be expected, in view of the NATO deliberations, the general paper's statement about Canada's position and role in the world represented a marked shift in the government's articulation of foreign policy. In November 1969, at the Liberal Party policy conference at Harrison Hot Springs, Mitchell Sharp offered a revealing insight into the attitude of the Canadian government when he stated: 'I would go so far as to say that public disenchantment with Canadian foreign policy in recent years is essentially the result of placing too much emphasis on role and influence and not enough on policy objectives and interests.'[39] In the general paper the government did not reject the idea that Canada should act as mediator when such an activity was required but rather what it regarded as the country's previous tendency 'to base foreign policy on an assumption that Canada can be cast as the "helpful fixer" in international affairs.'[40] Canada had neither the means nor the opportunities to satisfy these lofty aspirations.

This denigration of the 'helpful fixer' role echoed three frequently stated beliefs of the Prime Minister. The general paper's statement that 'What Canada can hope to accomplish in the world must be viewed not only in the light of Canadian aspirations, needs and wants but in terms of what is, from time to time, attainable'[41] was in keeping with Mr Trudeau's belief that Canada was a relatively small country and that its foreign policy should keep in mind its limited means. The general paper stated that foreign policy should be 'active' rather than 'reactive' as in the past,[42] another tenet of the Prime Minister, who had often deplored the fact that Canada's foreign policy had been based on reacting to world crises rather than on promoting the kind of objectives that were important to Canada. Finally, Mr Trudeau's belief in the need for selective specialization was reflected in the paper's statement that Canada could make its most effective contribution to international affairs by concentrating on the fields in which Canada excelled.[43]

Even the things that were *not* mentioned in the report reflected the thinking of the Prime Minister. In its 1971 Report to the House, the Commons' External Affairs Committee noted that the review appeared to have been intended to focus only on those areas Mr Trudeau described in his statement of May 29, 1968 as likely to require policy changes.[44] Issues such as the Middle East, Berlin, Viet Nam, and the

Strategic Arms Limitation Talks were not examined in depth, in keeping with Trudeau's belief that Canada's modest power precluded its influencing these matters, and that the country should concentrate on a relatively small number of issues of immediate importance to its basic national interests.

The most apparent and frequently criticized omission was the absence of a comprehensive analysis of Canada's relations with the United States, especially at a time when Canadian-American relations were arousing considerable public controversy in Canada. External Affairs Minister Sharp defended this omission on the grounds that the influence of the United States in all aspects of Canadian life was so great that no single paper could adequately treat such a complex subject.[45] But it is likely that the delicacy of this relationship, and the Canadian government's desire not to commit itself in advance on such issues as continental energy-sharing, played a major part in the decision virtually to ignore this subject. This is also consistent with the attitude of the Prime Minister, who had rarely expressed any great concern with Canadian-American relations, at least before 1971.

Indeed, Mr Trudeau's belief that a substantial degree of economic integration with the United States was not wholly undesirable was firmly expressed in the general paper in spite of the mood of economic nationalism within Canada. It stated that for the majority of Canadians 'the aim appears to be to attain the highest level of prosperity consistent with Canada's political preservation as an independent state. In the light of today's economic interdependence, this seems to be a highly practical and sensible evaluation of national needs.'[46] The policy recommended—'a judicious use of Canadian sovereignty whenever Canada's aims and interests are placed in jeopardy'[47]—was based on Mr Trudeau's selective economic nationalism. While aware that maintaining a proper balance between economic growth on the one hand and sovereignty and independence on the other would be one of the major tasks facing Canada in the next decade, the paper accepted, as did Mr Trudeau, that Canadian dependence on American industry and technology would 'continue to be a fact of life'. Had the government allowed itself to be influenced by articulate public opinion it would have advocated a much greater degree of economic nationalism.

The final aspect of the general paper that merits discussion is the role of public opinion. As Professor Gilles Lalande has noted, the seminars and discussions in which academics and businessmen were involved during the foreign-policy review were sector- and policy-oriented. 'Jamais à ma connaissance,' he told the Commons' Committee, '... il ne fut question, dans les termes retenus dans le premier fascicule, de buts nationaux, d'objectifs de politique étrangère et de mise en ordre de priorité de tels objectifs.*[48] The general paper was entirely a product of government deliberation, prepared without the participation of outside sources.

But the government frequently indicated that the views of the public would be sought *after* the paper was published, even though it did not solicit external advice during its preparation. Early in 1969 the Prime Minister said that once the review was complete, it would be discussed by Parliament and the public; then the government would consider changing its original proposals.[49] However, the press release that accompanied the publication of *Foreign Policy for Canadians* greatly narrowed the range of subjects open to public discussion: it excluded specific policy decisions such as the increase in foreign aid and offered for this purpose only the conceptual framework contained in the general paper. The sector papers apparently announced government decisions that would *not* be changed.

As the general paper contained few specific policy recommendations, it seems to have been written with the intention of educating the public rather than of soliciting its advice. 'In considering this policy report,' it said, 'Canadians should be asking themselves: "What kind of Canada do we want?"'[50] A more revealing explanation of the government's thinking was Mr Sharp's remark at the press conference that one of the purposes of the papers was 'to invite the public to think about foreign policy not as something apart from domestic policy but simply as a means of pursuing national policy by other means in the international environment.'[51] Since one of the government's main aims

---

* 'As far as I know, there was never any discussion of national goals, foreign-policy objectives, or the ordering of these objectives in terms of priorities, as was done in the first [general] booklet.'

ever since the inception of the review had been to eradicate what it regarded as the 'romantic' view of Canada's international role, its emphasis on national interests may have been in large part an attempt to make foreign policy more relevant to the Canadian public. Mr Trudeau's own approach to governing is to provide people with the 'incentive to think', whether by giving them the illusion of participation in policy formulation or by explaining policy in terms that have considerable public appeal, such as economic growth. To a large extent *Foreign Policy for Canadians* appears to have been an attempt by the government to remind the public of the importance of the national objectives that Mr Trudeau regarded as particularly essential.

The testimony of several informed witnesses, strategically placed and eminently credible, confirms that the striking similarity between the foreign-policy papers and Mr Trudeau's own ideas was not coincidental but purely intentional. Furthermore, the evidence presented in this study strongly suggests that Mr Trudeau's personal preferences and perceptions determined the degree to which other factors were able to influence the foreign-policy review. Changes in the external environment had decreased Canada's relative power, but it was the Prime Minister's view of the country's most important national interests that led to the widely publicized NATO cutback and the explicit condemnation of the 'helpful fixer' role. Economic problems necessitated the establishment of spending priorities and the curtailment of some government programs, but they did not determine which ones would be sacrificed—Mr Trudeau did. Furthermore, there is no proof that budgetary considerations played a major role in the 1969 NATO decision, and the decision to emphasize the trade-and-commerce aspect of external policy seems at least as much a response to the Prime Minister's own predilections as to domestic economic conditions. The criticism expressed by academic and Parliamentary commentators appears to have reinforced Mr Trudeau's 1968 view that something was wrong with Canada's existing foreign policy; but they found it far more difficult to influence the outcome of the review, for they recommended a continuation of the internationalistic role-playing of which the Prime Minister disapproved. The Departments of External Affairs and

National Defence were left with the authority to make little more than tactical decisions during the review, and in making even these they were often obliged to keep in mind the Prime Minister's personal preferences. The formulation of overall strategic policy was in the hands of the Prime Minister and those Cabinet ministers and personal advisers whose views coincided with his.

Notes

[1] Canada, Department of External Affairs, *Foreign Policy for Canadians*. Ottawa: Queen's Printer for Canada, 1970.

[2] *Globe and Mail*, January 23, 1969, p. 6; *Debates*, February 7, 1969, p. 526.

[3] *Debates*, May 8, 1969, p. 1435.

[4] House of Commons, Standing Committee on External Affairs and National Defence, *Report to the House respecting 'Foreign Policy for Canadians'*. June 1971, p. 42 (hereafter referred to as *Report, 1971*).

[5] *Foreign Policy for Canadians (Europe)*, p. 28.

[6] *Ibid*., pp. 27, 28, 30.

[7] See the *Globe and Mail*, October 25, 1968, p. 1; *Monthly Report*, January 1969, p. 17; *Globe and Mail*, January 25, 1969, p. 3.

[8] *Foreign Policy for Canadians (Latin America)*, pp. 22-4.

[9] See *Monthly Report*, June 1969, p. 192.

[10] John Hay, 'Canada drifts toward less political involvement in UN'. Saskatoon *Star-Phoenix*, June 20, 1970.

[11] *Foreign Policy for Canadians (International Development)*, pp. 8, 9, 10, 13.

[12] *International Canada*, May 1970, p. 109.

[13] *Debates*, December 1, 1969, p. 1425.

[14] John W. Holmes, *The Better Part of Valour: Essays on Canadian Diplomacy*. Toronto: McClelland and Stewart, 1970, pp. 213, 215, 217.

[15] See the comments to this effect made by Mr Trudeau in *Debates*, January 24, 1969, p. 4769.

[16] See John Paul and Jerome Laulicht, *In Your Opinion*, Vol. 1, Clarkson, Ontario: Canadian Peace Research Institute, 1963, p. 85.

[17] *Debates*, February 10, 1969, p. 5307; and February 12, 1969, p. 5424.

[18] *International Canada*, May 1970, p. 108.

[19] *Foreign Policy for Canadians (Pacific)*, p. 25.

[20] *Le Monde*, 21 février 1970, p. 4.

[21] *Foreign Policy for Canadians (Pacific)*, p. 10.

[22] Denis Stairs, 'Notes for Talk to External Affairs Departmental Conference', May 13-14, p. 5 (unpublished).

[23] Canada, Department of External Affairs, *Reference Papers*, 'Department of External Affairs', Revised August 1970.

[24] *Debates*, June 15, 1970, p. 8103.

[25] *Globe and Mail*, June 26, 1970, p. 6.

[26] John Gray, 'Ottawa Policy Marked by Self-Interest', *Montreal Star*, July 4, 1970, p. 14.

[27] *Foreign Policy for Canadians*, p. 9.

[28] *Minutes*, December 15, 1970, pp. 19–20.

[29] Peter C. Dobell, 'Canada and NATO', *Orbis*, Vol. XIII, Spring 1969, p. 317.

[30] *Foreign Policy for Canadians*, p. 32.

[31] *Ibid.*, p. 34; Toronto *Star*, June 26, 1970, pp. 1-2.

[32] *Minutes*, December 15, 1970, p. 28.

[33] *Foreign Policy for Canadians*, pp. 29–30.

[34] *Globe and Mail*, January 12, 1970, p. 7.

[35] *Minutes*, October 23, 1970, pp. 9, 10.

[36] *Foreign Policy for Canadians*, p. 10.

[37] *Ibid.*, p. 39.

[38] *Monthly Report*, December 1969, pp. 322-3.

[39] *Monthly Report*, November 1969, pp. 312-13.

[40] *Foreign Policy for Canadians*, p. 8.

[41] *Ibid.*, p. 6.

[42] *Ibid.*, p. 8.

[43] *Ibid.*, pp. 18-19.

[44] *Report, 1971*, p. 42.

[45] *Ibid.*, p. 38.

[46] *Foreign Policy for Canadians*, p. 10.

[47] *Ibid.*, p. 39.

[48] *Minutes*, February 2, 1971, p. 15.

[49] *Globe and Mail*, January 23, 1969, p. 6.

[50] *Foreign Policy for Canadians*, p. 42.

[51] *International Canada*, June 1970, p. 135.

7

Assessment

I. Reaction to the Policy Papers

Foreign Policy for Canadians had undergone a difficult period of gestation, and the reaction to its long-awaited appearance revealed once again that there was a wide range of views about the country's foreign policy. For some Canadians the government had recommended policies that constituted a dangerous departure from the past; for others, the papers offered few really significant initiatives and were merely an attempt to rationalize the maintenance of the status quo; still others looked beyond specific policy proposals and attacked the government's new philosophy and conceptual framework.

One of the most frequently expressed fears was that the denigration of the 'helpful-fixer' role meant that Canada would no longer take an active part in international mediatory and peacekeeping ventures. Andrew Brewin, the NDP foreign-affairs critic, commented that the general paper 'hints at a withdrawal from idealistically inspired world-wide involvements.' Peyton Lyon did not feel that the government had lost all desire to participate in such international activities, but he took issue with the fact that Canada's capabilities as a peacekeeper were downplayed and that the aversion of the Canadian public to such ventures was overemphasized. Some of the nation's editorial writers, on the other hand, saluted the government's recognition that a more modest approach to peacekeeping was necessary. 'The most exciting discovery', according to the Edmonton *Journal*, was 'the official abandonment of the pretence that Canada could, being allegedly uncommitted to any bloc, act as mediator, peacemaker, or leader of the so-called third world.' Although it is doubtful that even Howard Green or Paul Martin ever viewed Canada as the leader of the Third World, this statement shows how the exaggerated rhetoric of these two former ministers had entirely misled some Canadians. The Montreal *Gazette* was more accurate. It noted that there had never 'been such a role for Canada in the real world as that of the honest broker, although it has flourished in the imaginations of some politicians.' Christopher Young of the Ottawa *Citizen* summed up the government's attitude well when he wrote: 'We are not committing ourselves in advance to answer any summons in the name of peace. But we are ready to contribute if we judge that the operation has a chance of success.'[1]

Another focus of controversy was the government's decision to relegate peace and security—the supreme foreign-policy goal of all Canadian post-war governments—to the second tier of Canada's new policy priorities. The danger of isolationism was implied in Professor James Hyndman's comment that the new emphasis on national interests 'seems likely to involve some retrenchment from the marked internationalist policies pursued throughout the post-war era, a shift for a time to a more "introversive" approach.' Maxwell Cohen of McGill University noted that, contrary to the claims of the government, there might well be instances when Canada's national interests at home did not, and should not, coincide with its interests abroad. He noted the absence from the policy papers of 'a sense of the primacy, not of specific national objectives as such, but of how these legitimate claims fit into the even more legitimate requirements of a viable international community.' Some observers feared that if a conflict of interests ever arose in an area where Canada had a major economic stake, the government would not hesitate to sacrifice other themes for the sake of economic growth. *Foreign Policy for Canadians* did not explain how such a conflict of interests would be resolved, but its announcement of policy towards southern Africa seemed to indicate that a restrictive interpretation of national interests would prevail where Canada's purely national concerns—e.g. economic growth—came into conflict with its international responsibility to promote social justice. The decision to maintain trading relations with South Africa while continuing the embargo on the sale of military equipment was described by the government as a balancing of the two themes of economic growth and social justice; but critics were quick to charge that this approach paid little more than lip service to the latter. The government's policy papers were soon questioned by four members of the Committee for a Just Canadian Policy Towards Africa, who released their own 'Black Paper' calling for a termination of all Canadian trade with South Africa. Trade, they argued, was an instrument of foreign policy, not something that could be distinguished from it, and Canada was left in a morally untenable position by continuing to have economic relations with a country that openly practised racism. Moreover, since Canada's economic interests in South Africa were relatively limited, complete economic disengagement would not even be overly costly. To many the policy papers seemed to diminish Canada's traditional concern with social justice.[2]

The way in which economic growth was discussed in the general paper left a clear impression in the minds of most observers that it had become the government's main concern in the field of external relations. (Mr Sharp later claimed that this was not so.) The Toronto *Globe and Mail* was especially struck by this. 'Whether talking about Eastern Europe, Latin America, the Pacific, or Western Europe,' its editorial said, 'the report usually is concentrating on one point: dollars and cents.' The *Globe* went on to note that, though foreign trade and foreign policy were inseparable and should be balanced, the policy papers had 'tipped the scale toward the dollar and away from diplomacy.' The Canadian public had clearly become accustomed to viewing foreign policy with a touch of idealism and the new emphasis on economic growth was hard to accept. 'For a nation as rich as Canada to place economic growth as its first value choice', the Canadian Peace Research Institute charged, 'is a Philistine decision of the type the youth of this country are clearly rejecting.' Others feared that a 'dollar-diplomacy' image would be projected abroad and would lead to a loss of prestige and good will, particularly in the Third World. Dale Thomson and R. F. Swanson speculated that, if the economic growth of Canada was the government's prime objective, 'then much closer commercial and financial integration with the United States is indicated, or at least, primacy for relations with the more developed countries.' Needless to say, the Canadian Pulp and Paper Association and the Canadian Export Association supported the new priorities wholeheartedly. These two rather biased observers were virtually the only groups that did so among all those that expressed their views to the Commons' Committee on External Affairs.[3]

This is not to say that most of the critics of the new policy priorities did not recognize that Canada was obliged to accord great importance to economic growth in its foreign policy. As the government noted in the general booklet, Canada, which requires a growing economy if it is to play a responsible international role, is exceptionally dependent on international trade. What critics decried was not so much the government's emphasis on economic growth as its apparent de-emphasis of peace and security as a major objective of Canadian foreign policy. By putting economic growth in the first tier of priorities and peace and security in the second, the government had left itself embarrassingly vulnerable to charges that it was adopting an isolationist, self-seeking foreign policy. The government said in the policy papers that economic growth was the means by which Canada's other objectives of social justice, quality of life, and a harmonious natural environment would be achieved. The Winnipeg *Free Press*, however, reversed the priorities and, in the true Pearson tradition, wondered, 'without peace and security, how can we have much hope in other fields?'

The most intensive review of the policy priorities was the one conducted in 1970–1 by the Commons' Standing Committee on External Affairs and National Defence, which, in spite of its predominantly Liberal composition, issued a report that was clearly critical of the basic principles of the general paper. The Committee's perceptive analysis was that the relative importance attached to economic growth might have attracted less criticism if peace and security had received equal priority. It also said:

> Although the Committee has agreed that the paper's re-affirmation of national objectives is timely and useful, it considers that the paper over-emphasizes both the pursuit of national interests and the parallel in domestic and foreign-policy priorities. What is lacking, in the Committee's opinion, is a recognition of Canada's place in an increasingly interdependent world; what is needed is a more generous and responsible approach to the national interest of Canada interpreted in the broadest sense. The policy paper concludes with the following question to Canadians: 'What kind of Canada do we want?' In thinking about foreign policy, the Committee would submit it is also necessary to ask, as one witness did, 'What kind of world do we want?'[4]

Another criticism that was frequently heard during the analysis of the policy papers had to do with the lack of any substantial discussion of Canada's relations with the United States. The Edmonton *Journal* was one of many newspapers that were astounded that so crucial an issue as Canadian-American relations could have been dealt with in the policy papers in only a handful of sentences. American analyst Robert Osgood observed of this cursory treatment that 'In intellectual terms it seems to me like a tremendous gap.' Canadian commentators noted important practical implications of the omission. The *Globe and Mail's* interpretation was that Canada's foreign policy was destined to remain low key as long as the Canadian economy remained tied to that of the United States. The Ottawa *Citizen*, however, stated that the government's approach to the U.S. had been 'clear and realistic throughout the review, neither strident nor supine'—without revealing how it had come to this mysterious conclusion.[5]

In addition to critics who decried specific decisions and omissions, there were those who believed that very little of a concrete nature had resulted from the review. 'It seems almost incredible', exclaimed the Edmonton *Journal*, 'that it took the federal government two years to produce what appears to be a large number of platitudes—but few specific suggestions—concerning Canada's future foreign policy.' The Ottawa *Journal* agreed, complaining that most of the booklets 'suffer from stating the obvious, managing to sound like a cross between the

Canada Year Book and a public relations officer.' It said that the award for the most sophomoric of the pamphlets should go to the one on Latin America, which did little more than state the government's desire to seek improved relations with that continent. (This criticism could also have been made of the Pacific paper.) Claude Ryan in *Le Devoir* wrote that, in concentrating on areas in which the government wanted to develop new relationships, *Foreign Policy for Canadians* ignored many of the crucial world issues on which critics expected specific policies. Pointing to the little attention paid in the review to the Middle East, Viet Nam, and the question of military dictatorships in Latin America and Greece, Ryan wrote:

> Il est facile, avec tant d'oublis, d'affecter une mine sereine et de parler avec placidité des 'intérêts canadiens'. On est très loin, cependant, du monde réel, des pays déchirés par des luttes très dures, des peuples en quête de structures nouvelles. Les planificateurs fédéraux ont voulu se libérer du complexe de 'boy scout' qui caracterisa naguère la politique étrangère du Canada. Le 'réalisme' qu'ils ont substitué à l'ancien défaut est entaché d'une secheresse qui le rend presque étranger aux préoccupations des hommes de ce temps.*[6]

Many of the critics did not seem to realize that the Prime Minister placed far greater importance on the general paper than on the five sector booklets. It has been shown that the latter did little more than rationalize and fill in the details of decisions that had been made in the course of the review: to emphasize economic and social relations with Western Europe rather than military contacts, to pay greater attention to legal and social issues in the UN, to accord greater importance to

---

* 'It is easy, with so many things forgotten, to assume a serene attitude and to speak placidly of "Canadian interests". That takes us very far, however, from the real world, from countries torn apart by very severe struggles, from people in search of new structures. The federal planners wanted to free themselves from the "boy scout" complex that characterized Canada's foreign policy in the past. The "realism" that they substituted for the former defect is blemished by a dryness that makes it almost foreign to the preoccupations of modern men.'

foreign aid, and to improve relations with the countries of the Pacific rim and Latin America. What was really new about *Foreign Policy for Canadians* was the outline of the Prime Minister's foreign-policy philosophy presented in the general booklet.

The most interesting critical discussion centred on its conceptual framework and whether or not these six themes could be translated into specific policies.* According to Denis Stairs the drafters of the general paper, beginning (as the Prime Minister wanted) with Canada's national objectives, soon became caught up in 'a kind of infinite regress' that led to increased abstraction. The general framework was little more than 'an organizational defence mechanism' that served to deflect attention away from questions of substance.[7] This quality of abstraction may have been accidental—the result of the paper's having been passed from one civil servant to another, all of whom were forced to reach a consensus not only within departments but among departments, and then through the hands of cabinet ministers, who were well aware that the variety of foreign-policy views held by Canadians made anything more than vague generalizations highly dangerous. The lack of concrete policy proposals and the emphasis on abstract discussion of themes could also have been intentional, however, reflecting the Prime Minister's desire to educate Canadians about what he perceived to be Canada's basic national interests and principles. Whatever the reason for the particular character of the general paper (it was most likely a combination of the two possibilities described above), *Foreign Policy for Canadians* was a disappointment for anyone who had hoped for dramatic new announcements about the substance of Canada's external relations.

---

* Virtually the only Canadian academic who admired the conceptual framework and its presentation was K. J. Holsti, a respected international-relations theorist at the University of British Columbia, who said that in some ways the paper was 'a much better effort than most academic work', since it attempted 'to produce categories of analysis—for example, "objectives" and "roles", "sources" and "outputs" and so on.' He implied that the paper might very well have a beneficial effect on Canada's future foreign policy. (*Summary of Proceedings of a Workshop at the Meeting of the Canadian Political Science Association, St John's, Newfoundland, June 11, 1971.*)

II. The Impact of the Policy Papers

The year 1971 saw few dramatic changes in foreign policy that could be traced back to the conceptual framework outlined in 1970. Canada's main preoccupation during the year and a half following the completion of the review was with internal economic problems, which were aggravated by the imposition of the ten-per-cent American surtax in August 1971. With the exception of Canadian-American relations, foreign policy was not a matter of great public interest. Many of the academic critics who had been very vocal during the review process (among them Stephen Clarkson) seemed to lose all interest in foreign affairs and had turned their attention to internal problems.

It is possible to present some tentative conclusions about what the policy review meant and will mean in the future for Canada's external relations. The government has unquestionably followed the general booklet's guidelines by giving increased emphasis to the economic aspect of Canada's external activities. The protocol signed by Prime Minister Trudeau in the Soviet Union in the spring of 1971 increased the possibility of greater technological exchange and more extensive trade with the U.S.S.R. The integration of the departments involved in Canada's foreign relations—External Affairs; Industry, Trade and Commerce; and Immigration—progressed at a steady pace. The administrative and clerical 'support' services of these departments were integrated in April 1971, and foreign postings are now made by an interdepartmental committee chaired by the Under-Secretary of State for External Affairs rather than by each of the three departments acting individually. Whether integration will continue had not been determined by the end of 1971,[8] but it seems probable that, after an initial period of delay while the various departments struggle to save as much of their power as possible, there will be further amalgamation. There is little reason to maintain departmental separation, which in the past ensured the predominance of the Department of External Affairs in Canada's activities abroad, if the economic aspect of external relations is to receive equal, if not greater, priority than the political. For future foreign-policy formulation, this move towards integration is one of the most significant by-products of the whole review.

Initial fears that Canada's foreign policy would become almost exclusively economically oriented were unfounded. Situations where economic growth conflicted noticeably with other policy themes have been the exception rather than the rule. Even in the classic case of conflict, southern Africa, the critical reaction to the government's initial statement of policy encouraged it to swing the balance slightly more in the direction of social justice. Polymer, a Canadian crown corporation, was instructed in 1971 to divest itself of its profitable investments in South Africa, and the government made tentative proposals to increase its representation and foreign aid in the surrounding black African states. In the last half of 1971 economic considerations dominated much of the thinking about Canada's external relations, but this was largely because of the serious problems that had been brought on by the American surcharge, which adversely affected Canada's trading position with the U.S. (The general paper had predicted that trade restrictions imposed abroad would constitute a serious future problem.) A new government policy on foreign investment that was leaked in late 1971, though not as severe as some Canadians would have liked, was nevertheless based on the premise that, in some circumstances, economic growth might have to be sacrificed to protect other national values.

What the government has in fact done is to place greater emphasis on the economic aspect of external relations than had been the case in the past, but not to the extent that other considerations have been ignored. Canadians who read the 1970 policy paper might have realized that this was the government's thinking if the paper had been clearer in its terminology. When it referred to themes of 'highest priority' it conveyed the impression to almost all observers that it was ranking the six themes in order of importance to assist in future policy formulation. But the paper also explained the government's thinking by saying that it was giving 'greater emphasis than in the past' to the themes of economic growth, social justice, and quality of life—not that it was necessarily placing them above the other three themes of peace and security, sovereignty and independence, and a harmonious natural environment. There is a difference between 'highest priority' and 'greater emphasis than in the past', but by using both phrases almost interchangeably the government inadvertently created an erroneous impression of its intentions: 'emphasis' rather than 'priority' is the operative word. During the year and a half following the completion of the review, speeches and articles as well as the actions of government officials indicated that economic growth was not necessarily the new theme of Canada's foreign policy. In the prestigious quarterly *Foreign Affairs*, Ivan Head described Mr Trudeau's 'new society' as one that challenged the philosophy of unrestricted economic growth and placed 'increasing emphasis on the quality of life and the importance of human relations.' The Prime Minister's number-one adviser on foreign policy also set out to destroy the impression that economic growth had been permanently ranked ahead of other policy themes. 'They should not be listed in any given order,' he said, 'for this leaves the impression that they are related in a fixed and descending order of importance. Ideally, they should be illustrated schematically.'[9] Had the six policy themes been presented to the Canadian public with the aid of the hexagonal diagram (as they were to Cabinet), it might have been easier to show that they were not mutually exclusive and that emphasis given to each by the Canadian government would vary according to changing circumstances. The failure of the attentive public to interpret the government's thinking correctly was also due to the fact that peace and security had become so ingrained in the minds of most foreign-policy commentators as Canada's supreme goal that they found it difficult to accept any lessening in the importance of this objective. But for the most part the government must take the blame for an imprecise and unclear description of its real intentions. For a government that prided itself on its ability to communicate with the Canadian people, the public's misinterpretation of this important theme in *Foreign Policy for Canadians* must have been a great disappointment.*

---

* It is of course possible that economic growth was intended as the first priority in 1970 and that the contrasting rhetoric and actions of the government since then was a response to critical public opinion. Although one cannot determine with certainty

Just as subsequent events indicated that economic growth had not become the be-all and end-all of Canadian foreign policy, they also showed that the government did not intend to reduce Canada's participation in international peacekeeping. Its activities in this field remained unaltered: Canada continued to participate in the United Nations operations in India and Pakistan, the Middle East, and Cyprus; to maintain standby forces for possible UN service; and to work actively in the UN Special Committee on Peacekeeping Operations. It should be remembered that the sector papers implied a more active role for Canada in such activities than the general paper's denigration of the 'helpful-fixer' concept seemed to suggest. The European booklet stated that Canada's precise military role at any time would depend 'in part on the requirements for peacekeeping', and the United Nations paper said that Canada should continue to take an active part in negotiations concerning peacekeeping operations.[10] As it did. Prime Minister Trudeau played an important mediatory role at the Commonwealth Prime Ministers' Conference in Singapore in 1971, helping to find a compromise that prevented several African members from leaving the Commonwealth because of British arms sales to South Africa. The Commons' External Affairs Committee observed approvingly that, 'Faced with the inconsistency between the belittling of the "helpful-fixer" role in the policy paper and the Prime Minister's initiatives both before and during the Singapore Conferences,' it favoured 'the action rather than the theory.'[11] And Mitchell Sharp has agreed that one of the prime reasons Canada remained entirely neutral during the 1971 India-Pakistan war was the prospect that it might eventually be asked to serve in a peacekeeping or mediatory capacity.[12]

Mr Trudeau has never expressed the idea that Canada should not accord great importance to peacekeeping. Where this theme was con-

---

whether this was so, it is unlikely, since the Trudeau government has never been disposed to alter its policies to suit a small number of articulate academic critics and there is no indication that the Canadian general public had any interest in foreign policy. The idea that economic considerations should predominate in virtually all aspects of a country's foreign relations is so unrealistic that it is hard to believe the government could ever have seriously believed this.

cerned the foreign-policy papers were merely intended to attack the rhetoric of the past, not the substance of previous Canadian foreign policies—to present to the public the firm conviction of both the Prime Minister and the country's foreign-service officers that Canada's peacekeeping operations had to hold a reasonable promise of long-term success if future ventures were to avoid the fate of the International Control Commission in Indochina and the United Nations Emergency Force in Egypt. Above all, the Prime Minister wanted Canadians to realize that foreign policy should be based on the quest for specific national goals rather than on a vague desire to achieve prestige and glory.

Very relevant to the national goals of peace and security and sovereignty was the Defence White Paper, called *Defence in the 70s*, that was published in August 1971. Designed to elaborate on the military priorities that had been established in the NATO review of 1969, it contained few surprises. Though sovereignty remained at the head of the list of priorities, the White Paper did not announce any massive shift of military resources from the field of collective security in order to attain the 'independent' Canadian defence policy to which the Prime Minister had alluded in his press conference on April 3, 1969. Sovereignty was paid little more than lip service in the announcement that Canada should provide as much of its own aerial defence as possible; it was recognized, however, that American aircraft would still need access to Canadian air space unless Canada was prepared to increase drastically the size of its defence budget. What was described as 'defence of Canada's sovereignty' turned out to involve merely defence of Canada's territorial jurisdiction and aid to the civil authority. Emphasis was placed on such activities as the surveillance of foreign fishing fleets and the patrolling of coastal areas to detect signs of pollution; much was made of the non-military function of the armed forces in combatting natural disasters and pollution, and of the possibility that future civil disorders might necessitate the involvement of the CAF.

The defence priorities that were established in 1969, as they were explained in the 1971 White Paper, turned out to involve primarily a change in articulation for domestic consumption. The internal duties of the Canadian Armed Forces were increased, but participation in NORAD, NATO, and peacekeeping was continued. In fact the White Paper reaffirmed Canada's support for the collective-security alliances of NATO and NORAD. Forces committed to NATO were to be increased by two squadrons based in Canada in readiness for rapid deployment to Norway in case of emergency. It was decided that the Bomarc nuclear missiles had outlived their usefulness in North American air defence and should be retired, but the interceptor role of the Voodoo CF-101s, armed with nuclear warheads, was to be maintained. With the White Paper's clear statement that there was a role for Canada's armed forces in the seventies, the general uncertainty about the future of the CAF that the government had inspired in 1969 was largely ended.

However, the sector paper on Europe in the 1970 foreign-policy review confirmed the 1969 decision to reduce by fifty per cent Canada's contribution to NATO—a decision that almost certainly caused a temporary deterioration in Canada's relations with its North Atlantic allies. From their point of view Canada's unilateral reduction made it more difficult for them to resist public pressure at home to reduce the size of their own military contributions. The consensus in NATO, moreover, was that progress could be made in arms-limitation negotiations with the Soviet Union only if all member nations maintained a united front: it was agreed that unilateral reductions such as Canada's undermined the prospects for success.

This temporary loss of good will and diplomatic influence could have been avoided and the Trudeau government could even have carried out its reduction without offending Canada's allies had its tactics been different. Considering the fact that the Canadian troops were not indispensable from a military point of view, NATO countries might well have been receptive had Canada informed them that it would have to reduce its commitment because of public pressure or economic problems at home. Given sufficient notice the other countries could have redeployed their forces to fill the gap left by the Canadians; and, had the reduction been carried out with a minimum of publicity, the impression of a united western front could have been maintained. But the Canadian government did precisely the opposite:

it announced its cutbacks barely a week before the twentieth-anniversary meeting of NATO in April 1969. Furthermore, it openly questioned the value of NATO in the course of a lengthy public debate, led by Mr Trudeau, on the organization's value. The Prime Minister apparently wanted to emphasize the importance of his government's decision to downgrade NATO in Canada's defence priorities in order to encourage Canadians to think of foreign and defence policy in terms of issues and goals that were oriented to North America. As a result the Prime Minister caused a deterioration in Canada's relations with its western allies that took some time to correct.

Mr Trudeau's well-known suspicion of military forces may have obscured his understanding of their political function. He may have been unprepared for the serious deterioration in Canadian-European relations that resulted from his NATO cutbacks, for Canada's subsequent actions were designed to increase its contacts with the countries of Western and Eastern Europe. The 1970 sector paper on Europe paid great attention to the cultivation of economic, political, and cultural relations with Europe as an effective counterweight to the overwhelming presence of the United States. Between 1969 and the end of 1971 Canada signed a wide range of scientific, technical, and cultural agreements with several European nations; special efforts were made to attract European investment; and so many special missions were sent across the Atlantic that one opposition Member of Parliament suggested that a permanent welcoming committee should be established at the Ottawa airport to greet returning Cabinet ministers and Parliamentarians.[13] Government spokesmen now say that Canada is not nearly as worried about Britain's entry into the European Economic Community as it was a few years ago, for Canada's point of view and interests are now much better understood in Europe. It is probable that such contacts will continue to increase in the immediate future, for Mr Trudeau seems to view Europe as a valuable counterweight to the United States.

The Prime Minister's trip to the Soviet Union in 1971 was another indication of his desire to establish for Canada what he calls 'alternative sources of influence, of trade, of friendship.'[14] Unfortunately his ill-timed comment that Canada needed closer ties with the Soviet

Union to protect its national identity from the political, economic, and even military domination of the United States gave rise to speculation that Mr Trudeau was 'anti-American'.* However, we have seen in Chapter 3 that the Prime Minister is well aware that the United States is Canada's most natural ally and friend because of the common history, geographical propinquity, and basic values of the two countries. His major concern is that Canada should maintain a variety of outlooks and contacts and thereby preserve its own identity. His moderate approach to problems of foreign investment in Canada indicates that his government will continue to preserve those aspects of Canada that it considers unique and valuable, but that it will not succumb to growing nationalist sentiment by becoming in any way anti-American. As Ivan Head has explained: 'Inevitably any suggestion of change attracted the criticism that it was motivated by anti-Americanism. . . . One might just as well describe as a "horse-hater" the farmer who had switched to tractors in order to accommodate new conditions.'[15]

Canada's relations with the Third World have also increased since 1970 and this trend can be expected to continue. The government has announced its intention to send an observer mission to the meetings of the Organization of American States,** although the Latin-American diplomatic missions that were closed during the 1969 economy drive have not been re-opened. Canada's development-assistance program has continued to expand, particularly in French-speaking countries. In March 1971 Mitchell Sharp announced that Canadian aid to francophone countries in Africa had reached the same level as aid to Commonwealth nations on that continent.[16] The establishment of diplomatic relations with the People's Republic of China was announced only a few months after the publication of the foreign-policy papers, and Canadian officials are hopeful that Canadian trade with China will

---

* The imposition of the ten-per-cent American surcharge in August 1971 led to increased criticism in Canada that Mr Trudeau had allowed Canadian-American relations to deteriorate. This issue became the centre of a Commons debate in November 1971, when the Conservative opposition moved a motion of non-confidence in the government.

** The OAS approved the seating of this mission in February 1972.

increase in the years to come. The government appears to have concluded that a continuation of close relations with Europe in no way precludes increased Canadian contacts with countries of the Third World—an attitude that supporters of NATO repeatedly expressed throughout the foreign-policy review.

Although there have been some foreign-policy changes in the areas discussed in the sector papers, there is little evidence that the conceptual framework set out in the general paper has had any significant impact on the actual content of Canadian foreign policy. The changes that occurred—and many of them *have* been significant—were mostly announced during rather than after the policy review: the decision to establish diplomatic relations with China and the Vatican, the fifty-per-cent reduction in Canada's contribution to NATO, the emphasis on non-political activities in the United Nations, a large increase in aid to francophone countries, and a twenty-per-cent cut in the size of Canada's armed forces. The value of the conceptual framework lies mainly in assisting policy planners to analyse the many considerations involved in external issues; it can also be used to rationalize decisions. But it offers little assistance in the formulation of specific policies.[17]

The significance of the conceptual framework was that it indicated a changed emphasis in the foreign policy of Canada. The economic aspects of Canada's external relations are receiving greater attention than in the past, and the government's approach to peace and security is now being based at least as much on measures to promote disarmament and on foreign aid as on support to collective-security organizations. But the two-tier pattern presented in *Foreign Policy for Canadians* will not likely result in any one theme's becoming predominant, for the ability of a small country such as Canada to plan its foreign policy is limited. The general paper recognized this fact when it stated that the degree of emphasis placed on themes like sovereignty and independence, or peace and security, depends largely on the extent to which they are challenged; but because it also implied that previous Canadian foreign policy had been too 'reactive', critics were led to conclude that the priorities of the framework were to be rigorously applied. In fact this has not happened, for no one theme has become predominant to the exclusion of all others.

In the opinion of the Commons' External Affairs Committee, one of the most important results of the review process was that it brought to an end the mistrust and lack of understanding that had prevailed, at least since early 1969, between the Cabinet and the Department of External Affairs.[18] The department may now have realized that the conceptual framework was desired by Mr Trudeau more for domestic purposes than with any intention of radically altering established policy. Some of the external changes he did propose—especially recognition of Communist China and a greater discretion in accepting peacekeeping duties without adequate terms of reference—had long been favoured by many foreign-service officers. Mitchell Sharp stated that the publication of the foreign-policy papers 'has given the department a clear mandate from the government and a new sense of direction.'[19] The resentment of 1969 appears to have vanished from the department. Officials finally understood what the new Prime Minister wanted from them—a new emphasis in policy rather than a sharp break from the past. Once its goals were clearly established the department realized that it was again working in unison with the political leaders.

In spite of this apparent harmony, however, some members of the department have a rather different attitude. They feel that in some areas—particularly in Europe and NATO—previous policies and patterns of emphasis have been sustained, and that the Prime Minister was obliged to retreat from his earlier intention to downgrade both Europe and NATO in Canada's foreign policy. They speak with some smugness of the fact that traditional policies were in large part maintained and contend that they 'won' the battle for control of foreign policy. On the question of NATO they may be right, for we have seen that the Prime Minister appears to have been leaning in the direction of a larger NATO cut than actually occurred in 1969. As for Canada's relations with Europe, it is not clear that Mr Trudeau ever wished to decrease Canada's economic and cultural relations with the continent, for it was primarily the military relationship that concerned him; he spoke of giving more emphasis than in the past to other parts of the world, not of decreasing Canada's contacts with Europe.

The educational value of the review process on the Prime Minister and his Cabinet colleagues should not be disregarded. Few of them had previously had much experience in matters of foreign policy.

Their extensive discussions in Cabinet, and with academics and other interested persons, cannot have failed to make them more aware of the hard choices that were involved. The Prime Minister had initially been disposed to withdraw all Canadian troops from Europe—until he learned that those forces performed an important political function. It would be surprising if he did not also become aware that the duties of a diplomat involve far more than the communication of information. The Department of External Affairs appears to have re-established its credibility in the minds of a once-skeptical Prime Minister and Cabinet. In 1969 the department's budget had been frozen at $56 million, but by the fiscal year 1971-2 it approached $100 million.[20]

The Prime Minister has undoubtedly succeeded in his goal of asserting political control over the conduct of Canada's foreign policy, but he may have realized that this has dangers as well as advantages. On the positive side, when foreign policy is not the exclusive preserve of one or two key departments but rather is formulated with the interests of as many as fifteen different departments in mind, the need for centralized co-ordination is great. Civil servants find it difficult to intervene directly in the affairs of other departments, and so the often conflicting demands of different departments can be resolved only by the political leaders. But centralized control that consistently ignores the views of civil servants can have a detrimental effect on government efficiency by undermining the morale of the officials who must implement foreign policy. By exaggerating the importance of the 1969 NATO decision for domestic purposes and by openly ridiculing the civil service, particularly the Department of External Affairs, the Prime Minister damaged, at least temporarily, the relations between the Cabinet and the civil service. If policy is to be formulated and implemented effectively, these must be harmonious.

Since 1970 the Prime Minister has trod more carefully. Most of the overall 'strategic' decisions have now been made, and so Mr Trudeau and his advisers have become much less visible in foreign-policy formulation. The country's pattern of foreign policy for the seventies has been laid down, and Cabinet seems content to leave its implementation—as well as the day-to-day decisions that must be made—in the hands of the civil service. With a few notable exceptions (Canadian-

American relations, for example), the Prime Minister has turned his attention to domestic matters, in which he is more interested.* There is little doubt that the political leadership intends to maintain its control over important strategic decisions when they are required, but earlier fears that the civil service would lose all influence in policy formulation have been eased. The harmonious relationship between the Prime Minister and the Department of External Affairs that has long been a Canadian trade-mark appears to have been re-established, although the nature of this relationship has clearly changed from the days of previous Canadian governments.

III. Appraisal of the Foreign-Policy Review

If one considers only the policies it initiated, the foreign-policy review was hardly an unqualified success. Some important changes did occur before the end of the review process, but few more could be expected on the basis of the 1970 policy papers, and many important issues remained unresolved. There was little indication of the way in which the government intended to act in its dealings with the United States, and the thorny question of whether Canada should have close relations with military dictatorships in Greece and Latin America was conveniently ignored. The review did not discuss in any detail the alternative courses of action that might be open to Canada once American troops were withdrawn from Indochina and the need for some transitional mediatory body became apparent. And there was no substantial discussion of other major world issues—the Middle East, prospects for East-West détente, the future role of Japan and China in Asia—because the government chose to view international affairs in the light of what Canada could accomplish in the short term.

Was the whole review therefore a waste of time? The Ottawa *Journal* seemed to think so. 'All in all,' it said, 'the whole 25-month-

---

* The likelihood of a federal election in 1972 is undoubtedly another reason why the Prime Minister has paid less attention to external affairs, which is of interest to relatively few Canadians.

long review appears to have been unnecessary. The changes proposed would likely have been recommended by the professionals in the department anyway. But grant Pierre Trudeau and Mitchell Sharp this much: after a long and distracting search under the bed and into the skeleton cupboard, they openly admit they found nothing of ill repute or practice.'[21]

After looking at the whole review process, however, it becomes clear that Prime Minister Trudeau accomplished much of what he set out to do when he announced the review in 1968. His influence may well have exceeded that of all other sources combined, and was unquestionably the single most significant one. It was his influence that resulted in a new foreign-policy philosophy: Canada was henceforth to think in terms of achieving well-defined national objectives, and not to view contributing to the peace and security of the world as the primary goal of its foreign policy. It can be argued that this was not a substantial change, for peace and security remains one of the government's six national themes. Nevertheless there is a real difference in emphasis between what might be called 'Pearsonian internationalism' and 'Trudeauvian nationalism'. The former is typified by Prime Minister St Laurent's attitude during the 1956 Suez crisis, when he told his Secretary of State for External Affairs to do what he thought best. Pearson proposed the establishment of a UN peacekeeping force as the most effective means of ensuring peace, an action that aroused the ire of British sympathizers in Canada and may have contributed to the electoral defeat of the Liberal Party in 1957. Trudeau, on the other hand, resembles Mackenzie King in the way in which he sees foreign policy as a means of promoting his most important national interests. National unity was King's major concern, and many of his foreign-policy decisions were based on how they would affect this over-riding consideration.[22]

Commentators who have attempted to analyse Mr Trudeau's political philosophy have frequently assumed that because he describes himself as an anti-nationalist he must be an internationalist or a continentalist. The truth of the matter is that he is as committed to the defence of the Canadian 'nation-state' as he is opposed to nationalism of an ethnic nature.[23] He seems determined to pursue foreign policies that contribute to national unity in three distinct ways: by projecting abroad the cultural duality on which Canada is based, by promoting the economic growth that is necessary if regional disparities and discontent are to be ended, and by finding political, economic, and cultural counterweights throughout the world so that Canada does not become so dominated by the United States that it loses its distinct, pluralist identity. Viewed in this light, *Foreign Policy for Canadians* is very much the 'Trudeau doctrine'.

The failure of the policy papers to delve deeply into substantial foreign-policy issues was not an oversight but was completely consistent with Prime Minister Trudeau's approach to international relations. If national concerns such as unity and economic growth are to be the main objectives of Canada's foreign policy, what point would there be in discussing remote issues that do not immediately threaten these basic goals? In a revealing interview with James Reston of the *New York Times* in December 1971, Mr Trudeau confirmed that he is not particularly interested or knowledgeable about international events that do not immediately affect what he regards as Canada's most important national objectives:

> Well, you're starting with the aspect of politics of which I know the least and on which I can perhaps be the least precise—world affairs and international politics. I can only extrapolate certain Canadian experiences and feelings and sort of say, it must be the same thing elsewhere.[24]

Mr Trudeau's major achievement during the review was not so much to alter the substance of previous policy as it was to change its articulation. Critics of traditional Canadian foreign policy welcomed his rise to power in 1968, for they regarded him as a maverick who would lead Canada in dramatically new directions. They soon learned that the new Prime Minister was not going to initiate a radically new foreign policy and that he was primarily concerned with the way in which Canada's external relations were viewed by Canadians. Summarizing the 'new' Canadian foreign policy in 1971, Ivan Head chose to emphasize 'the absence of pretentiousness. Canada is not number one; it has little inclination toward chauvinism. . . . One may even hope that it may even have buried forever self-delusion.'[25] This was precisely the change that Trudeau desired. To accomplish it required some changes in policy—notably a North American orientation in defence policy—but most of all it required an in-depth review so that both those who participated and those who read its conclusions would realize that Canada was no longer the great 'world peacekeeper' that many had thought it to be. The Prime Minister's whole theory of participatory democracy is based on the notion that people must *feel* they are sharing in decisions if they are to realize that their high expectations cannot always be met. 'The only way of avoiding that increasing gap between the desire, the expectation, and the fulfilment', he has said, is 'by repeating the truth to the people and getting them to participate in the decision—not in order that it be better, but in order that they realize for themselves that their expectations cannot be fulfilled and that the problem is more difficult of solution than the dreams would reveal.'[26]

Whether the foreign-policy review altered the attitude of the Canadian public in the manner desired by Mr Trudeau is a question that cannot yet be answered conclusively. Judging by the critical reaction it aroused in the Commons' External Affairs Committee, the government's attack on the 'helpful-fixer' role seems to have been widely interpreted as a condemnation of the constructive internationalism of 'Pearsonian diplomacy', which was the last thing the government intended. There is undoubtedly a danger that repeated attacks on the excessive rhetoric used by some Canadians to describe previous policy might lead the government to play down much that was laudable about Canada's foreign policy in the 1950s and 1960s. Fortunately 'Trudeauvian nationalism' does not appear to be the narrow, isolationist nationalism that some first considered it to be. Its byword is the 'national interest', but there are considerable grounds for hope that Mr Trudeau will define this interest—in actions if not in words—just as broadly as Lester Pearson did.

The review had very definite costs—notably a temporary decline of morale in the Department of External Affairs and a lessening of Canadian influence among its allies—but if it succeeded in making the public aware of Canada's limitations in influencing the course of international events, it may have been worth the time and effort. In the last analysis, whether the foreign-policy review was a success or a failure will be determined by the extent to which Canada, while avoiding unrealistic rhetoric and expectations, is able to play a constructive international role in the 1970s.

Notes

[1] See Andrew Brewin, et al., *Behind the Headlines*, August 1970; Peyton V. Lyon, *International Journal*, Winter 1970–1; Edmonton *Journal*, 'Foreign non-Policy', June 29, 1970; Montreal *Gazette*, 'Foreign Policy: Some Myths Laid to Rest', June 27, 1970; Ottawa *Citizen*, June 27, 1970.

[2] James Hyndman, *International Journal*, Winter 1970-1, p. 17; Maxwell Cohen, *Behind the Headlines*, August 1970; Garth Legge, Cranford Pratt, Richard Williams, Hugh Windsor, 'The Black Paper: An Alternative Policy for Canada Towards Southern Africa', *Behind the Headlines*, September 1970.

[3] Toronto *Globe and Mail*, 'Dollar Diplomacy', June 27, 1970; *Report, 1971*; D. C. Thomson, R. F. Swanson, *Canadian Foreign Policy: Options & Perspectives*. Toronto: McGraw-Hill Ryerson, 1971, p. 150.

[4] *Report, 1971*, pp. 37, 43; Winnipeg *Free Press*, 'Six Faces of Foreign Policy', June 26, 1970.

[5] *Minutes of Proceedings and Evidence*, February 24, 1971, p. 10; Toronto *Globe and Mail*, June 27, 1970; Edmonton *Journal*, June 29, 1970; Ottawa *Citizen*, June 26, 1970.

[6] Edmonton *Journal*, June 29, 1970; Ottawa *Journal*, June 26, 1970; *Le Devoir* (Montréal), 27 juin 1970.

[7] Denis Stairs, 'Notes for Talk to External Affairs Department Conference', May 13-14, 1971, (unpublished).

[8] Television interview, CTV, 'Question Period', January 2, 1972. (Hon. Mitchell Sharp.)

[9] Ivan L. Head, 'The Foreign Policy of the New Canada'. *Foreign Affairs*, Vol. 50, No. 2, January, 1972, pp. 239–43.

[10] *Foreign Policy for Canadians (Europe)*, p. 24; *Foreign Policy for Canadians (United Nations)*, p. 17.

[11] *Report, 1971*, p. 25.

[12] Television interview, CTV, 'Question Period', January 2, 1972.

[13] Thomson and Swanson, *op. cit.*, p. 58.

[14] Transcript of the Prime Minister's remarks released by the Office of the Prime Minister, November 11, 1971.

[15] Head, *op. cit.*, pp. 238-9.

[16] Thomson and Swanson, *op. cit.*, p. 87.

[17] See *Report, 1971*, pp. 9, 43.

[18] See *Report, 1971*, p. 42; and Thomson and Swanson, *op. cit.*, p. 148.

[19] *Report, 1971*, p. 43.

[20] Thomson and Swanson, *op. cit.*, p. 149.

[21] Ottawa *Journal*, 'Foreign Policy Review: A Paper Tiger', June 26, 1970.

[22] See Thomson and Swanson, *op. cit.*, p. 9.

[23] I am grateful to Professor Ramsay Cook of York University for helping me make more precise the distinction between Trudeau's attitude towards the 'nation-state' and the 'nationalist-state'.

[24] Transcript of Prime Minister's Interview with James Reston of the *New York Times*, Office of the Prime Minister, December 21, 1971.

[25] Head, *op. cit.*, p. 252.

[26] Transcript of Prime Minister's Interview with James Reston of the *New York Times*, Office of the Prime Minister, December 21, 1971.

Bibliography

I. Government of Canada Publications

Canadian International Development Agency. *International Development*. Ottawa: Information Division, Canadian International Development Agency, June 1970.

Department of External Affairs. *Annual Report, 1970*. Ottawa: Information Canada, 1971.

————. *Foreign Policy for Canadians*. Ottawa: Queen's Printer for Canada, 1970.

————. *Statements and Speeches*, Numbers 66/47, 67/8, 67/9, 67/12, 67/40, 67/41, 68/8, 68/13, 68/16, 68/17, 68/19, 68/21, 68/22, 69/1, 69/3, 69/4, 69/5, 69/7, 69/8, 69/9, 69/11, 69/15, 69/16, 69/21, 69/22, 69/23, 69/24, 69/25, 70/1, 70/5, 70/6. (For a list of the titles and dates of these speeches, see Department of External Affairs. *English-Language Publications Available in Canada*. Catalogue No. 21, 1970.)

Department of National Defence. *Defence in the Seventies*. Ottawa: Information Canada, 1971.

————. *White Paper on Defence*. Ottawa: Queen's Printer for Canada, 1964.

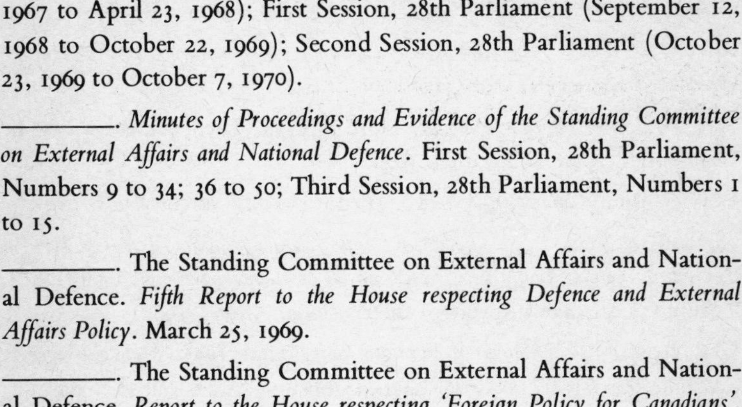

House of Commons. *Debates*. Second Session, 27th Parliament (May 8, 1967 to April 23, 1968); First Session, 28th Parliament (September 12, 1968 to October 22, 1969); Second Session, 28th Parliament (October 23, 1969 to October 7, 1970).

________. *Minutes of Proceedings and Evidence of the Standing Committee on External Affairs and National Defence*. First Session, 28th Parliament, Numbers 9 to 34; 36 to 50; Third Session, 28th Parliament, Numbers 1 to 15.

________. The Standing Committee on External Affairs and National Defence. *Fifth Report to the House respecting Defence and External Affairs Policy*. March 25, 1969.

________. The Standing Committee on External Affairs and National Defence. *Report to the House respecting 'Foreign Policy for Canadians'*. June 1971.

Office of the Prime Minister. *Press Release*. 1968 (July 29); 1971 (May 18, May 19, May 20, May 21, May 25, May 28, June 1).

II. Books

Clarkson, Stephen, ed. *An Independent Foreign Policy for Canada?* Toronto: McClelland and Stewart Limited, 1968.

Cleveland, Harlan. *NATO: The Transatlantic Bargain.* New York: Harper & Row, 1970.

Cook, Ramsay. *The Maple Leaf Forever: Essays on Nationalism and Politics in Canada.* Toronto: The Macmillan Company of Canada Limited, 1971.

Deutsch, Karl W. *The Analysis of International Relations*. Englewood Cliffs, New Jersey: Prentice-Hall, Inc., 1968.

________, and Edinger, Lewis J. *Germany Rejoins the Powers: Mass Opinion, Interest Groups, and Elites in Contemporary German Foreign Policy*. Stanford, California: Stanford University Press, 1959.

Eayrs, James. *Fate and Will in Foreign Policy*. Toronto: CBC Publications, 1967.

———. *The Art of the Possible: Government and Foreign Policy in Canada*. Toronto: University of Toronto Press, 1961.

Farrell, R. Barry. *The Making of Canadian Foreign Policy*. Scarborough, Ontario: Prentice-Hall of Canada, Ltd., 1969.

Fox, Paul, ed. *Politics: Canada.* Third edition. Toronto: McGraw-Hill Company of Canada Limited, 1970.

Gellner, John. *Canada in NATO*. Toronto: The Ryerson Press, 1970.

Gordon, J. King, ed. *Canada's Role as a Middle Power: Papers Given at the Third Annual Banff Conference on World Development, August 1965*. Toronto: Canadian Institute of International Affairs, 1966.

Granatstein, J. L. *Canadian Foreign Policy Since 1945: Middle Power or Satellite?* Toronto: The Copp Clark Publishing Co. Limited, 1969.

Harbron, John D. *This is Trudeau*. Don Mills, Ontario: Longmans Canada Limited, 1968.

Hébert, Jacques, and Trudeau, Pierre Elliott. *Two Innocents in Red China*. Toronto: Oxford University Press, 1968.

Hockin, Thomas A., ed. *Apex of Power: The Prime Minister and Political Leadership in Canada*. Scarborough, Ontario: Prentice-Hall of Canada, Ltd., 1971.

Holmes, John W. *The Better Part of Valour: Essays on Canadian Diplomacy*. Toronto: McClelland and Stewart Limited, 1970.

———; Burton, Bruce; and Hunt, Betty, *Power and Independence: The Relevance of Nationalism and Sovereignty in the 1970s and Beyond.* Toronto: Canadian Institute of International Affairs, 1970.

Lamarsh, Judy. *Memoirs of a Bird in a Guilded Cage*. Toronto: McClelland and Stewart Limited, 1968.

London, Kurt. *The Making of Foreign Policy.* Philadelphia: J. B. Lippincott Company, 1965.

Lyon, Peyton V. *Canada in World Affairs, 1961-1963*. Volume XII. Toronto: Oxford University Press, 1968.

———. *NATO as a Diplomatic Instrument*. Toronto: The Atlantic Council of Canada, 1971.

McLin, Jon B. *Canada's Changing Defense Policy, 1957-1963: The Problems of a Middle Power in Alliance*. Toronto: The Copp Clark Publishing Co. Limited, 1967.

Newman, Peter C. *Renegade in Power*. Toronto: McClelland and Stewart Limited, 1963.

________. *The Distemper of our Times*. Toronto: McClelland and Stewart Limited, 1968.

Paul, John, and Lanlicht, Jerome. *In Your Opinion*. Volume 1. Clarkson, Ontario: Canadian Peace Research Institute, 1963.

Peacock, Donald. *Journey to Power*. Toronto: The Ryerson Press, 1968.

Pearson, Lester B. *Peace in the Family of Man: The Reith Lectures, 1968*. Toronto: Oxford University Press, 1969.

________. *Words and Occasions*. Toronto: University of Toronto Press, 1970.

Rosenau, James N. *Public Opinion and Foreign Policy*. New York: Random House, 1961.

________, ed. *Domestic Sources of Foreign Policy*. New York: The Free Press, 1967.

________, ed. *International Politics and Foreign Policy: A Reader in Research and Theory*. Revised edition. New York: The Free Press, 1969.

Saywell, John, ed. *Canadian Annual Review*. Toronto: University of Toronto Press, 1967, 1968, 1969.

Shaw, Brian, ed. *The Gospel According to St Pierre*. Richmond Hill, Ontario: Simon & Schuster of Canada Ltd., 1969.

Smith, Denis. *Bleeding Hearts . . . Bleeding Country: Canada and the Quebec Crisis*. Edmonton: M. G. Hurtig Ltd., 1971.

Stewart, Walter. *Shrug: Trudeau in Power*. Toronto: New Press, 1971.

Thomson, D. C., and Swanson, R. F. *Canadian Foreign Policy: Options & Perspectives*. Toronto: McGraw-Hill Ryerson Limited, 1971.

Toronto *Telegram*. *Canada 70: A Summary Coast to Coast*. Toronto: McClelland and Stewart Limited, 1969.

Trudeau, Pierre Elliott. *Federalism and the French Canadians*. Toronto: The Macmillan Company of Canada Limited, 1968.

III. Articles

Brecher, Michael; Steinberg, Blema; and Stein, Janice. 'A framework for research on foreign policy behaviour'. *Journal of Conflict Resolution*, Vol. XIII, No. 1, March 1969.

Brewin, Andrew, *et al*. 'Foreign Policy for Canadians: Comments on the White Paper'. *Behind the Headlines*, August 1970.

Carrier, André. 'L'idéologie politique de la revue Cité Libre'. *Canadian Journal of Political Science*, Vol. I, No. 4, December 1968.

Cohen, Maxwell. 'The Arctic and the National Interest'. *International Journal*, Winter 1970-1.

Dobell, Peter C. 'Canada and NATO'. *Orbis*, Vol. XIII, Spring 1969.

________. 'The Management of a Foreign Policy for Canadians'. *International Journal*, Winter 1970-1.

Doern, G. Bruce. 'Recent Changes in the Philosophy of Policy-making in Canada'. *Canadian Journal of Political Science*, Vol. IV, No. 2, June 1971.

Eayrs, James. 'Dilettante in Power: The first three years of P. E. Trudeau'. *Saturday Night*, April 1971.

________. 'The End of Canadian Liberalism'. *Canadian Dimension*, Vol. 7, No. 5, December 1970.

Head, Ivan L. 'The Foreign Policy of the New Canada'. *Foreign Affairs*, Vol. 50, No. 2, January 1972.

Hilsman, Roger. 'Policy-Making is Politics', in Rosenau, ed. *International Politics and Foreign Policy*, 1969.

________. 'The Foreign-Policy Consensus: an Interim Report'. *Journal of Conflict Resolution*, Vol. III, 1959.

Holmes, John W. 'After 25 Years'. *International Journal*, Winter 1970-1.

Holsti, Ole R. 'The Belief System and National Images: A Case Study'. *Journal of Conflict Resolution*, Vol. VI, 1962.

Horowitz, Gad. 'The Trudeau Doctrine'. *Canadian Dimension*, Vol. 5, No. 5, June-July 1968.

Hyndman, James E. 'National Interest and the New Look'. *International Journal*, Winter 1970-1.

Jervis, Robert. 'Hypotheses on Misperception', in Rosenau, ed. *International Politics and Foreign Policy*, 1969.

Kissinger, Henry A. 'Domestic Structure and Foreign Policy', in Rosenau, ed. *International Politics and Foreign Policy*, 1969.

Legault, Albert. 'La nouvelle politique de défense du Canada'. *Le Devoir*, 25, 26 novembre 1969.

________. 'La position stratégique du Canada et la décennie 1970'. *International Journal*. Winter 1970-1.

Lyon, Peyton V. 'A Review of the Review'. *Journal of Canadian Studies*, May 1970.

________. 'Defence Policies Related to Foreign Policy'. *Special Studies prepared for the Special Committee of the House of Commons on matters Relating to Defence*. Supplement. Ottawa: Queen's Printer for Canada, 1964-5.

________. 'Sovereignty: Does it deserve to be our First Defence Priority?' *The Commentator*, May 1971.

________. 'The Trudeau Doctrine'. *International Journal*. Winter 1970-1.

McLellan, David S. 'The "Operational Code" Approach to the Study of Political Leaders: Dean Acheson's Philosophical and Instrumental Beliefs'. *Canadian Journal of Political Science*, Vol. IV, March 1971.

McNaught, Kenneth. 'Who Controls Foreign Policy?' *Behind the Headlines*, September 1954.

Reid, Escott. 'Canada and the Struggle Against World Poverty'. *International Journal*, Winter 1969-70.

________. 'Canadian Foreign Policy, 1967-1977: A Second Golden Decade?' *International Journal*, Spring 1967.

Stairs, Denis. 'Publics and Policy-Makers: The Domestic Environment of Canada's Foreign Policy Community'. *International Journal*, Winter 1970-1.

Stevenson, Garth. 'For a Real Review'. *Current Comment*. Ottawa: School of International Affairs, Carleton University, 1970.

Trudeau, Pierre Elliott. 'A l'ouest rien de nouveau'. *Cité Libre*, février 1961.

————. 'A propos de "domination économique"'. *Cité Libre*, mai 1958.

————. 'La Guerre! La Guerre!' *Cité Libre*, décembre 1961.

————. 'Pearson ou l'abdication de l'esprit'. *Cité Libre*, avril 1963.

————. 'Politique fonctionnelle'. *Cité Libre*, juin 1950.

————. 'Politique fonctionnelle II'. *Cité Libre*, février 1951.

————. 'Reflexions sur la politique du Canada français'. *Cité Libre*, décembre 1952.

————. 'Un Manifeste Démocratique'. *Cité Libre*, octobre 1958.

————, and Pelletier, Gérard. 'Pelletier et Trudeau s'expliquent'. *Cité Libre*, octobre 1965.

IV. Periodicals

International Canada. Toronto: Canadian Institute of International Affairs, January 1970 to December 1970.

Maclean's Magazine. September 1968 to July 1971.

Monthly Report on Canadian External Relations. Toronto: Canadian Institute of International Affairs, January 1968 to December 1969.

Time Magazine. Canadian edition. January 1968 to December 1970.

V. Newspapers

Edmonton *Journal*. June 29, 1970.

Le Monde (Paris). 21 février 1970.

Montreal *Gazette*. June 27, 1970.

Montreal *Le Devoir*. 27 juin 1970.

Montreal Star. December 23, 1967; July 4, 1970.

Ottawa *Citizen*. June 26, 1970; June 27, 1970; January 2, 1971; January 21, 1971.

Ottawa *Journal*. June 26, 1970.

Saskatoon *Star-Phoenix*. April 25, 1969; June 20, 1970; June 11, 1971.

Toronto *Globe and Mail*. January 1968 to August 1970; February 2, 1971.

Toronto *Star*. April 27, 1968; April 1, 1969; April 27, 1969; May 2, 1969; June 25, 1969; July 4, 1970.

Winnipeg *Free Press*. June 26, 1970.

Index

ABM (Anti-Ballistic Missile), 73-4
Acheson, Dean, 149
Africa, 11, 12
Allard, General, 18
Allmand, Warren, 133
Anderson, David, 151-2
Anderson, W. A. B., 125
Andrew, Arthur, 132, 179
Anti-Ballistic Missile (ABM), 73-4
Arctic, 131, 161, 186
Arctic Water Pollution Prevention Bill, 62-3
Asia, 11, 12
Avro Arrow: *see* CF-105

Bain, George, 56, 74, 85, 95-6
Ball, George, 33
Beaton, Leonard, 84
Belgium, 11
Benson, Edgar, 47
Berlin, 187
Biafra, 37
Blair, Gordon, 34
Bodin, Jean, 64
Bomarc missile, 16-17, 206
Brandt, Willy, 144
Brecher, Michael, 6-7, 28, 128, 148
Brewin, Andrew, 41-2, 134, 143, 194
Britain, 27, 207
Buchan, Alistair, 132

Cabinet, 87, 89-90, 92-3, 114-15, 150, 151-2, 154-7, 159, 177, 181, 184, 211
Cabinet Committee on Priorities and Planning, 81, 181
Cadieux, Léo, 45, 90, 137, 141-3, 144, 145, 146, 155
Cadieux, Marcel, 123, 124, 125
Cafik, Norman, 133, 151
Camp, Dalton, 39, 112-13, 118, 119
Campbell, Ross, 125, 126, 132
Canadian Armed Forces, 18, 19, 35, 107, 139, 141, 155, 161, 206
'Canadian Defence Policy—A Study', 157, 158, 159
Canadian Export Association, 197
Canadian Institute of International Affairs, 29, 36, 125
Canadian Institute of Public Opinion (CIPO), 34

Canadian International Development Agency, 71, 172
Canadian Peace Research Institute, 196
Canadian Pulp and Paper Association, 197
Caouette, Réal, 42, 143
CF-101 (Voodoo) aircraft, 16, 17, 206
CF-104 (Starfighter) aircraft, 16, 17, 149, 158
CF-105 (Avro Arrow) aircraft, 16
China: *see* People's Republic of China
Churchill, Gordon, 40
CIPO (Canadian Institute of Public Opinion), 34
Cité Libre, 55
Civil service, 87, 88, 90-2, 97, 148-50, 163, 211
Clarkson, Stephen, 28, 30, 31, 32, 111, 124, 129, 148, 201
Cleveland, Harlan, 141
Cohen, Maxwell, 195
Cold War, 10, 12, 15, 67, 73
Committee on Federal-Provincial Relations, 89
Commonwealth, 27, 32
Commonwealth Prime Ministers' Conference: London 1969, 85, 144; Singapore 1971, 70, 90, 204
Congo, 36
Conservative Party, 38-41
Cox, David, 124, 125
Créditiste Party, 42
Cross, J. R., 125
Crowe, Marshall, 88
Cuban Missile Crisis, 10
Curry, R. J., 125
Cyprus dispute, 36
Czechoslovakia, invasion of, 11-12, 38, 47, 67, 144, 159

Dare, Michael, 130
Davey, Jim, 81
Defence budget, 20-1, 30, 108, 121, 146-7
Defence in the 70s, 160-1, 205
Defence Production Sharing Agreement, 23, 32, 42, 46, 48, 110
Defence White Paper (1964), 17, 18-19, 22, 40, 107, 114; (1971), 160-1, 205
Denmark, 11, 24, 130
Department of External Affairs, 25-6, 91, 92, 112, 148, 149, 150, 156, 171, 175, 176-8, 184, 185, 190-1, 201, 211, 212, 215
Department of National Defence, 148, 149, 150, 185, 190-1
de Puyjalon, H. G., 125
Deutsch, Karl, 149
Dewhirst, G. H., 125
Diefenbaker, John, 16, 17, 36, 40, 48, 81, 94, 123
Dobell, Peter C., 125, 134, 162, 183
Douglas, T. C., 42, 142

Eastern Europe, 14, 40
East-West relations, 10-11, 106, 144
Eayrs, James, 22, 29, 30, 56, 109, 113, 118, 119, 124, 128, 129, 148, 149, 156, 162
Edmonton *Journal*, 195, 198
Egypt, 13, 36, 40, 42, 205
Europe, 11, 12, 14, 17, 47, 69, 71, 115, 130, 144; Canadian forces in, 12, 18-19, 23, 30, 38, 48, 107, 139, 141, 142, 150, 157-9, 162, 173, 211; Canadian relations with, 105, 169, 207, 210; Canadian role in 25, 26, 34, 72, 126, 133-4, 135-6, 151-3, 168; *see also* Eastern Europe, Western Europe
European Economic Community, 27, 207
External-Defence Report, 136-7, 147, 149

Fairweather, Gordon, 123
FLQ crisis, 161
Ford, Robert, 136
Foreign aid, 24, 29, 34, 40, 71, 109, 168, 172-3
Foreign Policy for Canadians, 2, 167, 189, 190, 194, 195-6, 199-200, 203, 209, 214
Formosa, 76
Foulkes, Charles, 130-1, 132
France, 11, 14, 68-9, 169

Galbraith, John Kenneth, 81
Gallois, General, 133
Gellner, John, 21, 130
Germany, 144
Golden, David, 131
Gordon, Donald, 29
Gordon, Walter, 32
Granatstein, Jack, 3, 29, 36, 111, 112-13, 117, 124, 129, 148
Greece, 44, 212
Green, Howard, 25, 38, 39, 195
Grey, R. Y., 125
Griffiths, Franklyn, 124

Hall Commission, 20, 21
Halstead, J. G. H., 125
Hanley, Charles, 32
Harkness, Douglas, 40, 129, 133, 142, 152
Harmel, Pierre, 132
Harmel Report, 10, 14
Head, Ivan, 88, 89, 137, 156, 157, 158, 203, 208, 214
Healey, Denis, 141, 144
Hellyer, Paul, 124
Hertzman, Lewis, 124
Hockin, Thomas, 29, 32, 112-13, 125, 126
Holland, 130
Holmes, John, 28, 29, 31, 32, 124, 125, 174
Honest John missile, 17
Horowitz, Gad, 61
House of Commons' Standing Committee on External Affairs and National Defence, 2, 31, 36-7, 168-9, 187, 197, 204, 209-10, 215
Howarth, G., 125
Hutchison, Bruce, 84
Hyndman, James, 195

ICBM (Intercontinental Ballistic Missile), 73
Ignatieff, George, 132, 171
India-Pakistan war, 204
Indochina, 205, 212
Information Canada, 95
Intercontinental Ballistic Missile (ICBM), 73
International Control Commission, 13, 25, 36, 205
Israel, 13, 40

Japan, 12, 212

Kent, Tom, 87
Kierans, Eric, 38, 46, 47, 90, 96, 123, 124
Killick, John, 125
King, Mackenzie, 94, 96, 213
Kissinger, Henry, 144, 149
Korean War, 21, 24

Lacrosse missile, 17
Lalande, Gilles, 125, 189
Lalonde, Marc, 81, 86, 87
Lamarsh, Judy, 114-15
Lamontagne, Maurice, 67
Lang, Otto, 124
Laporte, Pierre, 57
Latin America: Canadian relations with, 40, 48, 105, 109, 170-1, 212; Canadian role in, 31, 47, 76, 115
Lawson, R. W., 125
Legault, Albert, 130
Lewis, David, 42, 133, 134, 138
Lloyd, Trevor, 125
Luxembourg, 24
Lyon, Peyton V., 3, 5, 28, 30-1, 32, 84, 160, 162, 194

Macdonald, Donald, 46, 90, 115, 124, 147, 155
MacInnis, Grace, 42-3
McNaught, Kenneth, 28, 29, 128, 148
Manhattan, 74, 186
Marchand, Jean, 46, 90, 155
Martin, Paul, 13, 17-18, 25, 26, 106, 114-15, 195
Marzari, Frank, 125
Mathews, Roy, 125
MBFR (Mutual and balanced force reductions), 14, 143
Medicare, 20, 21

Middle East, 25, 187, 212
Montmorency Conference: *see* Policy Thinkers Conference
Montreal *Gazette*, 38, 195
Montreal *La Presse*, 38
Montreal Star, 38, 55-6, 182
Murray, Geoffrey S., 26, 117, 179, 182-3
Mutual and balanced force reductions (MBFR), 14, 143

Nasser, President, 13, 40
Nationalism, 2, 30, 39, 57-62, 65-6, 82, 110, 116, 117-19, 130, 140, 168, 176, 183, 213-15
NATO (North Atlantic Treaty Organization), 2, 10, 11, 13, 14, 15, 16, 17, 22-3, 32, 68, 75, 77, 121ff., 185, 209; Canadian role in, 1, 3, 4, 7, 12, 18, 19, 24, 26, 27, 28, 29, 34-5, 37-9, 40, 41, 42, 43-4, 45, 46, 47, 48, 71, 72, 73, 106, 108, 109, 110, 114, 116, 118, 190, 206-7, 210
NDP (New Democratic Party), 37, 41-3, 109
Nenni, Pietro, 145
New Democratic Party: *see* NDP
Newman, Peter, 5, 6, 78, 91, 125
NIBMAR doctrine, 77
Nigerian civil war, 13
Nixon, Richard, 66
NORAD (North American Air Defence Agreement), 15, 32, 33, 77, 132, 185; Canadian role in, 1, 3, 4, 19, 34-5, 38, 39, 40, 42, 45, 47, 72, 73-4, 107-8, 110, 116, 118, 128, 129, 131, 139, 160, 206
North Atlantic Treaty Organization: *see* NATO
Norway, 130
Nuclear weapons, 14, 16-17, 33, 35, 75, 107, 108-9; Canada's use of, 16-17, 25, 42, 142, 160

OAS (Organization of American States), Canadian role in, 31, 43, 76, 170-1, 208
Osgood, Robert, 198
Ottawa *Citizen*, 198
Ottawa *Journal*, 198-9, 212-13

PAG: *see* Policy Analysis Group
Parliament, 87, 93, 94, 97
Parti Québecois, 22
PCO: *see* Privy Council Office
Pearson, Geoffrey, 26
Pearson, Lester B., 3-4, 15, 16-17, 20, 21, 22-4, 25, 26, 29, 31-2, 37, 61, 62, 73, 75, 81, 91, 94, 106, 108, 111, 112, 113, 114, 115, 116, 123, 149, 172, 215
Pelletier, Gérard, 46, 90, 115, 155
People's Republic of China, 67, 72, 76, 84, 105, 212; Canadian relations with, 110, 174-6, 208; recognition of, 24, 38, 43, 75-6, 109, 116, 124
Pépin, Jean-Luc, 124
Pitfield, Michael, 89
Planning, Programming, and Budgeting System (PPBS), 82
PMO: *see* Prime Minister's Office
Policy Analysis Group (PAG), 2, 112, 178-9
Policy Thinkers Conference, 39, 112-13
Portugal, 44
Prime Minister's Office (PMO), 81, 86-7, 88, 93, 95, 97, 156, 157, 163
Priorities and Planning Committee, 89
Privy Council Office (PCO), 81, 86-7, 88, 93, 97, 157
Prud'homme, Marcel, 132-3

Québec, 21-2, 60, 63, 64, 74, 82

Regenstreif, Peter, 37
Reid, Escott, 29, 42, 111, 117, 148, 149
Reston, James, 214
Reykjavik declaration, 14
Richardson, James, 47, 124
Ritchie, A. E., 184
Robertson, Gordon, 86, 91
Robertson, Norman, 26, 111-12
Robertson Report, 26-7, 48, 105, 106, 107, 108, 115
Rosenau, James, 7, 8, 109

Ryan, Claude, 5, 199
Ryan, Perry, 133

Sabourin, Louis, 30, 125
SAGE detection, 16
St Laurent, Louis, 3, 48, 91, 94, 213
Schmidt, Helmut, 133
Schwarzmann, Maurice, 125
Servan-Schreiber, Jean-Jacques, 14
Sharp, Mitchell, 11, 12, 45-6, 71, 90, 92, 117, 124, 125, 126, 127, 136, 137, 147, 148, 155-6, 167, 175, 182, 183, 184, 187, 188, 189, 196, 204, 208, 210, 213
Skilling, H. G., 125
Smith, Denis, 57
Smith, Sidney, 48
Solandt, O. M., 131
Sommer, Theo, 130
South Africa, 44, 171, 196, 202, 204
South-East Asia, 13, 14, 15
Sovereignty, 62-5, 140-1, 155, 160-1, 168, 173, 185-6, 188, 205
Special Task Force on Relations with Europe: *see* STAFFEUR
Spencer, Robert A., 124, 125
STAFFEUR (Special Task Force on Relations with Europe), 135-6, 146-7, 149
Stairs, Denis, 28, 32, 112, 113, 178, 201
Stanfield, Robert, 39, 40, 41, 143
Starfighter aircraft: *see* CF-104
Steele, James, 32
Stevenson, Garth, 108-9
Stewart, Walter, 93
Strategic Arms Limitations Talks, 10, 188
Suez crisis, 117, 213
Swanson, R. F., 197

Taiwan, 76, 174, 175
Thomson, Dale, 197
Thorburn, Hugh, 125
Toronto *Globe and Mail*, 33, 37, 38, 182, 196
Toronto *Star*, 37, 38
Toronto *Telegram*, 37
Tremblay, Paul, 125, 136
Trudeau, Pierre Elliott: and his administration, 45-9; approaches to government, 5, 76ff., 85ff., 160, 190, 211-12; and his Cabinet, 89-90, 92-3, 154-5, 156-7, 158-9; and Canada's defence policy, 121-2, 139-41, 155, 160, 162; and Canada's international role, 69-78, 105, 110-11, 116, 128-9, 138-9, 155-6, 160, 162, 168, 187, 204-5, 210; and Canada's national interests, 83-5, 110, 118-19, 163, 214; and Canadian academics, 123-4; and China, 75-6, 84, 174-6; and the civil service, 85-6, 90-3, 122-3, 163; and the Commonwealth, 85; and the Commonwealth Prime Ministers' Conference: (London 1969) 85, 144; (Singapore 1971) 90, 204; and the defence budget, 145-6; and economic growth, 82, 183-5, 203; and economic nationalism, 66, 188; and Europe, 12, 162, 169-70, 207-8, 210-11; and foreign aid, 70-1, 172-3; and foreign policy, 84; and the foreign-policy review, 1-2, 4, 5-6, 48, 105, 109-10, 113-14, 115, 119, 167, 179, 181, 190-1, 199-200, 210-11, 213, 215; and Latin America, 170-1; and nationalism, 57-62, 79, 97, 214-15; and national unity, 82, 176, 182; and NATO, 71-3, 75, 114, 121-2, 137-41, 144-5, 148, 153-60, 207, 210; and NORAD, 71-4, 139; and nuclear weapons, 75, 160; and the OAS, 170-1; and the Pacific world, 173-6; and Parliament, 93-4; and the PMO and PCO, 86-7, 137, 157ff.; political philosophy of, 8, 54ff., 97, 115-16, 159-160, 183, 213-15; and public opinion, 95-6, 189, 215; and sovereignty, 62-5, 140-1, 155, 160-1, 185-6; and the Soviet Union, 67-9, 70, 201; and the UN, 171-2; and the U.S., 66, 188, 208

UNEF (United Nations' Emergency Force), 13, 25, 36, 40, 205

United Nations, 11, 13, 24, 27, 32, 71, 105, 171-2; Canadian role in, 1, 3, 4, 13, 18, 36, 39, 109, 111, 117-18, 148, 168, 204; Special Committee on Peacekeeping Operations, 204
United States, 6, 10, 13-14, 15, 23, 62, 74, 75, 97, 122, 129, 130, 144; Canadian relations with, 2, 4, 7, 15, 16-17, 23-4, 27, 28, 31-3, 35, 37, 39, 41, 42, 46, 47, 64-7, 72-3, 77-8, 109, 110, 130, 160, 172, 188, 198, 202, 208, 212, 214
U.S.S.R., 10, 11, 12, 14, 16, 45, 47, 67-8, 71, 72, 75, 97, 159; American relations with, 6; Canadian relations with, 77, 201; Trudeau's visit to, 67, 68, 83, 208

Vancouver *Province*, 38
Vatican, 43
Viet Nam, 15, 23-4, 26, 32, 33, 37, 174, 187; Canadian role in, 25, 36, 42
von Riekhoff, Harald, 28
Voodoo aircraft: *see* CF-101

Wahn, Ian, 127, 129, 133, 134, 152, 153
War Measures Act, 56, 57
Warnock, John, 28, 32, 113, 128-9, 148
Watkins Report, 66
Westell, Anthony, 114
Western Europe, 11, 12, 13, 14, 71, 105, 130, 169; Canadian relations with, 4, 143
West Germany, 11, 68
Whitehead, J. R., 125
Winch, Harold, 134
Winnipeg *Free Press*, 38, 197
Wright, H. H., 125

Yarmolinski, Adam, 130
Young, Christopher, 195